Praise for
America in Turmoil

"Required reading for policymakers on both sides of the political divide."
—**Mark Halperin**, American journalist, and publisher of *Wide World of News*

"Refreshingly sensible and original, John Briggs focuses on fixing problems, not fixing blame."
—**Bill Richardson**, Governor of New Mexico 2003–2011 (D)

"A wonderfully readable collection of trenchant essays addressing our society's challenges and offering non-partisan solutions."
—**William F. Weld**, Governor of Massachusetts 1991–1997 (R), and author of *Mackerel by Moonlight*, *Big Ugly*, and *Stillwater*

"A dispatch from a more civilized discourse … Briggs's intellectual integrity, reliance on data, and refusal to rely upon received wisdom sets his columns apart, and his insightful, engaging prose clarifies complex ideas without simplifying them."
—*BookLife*

"[*America in Turmoil*] is a must-read for students of politics and culture seeking a well-informed perspective on the recent events that have shaped the United States."
— *Readers' Favorite*

"A nuanced treatment of key issues affecting America, written from the perspective of a conservative (in the original meaning of that label), John DeQ. Briggs's *America in Turmoil* stakes out cogent and strong views on important topics."
—*IndieReader*

"Briggs allows readers from across the political spectrum to engage with the subjects and arguments of his essays without feeling alienated or unheard, always striving to encourage critical thinking and the development of a constructive dialogue."
—*Seattle Book Review*

AMERICA
★★★★ IN ★★★★
TURMOIL

ESSAYS *on* POLITICS, *the* ECONOMY,
SOCIETY, *and the* FUTURE

John DeQ. Briggs

Copyright © John DeQ. Briggs, 2023

All rights reserved. No part of this publication in print or in electronic format may be reproduced, stored in a retrieval system, or transmitted in any form or by any means, electronic, mechanical, photocopying, recording, or otherwise without the prior written permission of the publisher.

The scanning, uploading, and distribution of this book without permission is a theft of the author's intellectual property. Thank you for your support of the author's rights.

Distribution by Bublish
Published by JDeQB Publications

ISBN: 978-1-64704-731-3 (eBook)
ISBN: 978-1-64704-732-0 (paperback)
ISBN: 978-1-64704-733-7 (hardcover)

DEDICATION

This volume is dedicated to my family for allowing me the time, space and support to see this through and also to my fellow editors at *The Chesapeake Observer* who did me the honor of reading each chapter in real time and offering editorial support and encouragement.

PREFACE

This volume and its constituent pieces, each initially titled *Thinking about Things,* owe a debt to Vermont Connecticut Royster, for many decades the editor of the *Wall Street Journal* and the author in his later years of a regular column, usually published on the front page and on the far-right column, entitled "Thinking Things Over." My essays mimic his title with great respect and some trepidation, too, for perhaps being thought presumptuous. As I recall, perhaps incorrectly, his column came out most Wednesdays until 1986. The day his column came out was a day when I dedicated myself to a pleasant lunch in a congenial, reader-friendly environment and immersed myself in his column before moving to other pages.

He won many major journalism awards, including two Pulitzer Prizes, one in 1953 for editorial writing, and one in 1984 for distinguished commentary. He also won the Presidential Medal of Freedom in 1985 for his contributions to journalism and communications.

As my undergraduate Harvard club mate (and fellow poker player) Peter Kann put it (Peter Kann was CEO of Dow Jones at the time of Royster's death):

> In his editorials, columns and books, he articulated a profoundly principled conservatism, rooted in the lessons of history and his own uncommon good sense, that remains resonant in American society. His writings stand the test of time and will long be read for their erudition, eloquence and elegance.

In a 1967 book review, James Reston of the *New York Times* wrote that Mr. Royster's columns "compare favorably with the best essays being written in the language today." While comparisons with him do me no honors, I have always found his thinking, his writing, and his grasp of things to be impressive and worthy of much admiration. I can only aspire one day to be compared favorably with him in some small way.

John DeQ. Briggs
Easton, Maryland

CONTENTS

1. Money, Demographics, and Politics (September 17, 2019) 1
2. Questions for Presidential Candidates (October 28, 2019) 7
3. Annual, Decennial, and Other Observations (January 7, 2020) 12
4. Highlights of the Downward Spiral in American Education (January 21, 2020) 17
5. The Rise of Law and Decline of Politics (March 3, 2020) 22
6. Movies, Series, and Books (March 31, 2020) 29
7. The Next New Normal (April 28, 2020) 47
8. Lockstep Lockdowns and L'Affair Flynn (May 26, 2020) 51
9. The Ecstasy of the Mob. Virtue Signaling, Moral Clarity, and a Letter from Istanbul (June 20, 2020) 59
10. A [New England] Republican's View of Policies for a Unified Way Forward (July 4, 2020) 67
11. A Positive Path Forward (August 18, 2020) 78
12. The Politicization of the American Judiciary (September 28, 2020) .. 94
13. The Biden Family Business, Ethics, and the Rule of Law (November 3, 2020) 103
14. Winners, Losers, and Survivors (November 10, 2020) 108
15. Ruminations on the Biden Justice Department (December 8, 2020) 112
16. What Will They Do without Trump to Bash? (January 5, 2021) 118
17. On American Diversity and Its Origins (April 13, 2021) 123
18. With Mainstream Journalism Mostly Dead, Where Can One Find Real Journalists? (June 8, 2021) 144

19. The Present Ambiguity of July 4, the Rise of China as the CCP Hits 100, the Decline of the United States as a Serious Power, and the Politics of Everything (July 7, 2021) 154
20. While You Were Out (August 16, 2021) 158
21. Afghanistan, Mr. Biden, and Coming Full Circle (September 11, 2021) 173
22. Mr. Magoo as President and the Collapse of the President's Poll Numbers (October 12, 2021) 190
23. Would Anyone Today Actually Fight to Preserve the Union?: A Thought Experiment (November 2, 2021) 197
24. Societal Respect for the Rule of Law Is in Trouble (January 10, 2022) 203
25. Ruminations on the Need for Universal National Service (February 14, 2022) 213
26. The Tragedy of Ukraine and the Incompetence of American Strategy and Leadership (March 14, 2022) 221
27. Politics, Abortion, Guns, the Economy, Foreign Policy, and more (June 27, 2022) 227
28. The Beginning of the End Days for Mr. Biden within His Own Party? (July 11, 2022) 241
29. How Quickly Things Change (September 6, 2022) 245
30. Our Hugely Interesting 2022 Midterms (November 21, 2022) 258
31. A Year of Dark Clouds, Silver Linings, and Mysteries (January 10, 2023) 270
32. Forward to the Past with the GOP (March 7, 2023) 280

1

Money, Demographics, and Politics

September 17, 2019

This is my inaugural column. My column will be called "Thinking about Things." I do not know what I will be thinking about any given day, week, or month. In general, these days I tend to think about the ongoing breakdown and accelerating dysfunction of our political parties and, more broadly, our entire political system. I intend to think and write about these things (among others) in small bites, and in a reasonably orderly way. I expect to stay grounded in facts to support views. But along the way, I expect to digress into tangential matters of interest. Today, the tangent is in the title.

Money: Where It Goes

The expenditures of our country are hiding in plain sight on this mesmerizing website.[1] The captivating first page will tell you at a glance that federal spending is approximately $4.5 trillion; federal tax revenues are approximately $3.5 trillion; the US national debt is more than $22.5 trillion; the ratio of federal debt to GDP has increased from 34.7 percent in 1980 to 105.6 percent today; and much more. And you can see that total student loan debt is more than $1.6 trillion while total credit card debt is just a smidgen over one trillion dollars. Such numbers are at the center of most policy issues.

Here are the largest budget items: Medicare/Medicaid nearly $1.2 trillion; Social Security a little over $1 trillion; defense spending $643 billion; interest on the national debt $380 billion; income security (welfare/food stamps $299 billion; federal pensions $287 billion; food/agricultural subsidies $156 billion. These numbers come to $3.96 trillion). Given total federal spending of $4.5 trillion, the stubborn mathematics of it all is that the spending identified above amounts to 88 percent of the federal budget. And, of course, the entitlements (Medicare/Medicaid; Social Security; interest on the national debt; income security; and federal pensions) are growing relentlessly at a rate in excess of the growth of available federal revenues.

In the face of these daunting numbers, which have been trending this way for some time, it is astounding that no political party seems concerned or committed to any semblance of financial rectitude. Fiscally responsible budgeting used to be the province of the Republican Party and conservatives generally. This is no longer true. Financial responsibility has never been the province of progressives or the Democrats.

Money: Who Provides It

Tax data are important to any understanding of spending policies; the data are also fascinating. Data from the Congressional Budget Office tell us that total federal tax revenue is a bit more than $3.5 trillion and this includes income taxes, payroll taxes, corporate taxes, excise taxes, and all other federal taxes.[2] About half of this total amount comes from income taxes. More than a third comes from payroll taxes. Here are some highlights about income taxes from the Tax Foundation.[3]

- ★ The top 1% (1.4 million tax returns) paid 37.32% of all federal income taxes in 2018, and the average tax rate was 26.87%.
- ★ the top 5% (7.04 million tax returns) paid 58.23% of all federal income taxes in 2018, and the average tax rate was 23.49%.
- ★ The top 10% (14.08 million tax returns) paid 69.47% of all federal income taxes in 2018, and the average tax rate was 21.19%.
- ★ The top 25% (35.2 million tax returns) paid 85.97% of all federal income taxes in 2018, and the average tax rate was 17.84%.
- ★ The top 50% (70.44 million tax returns) paid 96.96% of all federal income taxes in 2018, and the average tax rate was 15.57%.

"The top 1%" is a construct that varies very much from state to state and is based on *household* income not *individual* income. In the US writ large, a family needs an income of $421,926 to be in the top 1%. But in New Mexico, this number is just over $250,000, while in Connecticut, it is just over $700,000. But the average income of the top 1% nationwide is "only" $1.32 million. State-by-state and other data of interest can be found online at various easy-to-find sites.

To be sure, there are thousands of households in the top 1% who may enjoy incomes (and net worth) well in excess of $20 to $50 million and even into the billions. These individuals likely include Hollywood stars, many professional athletes, highly paid media personalities, CEOs of certain public companies, and a good number of elected politicians who have managed to parlay public service into vast personal wealth.

It is not particularly clear as a matter of policy why these mega rich or super rich should be taxed at the same rate and in the same manner as a family of four with an income of $425,000. And it is not clear why the capital gains rate should be so far below the ordinary income tax rate. There are legitimate policy questions lurking in these areas. But however they are addressed, more taxing of "the rich" (whatever that might turn out to mean) will be neither a short-term solution to the nation's financial problems nor represent an endless cache of riches that can fund the progressive dream of debt forgiveness, free education, and free health-care services for future generations. There is also the question of the unintended consequence of tax policy serving to smother family businesses. Still, funding even the current deficit requires that the funds come from somewhere, and increasing taxes on the mega rich might make a dent in the deficit while creating more social cohesion. But absent a broader tax increase or a national sales tax, our nation cannot afford the obligations to which it has committed itself already, much less those obligations that demographics suggest might soon become politically popular.

So, let us turn to the stubborn truths of demographics.

Demography Is Destiny

Many aspects of the American future are obvious to anyone who cares to look. We can look at the current population and its ethnic/racial/religious/

national makeup; we can look at the birth rate of each discrete segment of the population; and we can look at immigration patterns for the same categories of people. Pew research data[4] show the accelerating impact of Asian, Hispanic, and other nonwhite populations. The data reveal several points of consequence for the medium and longer term.

First, there are wide gaps between the generations on many social and political issues. Millennials (born from 1981 to 1996) and other relatively young people are far more likely than their elders to hold liberal views on most political and social issues. Most do not identify with any political party, and more than half self-identify as political independents.

Second, the 2016 electorate was the most diverse ever, and the 2020 electorate will be even more so. Millennials are the most racially diverse adult generation; 43% are nonwhite. They are supposedly the "best educated" of any generation, although the nature of that education will be the subject of a future column. This is a generation burdened with much of the $1.7 trillion in student debt, many of whose members still live at home. It is a generation that may not have the wherewithal to produce an income sufficient to retire the debt. It is a generation more dependent on government support than any other.

Third, Millennials this year surpassed baby boomers (those born from 1946 to 1964) as the largest US adult generation. Millennials struggle financially, pay less in taxes, and do not contribute substantial amounts to the Social Security system. Baby boomers pay substantially more tax, are moving into Medicare at the rate of roughly ten thousand people per day and will also be drawing down Social Security entitlements while paying little or nothing into the Social Security system.

Politics and Policies: Cognitive Dissonance

The Democratic Party, increasingly dominated by progressives, seems fully prepared to tax the incomes of the rich, to tax wealth itself, and to add trillions of dollars to annual federal spending. And like it or not, given the demographic trends it is difficult to envision a future in which a majority of voters will ***not*** support much of the progressive agenda despite the vast public and private expenditures required.

The seismic demographic shift provides an enormous challenge to "conservatives," however they may today be defined. Their natural constituency is steadily declining. Yet there has been no coherent Republican or conservative response to the circumstances, other than what might be called "Trumpism." However, Trumpism does not bring together any particular set of consistent policies but rather represents at its best a series of ad hoc reactions to world and national events. It is also dependent on a declining base that will be overwhelmed by the ascent of immigrants and younger generations with little affinity for conservative principles but a natural affinity for "free stuff."

Yet there are multiple points of consensus across the country that conservatives might consider embracing as positive policy that could capture majorities in contestable jurisdictions. For example:

- *On immigration*: there is broad agreement on the need to develop an actual national policy on immigration that would welcome desired skills (including unskilled labor in many cases), while barring or limiting those with undesired skills from entry. Surely we can agree on country-by-country quotas and on some requirement that immigrants become integrated into our educational, language, and cultural systems. Immigrants who cannot or will not integrate simply re-create the tribal systems from which they came and do not seem desirable candidates for citizenship.
- *On entitlements*: a conservative agenda could substantially reduce expenditures for Medicare, Medicaid, Social Security, food stamps, and other such welfare by (a) ratcheting up over time the age of entitlements to age seventy or so; (b) requiring some form of state or national service for the unemployed, perhaps related to infrastructure maintenance or rebuilding; and (c) means testing, Social Security, and Medicare benefits.
- *On China*: addressing the PRC's routine theft of American Intellectual Property in ways that are aggressive but that do not create nearly uncontrollable trade wars to the detriment of American consumers. There are WTO and other remedies less disruptive than engaging in a broad-gauged trade war.
- *On climate change*: acknowledge that climate change is occurring, while also acknowledging that the United States cannot unilaterally make the slightest difference, if indeed any difference can

be made—even through multilateral action by the most populous countries in the world, including China, India, Brazil, and so forth).
- ★ *On guns*: accept and embrace *some* form of gun control. Rather than opposing any and all forms of gun control, conservatives might be far better off embracing *agreeable and uniform* approaches to *state* gun control. At some point soon, the annual slaughter of children by armed madmen using large-magazine weapons will produce a series of progressive policies that may reflect the emergent popular will.
- ★ *On criminal justice reform*: the Republicans (or at least the Trump administration) seems to have been more serious than the Democrats (but not the Progessives), and there does seem to be broad consensus that we should not be the country that incarcerates more citizens than any other country.

The list could go on and on.

This column will think about and address these and other similar things in a considered way and, in the fullness of time, make modest or immodest proposals for course changes both inside and outside political parties.

2

Questions for Presidential Candidates

October 28, 2019

As an interested voter, it has been depressing to see the debate moderators continue to skim the surface of policy questions without coming close to addressing the implications of the answers to those questions. The moderators have also failed to challenge candidates on matters on which, in more normal times, one hopes the candidates would want to be challenged. Here are questions, not in any divinely inspired order, that I would like to see each of the Democratic (and Republican where applicable) candidates answer. Few candidates will answer these questions, but their manner of avoiding them would itself be informative.

On Unifying the Country. The country is now seemingly more divided than at any time over the last one hundred years. Some sixty-three million Americans[5] voted for President Trump, a great many of whom still apparently support him. Can you address them now and tell them why they should vote for you in the general election, and how it is that you will try to address their concerns and also seek to unify the country?

On Foreign Policy. Virtually all of you have decried the way President Trump has carried out foreign policy in this country, whether it be with respect to China, North Korea, Europe, or more recently, Turkey/Syria/the Kurds. Putting to one side, if you can, your distaste for Mr. Trump and the manner in which he uses Twitter and other media to announce and effectuate policy changes, do you believe that:

- frontally addressing the long-standing Chinese theft of intellectual property from American companies was a necessary or desirable course of action?
- demanding that NATO members contribute their agreed share for the finances of NATO, as had been done by all past presidents, was a mistake?
- opening a dialogue with Kim Il Sung of N. Korea made nuclear war more likely than the absence of such dialogue?
- the United States should remain in Syria indefinitely and, if so, to what end?

On a Taxpayer Bailout for Student Debt Voluntarily Incurred. Much has been said about student debt during the campaign. Student debt stands at $1.7 trillion, or $37,200 per indebted student. The average total cost of public colleges is $25,299 (in-state); $40,940 (out-of-state); and $50,900 for private colleges. These costs have roughly tripled since 1977–1978.[6] For decades now, college tuition, both private and public, has increased at an annual rate of 8%, doubling about every nine years. This has been far in excess[7] of the nationwide cost of living. Students can procure their own loans without parental consent.[8] And under federal bankruptcy law, student debt is not dischargeable in bankruptcy. Like tax obligations, student debt remains forever.

Public and private colleges and universities are the direct beneficiaries of the student loan program. The ready availability to colleges of billions of loan dollars each year eliminates or relaxes pressures on colleges to moderate price increases or ensure that students enjoy success postgraduation. Many Democrats seem to support policies that would forgive all of the outstanding student loan debt and provide future for all students with a "free education."

Taking into account the circumstances, would you support a change in federal law that would not only make student debt dischargeable in bankruptcy but also require the colleges who took the funds to be responsible for some percentage (say, 35%) of the bankrupt students' obligations on unpaid loans? Would this not avoid requiring citizens who did not go to college financing those who did? Would it not also give colleges a greater stake in monitoring the debt level of students and hence limiting tuition costs somewhat, as well as giving them a real stake in the success of their students postgraduation? How would merely eliminating the student debt with taxpayer funds address any of those problems?

On the Economy. One of the few things that does not seem to be in serious dispute is that unemployment [9] has not been this low since 1969; median 2018 household income in the United States was $62,000, the highest ever;[10] and the poverty rate (12.3%) has fallen to its lowest point since 2014 (12.3%).[11] What will you say to people across the political spectrum to assure them that your stewardship of the economy will not upend the economy by raising taxes, creating more unemployment and reducing the incentives for business investment in this country, all to the detriment of union retirement funds, 401k plans, and other retirement funding sources that depend on invested assets?

On Impeachment. Each of you has been forthright, and for quite a while, that you believe that President Trump should be impeached. If Mr. Trump is as horrible as you and many others say, would it not be wise for the American people to remove him from office through the upcoming electoral process rather than for the people who elected him to be denied the opportunity to vote him out of office in a democratic process?

- ★ If the outcome of a Senate impeachment trial divides almost completely along party lines, how could an impeachment process unify the country, and how could it be taken by the electorate as anything other than a thoroughly partisan process? Why is that a desirable outcome?
- ★ If the proceedings in the House of Representatives have a purpose, should that purpose not include a good degree of transparency so that the electorate, especially Republicans, can be fully informed of the conduct that is said to warrant impeachment? Absent such support, how could impeachment be a healthy political process?

On the Federal Debt. Other likely indisputable facts are that the federal debt of more than $74 trillion ($874,000 per family) and the Federal budget deficit of more than $1.2 trillion (106% of GDP) are the highest they have ever been. This is unusual given the historically strong economy, inasmuch as a strong economy is usually an occasion for *reducing* the federal deficit. What will you do as president to bring the debt-to-GDP ratios back to the levels that existed, for example, between 1980 and 2000 (34.7% to 56%)?

Also, the persistent low interest rates since the financial collapse have facilitated the creation of more and more federal debt. What would you do about the debt if interest rates were to double or triple, thus making interest on the federal debt a much greater part of the federal budget (it is now $3.5 trillion or about 4.5% of the federal budget)?

On Health Care. You and many other elected politicians demonize health insurance companies. But are you aware that spiraling health costs are driven by providers of health care services, not by insurance companies, and that insurance company margins are very small compared to most businesses? These circumstances, and their relationship to government-sponsored health care and private health care, present serious policy questions.

Many providers (physicians, and some hospitals) cannot afford to accept Medicare patients because Medicare reimbursement rates can be at or below the actual cost of services and hence may not permit providers to be profitable.

Nearly all providers are profitable because private insurance companies subsidize Medicare. For example, where Medicare will pay only about $80 for a particular service, private insurance companies will pay something like $140 for that same service on behalf of their subscribers.

- If elected, what would you do to control the high cost that providers charge for their services?
- If elected, what actions would you take to relieve private insurance companies of the burden of essentially being required to subsidize Medicare patients?
- If this were done, are you aware how much more expensive Medicare would be?

On Social Security. The Social Security Trust Fund will be insolvent by 2035, only sixteen years away. This means the program will be insolvent when today's fifty-one-year-olds reach retirement age and today's youngest retirees turn 78. At that point, all beneficiaries will face a 20% across-the-board benefit, which will grow to 25% over time.[12]

- ★ You have been able to advocate for remedial legislation. Why have you not done so?
- ★ Could this problem not be solved by increasing by, say, two months each year, the age for eligibility of benefits? Why would it not make sense to defer citizens' access to benefits until age 68, or perhaps even 70, given that life expectancy is so much longer, and many people do not retire until well after age 65?

On Immigration Policy. Are you in favor of having a comprehensive immigration policy for the United States?

- ★ Is there something wrong with having quotas by country, by profession, or other categories that permit the nation to align immigration allowances with national needs and interests?
- ★ Is there something wrong with requiring immigrants to demonstrate that they will have gainful employment as a condition of nontourist entry, as is the case in most other countries?
- ★ You and others have made the point, and correctly, that no person in this country, including the president, should be above the law. So why is it that you believe that undocumented or illegal immigrants should be above the law and protected from federal law enforcement in hundreds of sanctuary jurisdiction?

On your vote: If you could not vote for yourself as president, for whom would you vote? If you had to vote for a candidate from the other political party, which one would you vote for?

3

Annual, Decennial, and Other Observations

January 7, 2020

As we begin the 2020s, I find myself reflecting on the last year, the last decade, the last quarter century, and even the last century. This column curates a selection of writings of interest on these things and offers some of my views as well.

The last year was dominated by impeachment fever and fractious fighting within the Democratic Party over the 2020 presidential nomination. These things almost make us forget so much else, such as the Mueller Report, which fizzled; the IG Report (executive summary and entire report here),[13] which did not fizzle and may foretell criminal proceedings against various high-ranking members of the intelligence and law enforcement communities; the revelation that rich Hollywood celebrities and others bribed their way into brand-name colleges for their underachieving children; the "blackface" scandals of Virginia Democratic officials; Jussie Smollett's strange escape from responsibility for his faked claims of racial torment in Chicago. These events and much more are remembered in the annual and always hilarious Dave Barry reminiscence about the past year. For those of you who may not have seen his 2019 Year in Review, it is right here.[14] It is a surefire way to get you thinking about the year in a healthy state of mind.

Other articles have commented on various aspects of the year. Suffice it here to say that the administration has confronted China in a more serious way than ever before, especially with respect to the theft of intellectual property and other serious trade and nontrade issues. There has been a rare and refreshing sense of near bipartisanship about the confrontation with the PRC over issues of unusual importance to the proper functioning of a competitive, market-based economy. The same cannot be said of any other aspect of foreign policy. Once upon a time, partisanship ended at the water's edge. Partisanship is now worldwide and knows no bounds. Both parties have involved foreign countries and political parties within countries in their own partisanship, which cannot help but degrade international relations and make it difficult for the nation to sustain coherent long-term policies.

One of the most important events of the last several years might have been the revelation last month regarding the false reports on the Afghanistan war provided to the American public by every administration going back to the beginning of the century. The erroneous reports came from every organ of government but most notably the State Department, the Defense Department, the intelligence community, and of course, the White House. Congressional oversight committees did their part to suppress much of what they knew. This was bipartisan obfuscation undertaken to avoid admitting that our policies in Afghanistan have been a failure from the day that Osama bin Laden escaped the country. The full reports (in six parts) may be found in this footnote, which will take readers to the Washington Post series.[15]

But almost as shocking as what they detailed is that the whole issue disappeared from newspaper front pages the day after it had dominated the headlines. What came back to the front page was the impeachment circus. The implications of our nation being unable to confront or address matters of great seriousness to focus instead on fractious partisanship is surely a sign of a nation in decline.

Right here[16] is a link to a podcast called *The Argument* put out by three columnists from the *New York Times*. A few minutes into it you get to the remarks by Ross Douthat linking the Afghanistan papers, the Iraq war, the financial crisis, and the general loss of massive credibility by the establishment elite of both parties, including those who testified for the Democrats during the House impeachment proceedings. He has also written about these things. See the Afghanistan papers, Americans' distrust in the experts who testified against Trump,[17] and the political establishment's loss of credibility.[18] These are valuable insights into the underlying reasons why a majority of both Democrats and Republicans reject their parties' "values" of the near past. All of this explains Trump, Sanders, and Warren as much as anything.

Then there was the incessant frothing about income and wealth inequality in America. The left seems ready to throw out the baby with the bathwater (get rid of capitalism) to address the issue. The right tends to deny that there is much of a problem. But there really is a problem, if not one of economics then at least a problem concerning optics and politics. Many Republicans (Trump supporters) and a majority of the Democrats (Sanders and Warren supporters) are politically motivated to address in some way the matter of income or wealth disparity. In this toxic political environment, it does not matter that virtually *all* Americans are in the top 1% worldwide. What seems to matter is that the top 1% in America have an outsized influence in politics (of both parties) and elsewhere. We are becoming a nation of people motivated more by jealousy and envy than by aspirational values.

That this concern arises in a setting of unprecedented full employment, economic growth, and stock market wealth is perhaps not surprising. My favorite economist, Robert Samuelson, has recently pointed out that important updated data show that a massive portion of all of these economic gains have found their way to the rich and the near-rich. See *Our Lopsided Prosperity*.[19] As Samuelson observes, the great and real danger here is social and political. The rich and the near-rich feel stigmatized unfairly for their successes, while many Americans below the top tier resent that their hard work has not given them the security and stability to which they feel entitled. This whole family of issues, along with those surrounding the impeachment theater, are likely to dominate the presidential campaign of 2020, which at the moment looks as if it could end up presenting all but the oldest of us with the first brokered convention during our lifetime.

The past decade (and even earlier) is especially interesting, and there have been a number of thoughtful columns from across the political spectrum providing insight. A refreshing reminder of important events occurring during the early years of the last decade is recorded in a *Washington Post* column by David Zak, entitled "The Decade has Ended but It Will Never Be Over."[20] Among other things, it is a reminder of just how undeveloped social media platforms were just a decade ago.

Worthy of note, too, are six short columns providing their own characterization of the last decade, described variously as the decade of unraveling, sharing, dissonance, anxiety, ouroboros, and retreat. Some of these observations are humorous, others serious. All are less than two hundred words and can be found here.[21] The final and (in my view) best is Robert Samuelson's column characterizing the last decade as the end of the "American Century." In a sense, the American Century began at the end of World War I in 1919, and it seems now to be the dawn of the Chinese Century. The spirit of nationalism that in part animates Trumpism will fight this, but just as the British Empire finally gave way to American domination of the post–World War II world stage (as evidenced most starkly by Eisenhower's refusal to support the British, French, and Israelis over Suez in 1956) so it seems likely that China, with help from Russia, Iran, and others will dilute substantially American influence in the western hemisphere over the next few decades.

There is another noteworthy Douthat column entitled "The Decade of Disillusionment,"[22] looking at the last thirty years as a triptych: the decade between the fall of the Soviet Union and 9/11; the decade thereafter; and then the decade just concluded. There is much in the column one might disagree with, but there is probably much more one might agree with. The '90's brought American dominance worldwide, and as Francis Fukuyama famously predicted, "the end of history." The aughts brought this notion to an end with 9/11 and follow-up events, most notably in Iraq and Afghanistan. And with those wars begun, and still in many ways going on, that decade pointed in a far different direction than the 1990s.

And the election of Barack Obama toward the end of the decade, for very complex reasons, brought us the beginning of unprecedented partisanship (the president's birth issue and the Tea Party, among other things) that has gotten much worse in the intervening four years. It began the era of "no compromise," ending up with the stunning 2016 electoral rejection of the professional political class, whether Republican or Democrat. Since then, it has been impeachment talk and, eventually, actual impeachment by the House focused on a phone call. An inappropriate phone call, yes, but unlikely ever to be found a hanging offense by the Senate. Indeed, as I write this on January 3, 100% of the Democratic Party presidential candidates have condemned the administration's termination of Iran's General Soleimani, in part on the ground that the president failed his constitutional duty to inform the Congress of his intended action. One senses that even this action may end up as a new article of impeachment in some fashion. Quite a distasteful spectacle that the termination of a man as dangerous as Bin Laden should become a faux issue in the Democratic primary.

Finally, on the decennial front, there is a whole decade's worth of Dave Barry annual reviews that should keep everyone in good spirits for a while: *Dave Barry 2009–18*.[23]

And so, as we enter the fourth decade after the collapse of the USSR, our national direction is up for grabs. But what is certain is this: about half of the citizenry will be angry. It has been said that our democracy depends on the consent of the losers. For at least the last few election cycles that consent has been denied and it will probably be denied after November 2020. So, despite the highest economic growth and lowest unemployment in a half-century, the road ahead is full of potholes and fraught with danger. Even more important than addressing the green planetary issues is the matter of addressing our broken political system. Future columns will address this both with brevity and with a couple of specific proposals that might work. Without repairing the political system, even the most sensible and well-intended policies, whatever they might be, cannot be agreed, pursued, or advanced.

4

Highlights of the Downward Spiral in American Education

January 21, 2020

It is difficult for me to think about education in America these days without thinking about how much has changed and how much seems to have been lost. I was recently asked to submit some reflections to my alma mater, Harvard College, on the occasion of my upcoming fifty-fifth reunion. What is set forth below is both an excerpt from and an expansion of those ruminations. There is more to say in a further effort down the road.

What I said in my essay was that I had neither the will nor the energy to put down on paper all the many things that have so defiled the American educational system. But the main points I mentioned implicated the watering down of the curricula, the absence of any common knowledge base among recent graduates of all colleges, the coddling and closing of the American mind (which begins and is sustained on college campuses such as Harvard), the insidious growth of cancellation history and historical revisionism, and the scandalous ways in which influential parents pry open the doors of brand-name schools for their inadequate children. These and many other aspects of higher education all bode very poorly for the future success of current undergraduates and for the country as a whole. Indeed, to the extent that our democracy depends upon a well-informed electorate to be successful, there is reason to doubt the long-term success of our entire system.

Many bright and talented young people will enter a world without adequate preparation, and without any expectation that they will ever have to make sacrifices. The strong pull of individualism, divorced as it has become from social responsibility, is breaking social bonds of family, community, church, employer, and the polity in general. Places like Harvard may think they are preparing young people for a life of contribution to causes greater than themselves, but from afar it looks more as if these young people are being prepared for a life of narcissistic self-absorption, unburdened by exposure to even the mildest of unwelcome points of view, and where they enjoy nearly unlimited rights while shouldering few if any actual responsibilities.

The current state of affairs has been building for many decades. Allan Bloom's *The Closing of the American Mind* was published in 1987, more than three decades ago. Bloom was a professor of philosophy at Cornell, and at the risk of gross oversimplification, a major premise of the book was that a "moral relativism" had taken over American universities and constructed barriers to notions of truth, critical thinking, and genuine knowledge. The book's subtitle is *How Higher Education Has Failed Democracy and Impoverished the Souls of Today's Students.* While no substitute for the book itself, here is a handy summary of its main points from Wikipedia, a kind of twenty-first-century substitute for Cliff's Notes.[24] The link in the notes contains several summaries of different reviews of the book by substantial supporters and opponents of the book's premises. For me, that book was the opening salvo in the academic theater of the culture wars.

Flashing forward to the present time we find more familiar critiques, such as in *The Coddling of the American Mind* by Greg Lukianoff and Jonathan Haidt, published in 2019, but anticipated in their lengthy 2015 article in *The Atlantic*.[25] and Anthony Kronman's 2019 *The Assault on American Excellence,* summarized in a *Wall Street Journal* op-ed piece, "The Downside of Diversity."[26]

Coddling is more up to date than *Closing.* It focuses on uniquely modern transgressions such as "microaggressions," most typically in the form of "offensive speech or conduct." For example, some campus guidelines condemn as a microaggression asking an Asian American or Latino American questions like "Where were you born?" because this implies that he or she is not a real American. These are not isolated matters. The deans and department chairs at the ten University of California system schools were presented by administrators at faculty leader-training sessions with examples of microaggressions, including "offensive" statements such as: "America is the land of opportunity," and "I believe the most qualified person should get the job."

The 1980s movement chronicled by Allan Bloom sought to restrict speech (hate speech aimed at marginalized groups) but also challenged the literary, philosophical, and historical canon, seeking to widen it by including more diverse perspectives. But now, decades later, the current movement is largely about emotional well-being. It presumes an extraordinary fragility of the collegiate psyche and therefore elevates the goal of protecting students from psychological harm. This movement seeks to punish anyone who interferes with that aim, even accidentally. *Coddling*'s authors conclude that this new protectiveness may be teaching students to think pathologically rather than critically. Both politically and collegiately students and others are encouraged to make moral judgments largely unhinged from critical thinking. And part of what we do when we make such moral judgments is to express allegiance to "a team." This further interferes with our ability to think critically, insofar as acknowledging that the other side's viewpoint has any merit runs the risk of being labeled a traitor by one's "teammates."

So, we get to the difference between critical thinking and emotional reasoning. Critical thinking requires grounding one's beliefs in evidence rather than emotion and learning how to search for and evaluate evidence that might contradict one's initial hypothesis. But little about campus life today fosters critical thinking. This seems to be true in the larger world as well. Instead, emotional reasoning increasingly dominates social and political debates and discussions. And a claim that someone's words are "offensive" is not just an expression of one's own subjective feeling; the speaker is publicly charged with objective wrongdoing. In this case, the speaker must apologize or be punished by some authority for committing an offense. The authors provide examples of punishments meted out to faculty and students alike for what seem like the most trivial of verbal or literary "offenses" (including reading a paperback book against the KKK but with a cover depicting a Klansman).

Federal law and regulation have amplified the problem. In 2013, the Department of Justice and Department of Education greatly broadened the definition of "sexual harassment" to include verbal conduct that is simply "unwelcome." One result is that universities, fearing federal investigations, now apply this same standard not just to sex but to race, religion, and veteran status as well. As the *Coddling* authors put it: emotional reasoning is now accepted as evidence.

Kronman's *The Downside of Diversity* begins with the following sentence:

> "Diversity" is the most powerful word in higher education today. No other has so much authority. Older words, like "excellence" and "originality," remain in circulation, but even they have been redefined in terms of diversity.

Kronman is not against diversity in every sense but only in the sense that it should not be rooted in racial, ethnic, religious, gender, or sexual identity. Rather, it should come in the form of diversity of thought. The lack of diversity of thought allowed on campuses is probably the most stunning feature of the twenty-first-century American college and university (and increasingly other corporate and governmental institutions), at least in my judgment. The demand for diversity has steadily weakened the norms of objectivity and truth and substituted for them a culture of grievance and group loyalty. One of the points Kronman makes, which ought not be controversial, turns out to be just that:

> Whatever else it may be, the truth is not democratic. We don't decide what is true in mathematics or history or philosophy by a show of hands. The idea of truth assumes a distinction between what people believe it is and the truth itself. Socrates drove this point home in every conversation he had. It might be called the Socratic premise of all intellectual inquiry.

The damage to the academy is obvious. But even greater is the damage to our democratic way of life, which needs all the independent mindedness its citizens and leaders can summon—especially at a moment when our basic norms of truthfulness and honesty are mocked every day by a president who respects neither. Especially interesting reviews of this book are here [27] and here.[28]

And then there is the student debt fiasco, which I have previously discussed in these pages. Stunningly, undergraduates can obtain massive loans without parental consent. The total amount of outstanding student debt is $1.7 trillion.[29] This exceeds all the credit card debt in the United States put together. This tsunami of readily available cash permits colleges to increase their tuition, room, board, and other fees nearly in lockstep and at a rate of increase that far exceeds any known cost of living index. These loans, like tax obligations, are not dischargeable in bankruptcy either.

At the risk of wading into a fierce political issue, it makes no sense to me to ask people who never went to college, and others who worked while in college to avoid the debt, to take responsibility for paying off the obligations of those who volunteered to incur debts to receive their education. This is an extreme example of moral hazard, something that seems to have become passé. Better to allow this obligation to be discharged in bankruptcy and then to make the educational institution that received the funds responsible for some portion of the defaulted debt, say, 35 to 50% or so. This is a market-based approach that would provide colleges and universities with some interest in the success of their students and an incentive to minimize their debt.

As with so many things in this country these days, there are enormous economic interests at stake. And there is no political will to address the problem using more than a few words on a bumper sticker or in a political slogan. Sensible solutions are, as a result, unlikely. And higher educational institutions have a large financial interest in being part of the problem rather than being part of a solution.

It would be nice to see our colleges and universities do something useful to address the actual problems that beset America, including decreasing the cost of education, educating students in ways that make them share some important basic foundational material, and more generally to inculcate a set of values that can enthusiastically accommodate a broad spectrum of political views from left to right (or right to left).

The strength of our democracy depends on a well-educated voting population, something that is being lost bit by bit and day by day. One suspects (or at least I suspect) that a frightening number of actual voters in America could not pass the same test that immigrants must pass to acquire citizenship. The way that universities have permitted the arts and the humanities to disappear almost completely from school curricula strikes me as subtle evidence of an enormous problem: a disconnect from education writ large. I have my doubts that even our most esteemed educational institutions are up to the task. But hope springs eternal.

5

The Rise of Law and Decline of Politics

March 3, 2020

I have recently finished reading an extraordinary book by Jonathan Sumption entitled *Trials of The State and the Decline of Politics*. It is one of those rare books that is as trenchant as it is short (it is about 125 pages). The book, published late last year in Great Britain, is essentially a publication of five separate lectures broadcast on BBC Radio 4 during the summer of 2019. Sumption is a British judge and historian who served as a justice on the UK Supreme Court from 2012 the 2018 and is only one of five people to be promoted directly from the bar to the highest court. According to one of the blurbs on the dust jacket of the paperback copy, his shaggy white hair covers "the biggest brain in Britain." But there is nothing intimidating about the book, which is written with unusual simplicity and clarity. And while much of the focus of the book is on law and politics as they evolved in the United Kingdom, the book has considerable explicit and implicit relevance to law and politics today in the United States.

The book comprises five chapters: (1) "Law's Expanding Empire," (2) "In Praise of Politics," (3) "Human Rights and Wrongs," (4) "Lessons from America," and (5) "Constitutions, New and Old." The very first sentence is attention grabbing: "In the beginning, there was chaos and brute force, a world without law." He goes on to point out that in the mythology of ancient Athens, Agamemnon sacrificed his daughter so that the gods would allow his fleet to sail against Troy. His wife murdered him to avenge the deed, and she in turn was murdered by her son. Athena, the goddess of wisdom, put an end to the cycle of violence by creating a court to impose a solution in what today we would call the public interest: a solution based on reason, on the experience of human frailty, and on fear of the alternative. Aeschylus in the *Oresteia* trilogy had Athena justify her intervention in the world of mortals as follows: "Let no man live uncurbed by law, nor curbed by tyranny."

The expansion of law, especially in the last century, is one of the most significant phenomena of our time. And in this country, even more so than in Great Britain, the law touches nearly everything. The law has more power than the family regarding the well-being of children. The law has more power over social behavior than most churches and increasing power over commerce at every level. The expansion of individual and group constitutional rights has placed matters before courts that, in virtually every other developed country in the world, are handled by legislatures and hence have the power of real political legitimacy.

Further, the proliferation of administrative agencies within the federal government has permitted elected officials to avoid voting for or against whatever it is that those administrative agencies do by regulation on a day-to-day basis. This protects them against the anger of voters and makes all forms of regulation—whether of individuals, farms, factories, or other enterprises, a matter for adjudication by the courts. This somewhat subtle abandonment of responsibility by elected officials in favor of the work of agencies and courts has contributed to massive divisiveness in societies around the world but especially in the United States. The active membership in political parties has been abandoned to small numbers of activists who are increasingly unrepresentative of those who vote for them. One effect has been to obstruct the ability of parties to function as instruments of compromise and to limit the range of options on offer to the electorate. Sumption finds this a "dangerous position."

Sumption addresses uncomfortable truths, one of them being that an important object of modern democratic constitutions is to treat the people as the source of legitimacy, while placing barriers between them and the levers of power. They do this in order to contain the fissiparous tendencies of democracy and to counter its inherent tendency to destroy itself when majorities become a source of instability and oppression. One of these barriers is the concept of representation, and the other is law, with its formidable bias in favor of individual rights and its corps of professional judges who are not accountable to the electorate for their decisions.

We learn that in Great Britain, as in the United States, if you were to sit in on an appeal in the UK Supreme Court on a question of public law, you would notice that in addition to the advocates of the parties, there are numerous lawyers representing "interveners," or what in the American system we call *amici curiae* or "friends of the court." As here, these are nothing more than very expensive lobbyists. They are typically single-issue pressure groups with highly specific political agendas. Often, if not always, they present agendas that the legislature has refused to adopt but could still be imposed through the courts. Their presence is symptomatic of a profound change in the constitutional role of the courts. As Sumption puts it: "To adapt the famous dictum of the German military theorist Clausewitz about war, law is now the continuation of politics by other means." Sounds very familiar.

In Britain, judges have been nominated by a nonpolitical commission since 2006. But there are demands that they should be subject to political scrutiny before their appointment takes effect. Sumption believes that the political character of much of their work will sooner or later make these demands irresistible. And he points out that in United States the result has been the appointment of judges *because* of their identification with known political positions. He fears that in Great Britain, such a change would transform the entire nature of the legal process and discredit the judges who work in it as has already happened to a nontrivial extent here.

And so, he gets to the heart of the matter about what is going on in the judiciary in this country. He believes that the judicial resolution of policy issues undermines the single biggest advantage of the political process, which is to accommodate the divergent interests and opinions of citizens. And even though politics in Great Britain and the United States may not be doing a good job of accommodating these divergent interests, the courts do not "accommodate" at all: they decide in the context of what in most cases is a zero-sum game. Given that successful democracies depend on the consent of the losers, constant recourse to the judiciary on vital matters of social or economic policy creates losers who simply will not accept the system anymore. One would have to have been under a rock for many years not to see this happening all around us right now.

Thus, here we are, one fifth of the way through the twenty-first century, watching presidential candidates of both parties seeking votes on the basis that they will appoint judges whose opinions will be in the interests of those who vote for them. We see a president suggesting that at least two respected

Supreme Court justices should recuse themselves in matters involving his administration; we see individual justices aligning themselves closely with one or another political party's interest groups; we see senior legislators still fulminating at the confirmation of a Supreme Court justice whose legitimacy they do not accept and whom they would not hesitate to impeach if they could; we see senior legislators scheming to "pack" the Supreme Court in another administration; we see individual justices making political comments that become public, demonstrating obvious political leanings; and then we see Chief Justice Roberts seeking (lamely and ineffectively in my opinion) to suggest that "we do not have Obama judges or Trump judges, Bush judges or Clinton judges. What we have is an extraordinary group of dedicated judges doing their level best to do equal right to those appearing before them. That independent judiciary is something we should all be thankful for."

There was a time when this may have been so, but that time passed no later than 1986, when Judge Robert Bork was denied a seat on the Supreme Court solely for political reasons. That time may have passed even earlier than that, but the name "Bork" quickly became a verb and is still in common use. Judges whose views are too pure (or too impure) get "Borked" by the Senate.

There are at least two approaches to mitigating the current or looming catastrophe, and they are uncomplicated in their own way, albeit hugely controversial. One approach is to begin to limit the breadth or number of certain constitutional rights and remit them back to legislatures where they probably should have been resolved in many cases. To pick an example of something that has created much discord, the constitutional right to privacy was discovered in a 1965 criminal case involving poor Mr. and Mrs. Griswold. They were famously prosecuted by the great state of Connecticut for using contraceptives in the privacy of their own bedroom in their own home, a practice criminalized in 1879 by the Connecticut legislature.

The stupendous idiocy of the State of Connecticut for bringing the case notwithstanding, the existence of an archaic and stupid statute enforced by foolish prosecutors was not a sufficient basis for elevating the right of privacy to a constitutional level. But the Supreme Court did just that in *Griswold v. Connecticut.* The court, by a 7–2 margin, found a right of marital privacy to be within the penumbra of the specific guarantees of the Bill of Rights. The expansion of this and other allied rights thus removed from legislatures any ability to mediate various social issues to a political resolution.

Why this point is broader than it might sound is shown by a brief digression into one of the underpinnings of Brexit. Few Americans are likely to know very much about the European Convention on Human Rights, much less Article 8 thereof. I certainly knew little about it until spending several years in Brussels practicing law before the European Commission, and this sensitivity was much sharpened by reading Sumption's book. To make a long story very short, the European Convention on Human Rights (ECHR) was adopted by the British parliament through Britain's Human Rights Act of 1998. It came into effect in 2000. That parliamentary law empowered, indeed mostly obliged, British courts to strike down any rule of common law, regulation, or government decision found to be incompatible with the Convention. It required the courts to apply muscular principles of interpretation to statutes with a view to making them conform with the Convention. If interpretation of this kind was not possible, then an act of parliament could be declared incompatible with the Convention. Furthermore, the Human Rights Act *required* the British courts to take account of the rulings of the European Court of Human Rights, the international court set up in Strasbourg to interpret the Convention.

While many in Britain disliked being told how to conduct their affairs by a foreign court, the deeper and more nuanced objection to the entire process derived from the impact that the European Convention and the Human Rights Court had on the way that Britain made laws for its own society. Notably, the ECHR was drafted in the aftermath of the Second World War, under the shadow of the Gestapo and the concentration camps of the Third Reich. Initially created to address notions of "inhuman or degrading" treatment, these notions expanded over time. But Article 8 of the Convention involved miles of mission creep. For example, Article 8 now protects the human right to private and family life, as well as the privacy of the home and of personal correspondence. The Strasbourg court developed this human rights expansion into what it today calls a "principle of personal autonomy."

Sumption points out that a very similar development has occurred in the United States courts in relation to the right to liberty under the Fourteenth Amendment (and of course the right to privacy created in *Griswold* and its progeny). Much like the expansion of individual and group rights in the United States under the US Constitution, the Strasbourg court has held that a vast range of issues to be covered by Article 8, including: the legal status of illegitimate children, immigration and deportation, extradition, criminal sentencing, abortion, artificial insemination, homosexuality, same-sex unions, child abduction, the policing of public demonstrations, planning and environmental law, eviction for nonpayment of rent, and much more. None of these intrusions on personal liberty have been agreed by the signatory states. They are all extensions of the text of Article 8, which rest on the sole authority of the judges of the Strasbourg court. This came to be seen in Britain as what it was: a form of nonconsensual legislation. This great expansion of "fundamental human rights" transformed the ECHR from an expansion of noble values almost universally shared into something meaner. As Sumption puts it:

> It has become a template against which to assess most aspects of the ordinary domestic legal order, including some highly disputable ones. The result is to devalue the whole notion of universal human rights.

This brings us to a very similar proposition here in the United States. Human rights law, or simply the declaration of individual rights based on nonstatutory or non legislative sources, transforms controversial political issues into questions of law for the courts. To quote Sumption again:

> If we are going to deal with fundamental human rights in a way that has such radical implications, then we need to have a very clear idea of what a fundamental human right really is. In particular, we have to distinguish a fundamental human right from something that is merely a good idea.

It was in part this slow and inexorable loss of control or influence over their own lives and liberty in various spheres that motivated many Britons to choose Brexit over remaining in the European Union. It would be a mistake for American citizens not to appreciate that something of the same dynamic brought about the election of Mr. Trump in 2016 and may well do the same for Mr. Sanders (or Mr. Trump again) in 2020.

 A second approach is to reduce substantially deference that the federal courts are today obliged to give to decisions of federal administrative agencies and the hundreds of thousands of pages of regulations that each of these agencies promulgates every year. But reducing that deference would clog the courts and, in any case, would not be complete without at the same time making elected officials in the House of Representatives and the Senate politically responsible for the enactment of those regulations. Just requiring elected officials to vote for or against these regulations could have a substantial impact on the ability of otherwise unaccountable agencies to regulate our personal, social, economic, and other affairs. Much has been written on this, and it is not a short topic, but it is conceptually simple.

The main if not only point of these approaches would be to return the judiciary to something much more akin to "calling balls and strikes": to get judges out of the business of having such a deep commitment to one or another political party and to try to take ideology out of the judiciary and to leave as much of it as possible in the legislatures.

These things may not happen in my lifetime, but if they do not happen in the lifetime of the next generation, we should not be terribly surprised to see both law and politics continue their precipitous downward trajectory.

6

Movies, Series, and Books

March 31, 2020

Like everyone, I have been deluged with a tsunami of information about COVID-19. Each day the news delivers an endless Möbius strip of virus news, one day pretty much like the prior day but with slight differences. The cable opinion and media op-ed pieces hurling blame diatribes are the differences, and their onslaughts continue as if this were the normal response to a public health and economic catastrophe, teaching us at least two things: (1) there is no politician alive who will not seek a political advantage from a crisis, no matter how catastrophic (interesting opinion piece on that score here[30]) and (2) sadly, COVID-19 confirms what has been said for a few years now—we have devolved into an unserious nation. We have a strong bipartisan preference for fixing responsibility and blame rather than fixing problems. Nero fiddled while Rome burned. In this country, our officials (and media-siloed supporters) prefer simply to squabble while the systems begin to collapse.

So, here we all are, more or less under house arrest. As a result, I have been thinking about how to pass the time and how I can make a modest, positive and practical contribution to readers. So, I offer up my own curated selection of movies, binge-worthy series, and books all of which I heartily suggest are worthy of your attention. By the highly subjective standards of our household, they are all either five-star or four-star. I start with movies since these tend to be two hours or less and do not necessarily demand long-term attention or commitment. Here goes. Fasten seat belts.

Movies

Unexpected Jewels

1. *The Pope of Greenwich Village* (1984)
2. *The Mission* (1986)
3. *Cider House Rules* (1999)
4. *Memento* (2000)
5. *The Painted Veil* (2006)
6. *The Illusionist* (2006)
7. *In Bruges* (2008)
8. *The Grand Budapest Hotel* (2014)
9. *The Green Book* (2018)

Lasting Favorites (much older stuff)

I'm not going to include well-known super-good movies such as *The Godfather* (I and II) or *The Shawshank Redemption*, among others, on the assumption that everyone alive knows about them. But like those gems, the following are movies I tend to watch even if I bump into them mid-movie. I lump several of the Tom Hanks movies together even though they are not all equal. I put *Saving Private Ryan* at the top of my Tom Hanks list. Hard to believe that was twenty-two years ago!

1. *The Princess Bride* (1987)
2. *Stand By Me* (1986)
3. *Goodfellas* (1990)
4. *Pulp Fiction* (1994)
5. *Moulin Rouge* (2001)
6. *Chicago* (2002)
7. Our favorite Tom Hanks movies
    a. *Big* (1988)
    b. *Sleepless in Seattle* (1993)
    c. *Apollo 13* (1995)
    d. *Toy Story* (all four: 1995. 1999, 2010, 2019)
    e. *Saving Private Ryan* (1998)
    f. *The Green Mile* (1999)

    g. *Cast Away* (2000)
    h. *Bridge of Spies* (2015)
    i. *Beautiful Day in the Neighborhood* (2019)

Others Hard to Categorize, but Very Good

1. *Body Heat* (1981)
2. *Midnight Run* (1988)
3. *Slumdog Millionaire* (2008)
4. *Inglourious Basterds* (2009)
5. *Life of Pi* (2012)
6. *1917* (2019)
7. The Boston movies (I like the Affleck movies the best and of those probably *The Departed* the most)
    a. *Good Will Hunting* (1997)
    b. *Mystic River* (2003)
    c. *The Departed* (2006)
    d. *The Town* (2010)
    e. *Shutter Island* (2010)
    f. *Gone Girl* (2014)
    g. *Spotlight* (2015)
    h. *Manchester by the Sea* (2016)

Binge-worthy Series from Around the World

The United States

The breakthrough for this format was *The Sopranos*, which ran six seasons from 1999, eighty-six episodes in all. Organized crime boss as human with family. Then came *Mad Men*, which started in 2007 and lasted for seven seasons and ninety-two episodes, but the first three to four years were the best. Madison Avenue in the 1960s. The year 2008 brought us *Breaking Bad*. Cancer-stricken high school chemistry teacher becomes producer of high-quality crystal meth and gets deep into organized crime. The series lasted five years (sixty-two episodes). I believe this is the best television series ever produced anywhere in the world, ever!

A strong and memorable character in the series was a criminal lawyer named Saul whose billboard was *Better Call Saul*. A spinoff of that name began in 2015. It is a superb prequel showing how he came to be the character in *Breaking Bad*. Compelling, and now in its fifth season (forty-six episodes).

Game of Thrones, eight seasons from 2011 to 2019, seventy-three episodes. You will either love it, hate it, or not understand it. I loved it. Then of course there is *Homeland*, which was superb for three to four seasons but tails off a bit later. It was based on an Israeli thriller *Hatufim* (2011–2020). Eight seasons, ninety-one episodes. Sort of espionage thriller, but more.

My favorite American production after *Breaking Bad* is *The Americans*, which I found scarily addictive. Russian KGB agents posing as US citizens with children they were required to produce to protect their cover. They end up living in suburban Virginia across the street from the FBI agent (and his family) charged with finding Russian "illegals." Seven seasons from 2013 to 2018, seventy-five episodes. Constant tension. You end up fearing for the Russians if not affirmatively rooting for them. Brilliant.

An especially worthy shorter series is *Fargo,* three seasons, thirty episodes from 2014, 2015, 2017, and a fourth season in the works for 2020. Each year a different story and different cast. All excellent, but the first season especially so for Billy Bob Thornton fans like me. *Goliath* is another Billy Bob Thornton series. Solo lawyer fights big boys. Excellent. Three seasons, twenty-four episodes, with a fourth season in the offing.

The Wire was a sleeper when it first came out. Today it is thought to be one of the finest American series ever produced. And it all takes place in the 410 area code in Baltimore and environs. Familiar places and people. All-star cast and program. Many people watch the entire series again a year later just to be reminded how much they loved it. Each season takes on a different feature of Baltimore: drugs, politics, the press, the harbor, etc. Hard not to watch at least two episodes at a time. Sometimes three.

A current offering, *Ozark,* just began season three this last weekend. Corrupt but engaging and clever financial advisor forced to leave Chicago after a money laundering scheme goes wrong. He takes his family to a small town on Lake Ozark to hide out. But he is found and must make amends to a Mexican cartel by laundering huge amounts of their cash, no easy feat. A touch of *Breaking Bad*, but quite different and right now the most popular thing in the land after a slow viewership start. Three seasons so far, thirty episodes.

A hidden gem is the first season of *True Detective* starring Matthew McConaughey, Woody Harrelson, and other excellent actors. The season is set in Louisiana and follows a pair of Louisiana state police detectives in their pursuit of a serial killer over a seventeen-year period. The second season set in Los Angeles is ordinary and forgettable, but it returns to quality in the third season, with the episodes set in the Ozarks. Each season is eight episodes. There is no connection between the cast or the storyline season to season. But it is really just the first season that puts the program on this list.

Big Little Lies is upscale soap opera with a cast of best actress winners, including Nicole Kidman, Meryl Streep, and Reese Witherspoon. Set in Monterey, it is a dark comedy murder mystery. Not great drama or a great story, but great acting. Light, frothy, a fine escape as was *Revenge* (although that had little acting talent to speak of and a weak storyline). Two seasons (2017–2018), fourteen episodes.

Ken Burns series like *Baseball* and *Vietnam* are nearly always binge-worthy. These two especially.

Britain

Downton Abbey reminded my family of the fine offerings of British filmmaking. It started in 2010 and ran six seasons, fifty-three episodes. Starts in 1912 and ends well after WWI and the start of the decline of the landed gentry and the splendid country houses. An updated and higher quality variation on the old *Upstairs Downstairs* series that ran from 1971–1975. Also, now a movie, but the series is must-see TV.

Once one begins to explore British television series (via Britbox, Acorn TV, BBC America, Netflix, Amazon Prime, and others), there is too much to mention here. Many but not all of the series are murder mysteries of one sort or another. The granddaddy of these is *Midsomer Murders*, now in its twenty-first year and still going strong. It began in 1997, and thus far there are 124 episodes, most of which are ninety minutes long, and so each is almost movie length. The shows are engaging but not too demanding. And one can watch an episode ten years later (or two years later) and enjoy it as much as the first time since one can never remember the vital details of any one episode.

Even before that was *Prime Suspect*, which starred a young Helen Mirren as a female chief inspector in London's Metropolitan Police Service. It lasted seven seasons but only two episodes per season. It ran from 1991 to 1996 and then 2003 and 2006. Really good!

The Crown, still ongoing, has thus far served up three seasons and thirty episodes following the reign of Queen Elizabeth from her youth until the recent past. It is a drama, not a biography, but it seems broadly faithful to historical fact. If that sounds dull, it is not. It is simply spellbinding. For its genre, this is in a class of its own. *Queen Victoria* is a similar genre but not quite as superb. Three seasons. Twenty-five episodes.

Wolf Hall, released in 2015, is just one season, six episodes and it leaves one waiting anxiously for another to continue the saga. Based on Hillary Mantel's *Wolf Hall* and *Bring up the Bodies,* it follows the career of Thomas Cromwell and is faithful to the main historical events of the period under Henry VIII between 1529 and 1536, covering the downfall of Katherine of Aragon, Cardinal Woolsey, Thomas More, and in 1536, the beheading of Ann Boleyn. We burned through it in two evenings. The final book in the trilogy, *The Mirror and the Light,* just came out. I have not yet read it, although the ending is not a mystery. Thomas Cromwell himself goes to the block in 1640. But the story between his beheading and that of Ann Boleyn in 1736 is apparently the range of the third volume.

Foyle's War is a hidden gem that started in 2002 and lasted eight seasons, but only twenty-eight episodes. Michael Kitchens, a superb actor, is Chief Superintendent Foyle in Hastings, Sussex. The lovable Honeysuckle Weeks (great name, by the way) is his driver Samantha. The series begins with a murder victim found in the rubble of a bombed building after a German raid on London in 1940. Crime solving during wartime. The series progresses with various British-centric war events chronologically in the background. Totally addictive. Another war-related show that engages is *The Bletchley Circle,* two seasons, seven episodes about four women who worked as code breakers. The series evolves into early 1950s detective work. Very good stuff.

Other really good British crime drama offerings include *Luther,* starring Idris Elba (who also features prominently in *The Wire*). Five seasons 2010–2019, twenty episodes. Then there is *Sherlock,* a twenty-first-century hi-tech Sherlock Holmes played by Benedict Cumberbatch. Four seasons, twenty episodes. Back in the USA, there is also a competing Sherlock, *Elementary,* seven seasons starting in 2012 and 154 episodes. Set largely in New York. Uneven, but mostly very good.

Back in Britain we have *Happy Valley,* set in West Yorkshire. Started 2014. Two seasons, 12 episodes. Sad to see it end. Ditto *Broadchurch* (2013–2017, twenty-four episodes) and *Vera* (2011–2020, forty episodes). All excellent classic British mysteries. *Murder in Paradise* is a frothy mystery series. Unserious and almost comedic. Filmed in the Caribbean. Light but pleasant entertainment. One gets attached to the characters.

The Night Manager, a six-hour rendering of the John le Carré novel of the same name, is my all-time favorite short series. Even the opening credits are masterful. I find John le Carré to be an outstanding writer in any genre, and his novels are impossible to squish into a two-hour movie. Their depth and complexity demand several hours of immersion in his many-layered story and the characters. This one is near perfect in doing just that. But see also the 1979 seven-part series of *Tinker, Tailor, Soldier, Spy* starring Alec Guinness as George Smiley. While slightly dated, it is the perfect melding of actor and character.

One of the most popular series ever in Britain is *Line of Duty*, which began in 2012, and ran five seasons with twenty-nine episodes. It is focused on an anticorruption unit called AC-12. It gets into the deep-rooted corruption involving the police and organized crime. Riveting.

The Honourable Woman, a 2014 eight-episode political spy thriller set in the Middle East. Hard not to blow through it in three days.

Not all British television is police and spies. There is medical humor in *Doc Martin*. Short (thirty-minute) episodes are quite a rarity these days. You cannot help becoming very attached to all the recurring (and quirky) characters. Wonderful. Nine series, seventy episodes. There is also *Mr. Selfridge,* a period drama about Harry Selfridge and his department store in London set from 1908–1928. Four seasons, forty episodes. Similarly themed is the costume drama *The Paradise,* coproduced by the BBC and Masterpiece. It is set in 1875 London and revolves around the lives of the store's owner and employees. As good as, but not as successful as, *Mr. Selfridge.* Two seasons, sixteen episodes.

Then there is *Outlander* (2014–2020), involving time travel. Do not let this be off-putting. Married British nurse (1946) visiting Inverness during postwar deferred honeymoon finds herself hurled back in time to the same area a couple of years before the 1746 Battle of Culloden. She is eventually smitten by a young Scot, a Highlander Jacobite leader from Clan McKenzie. It has some *Back to the Future* qualities but is not comedic at all. Serious drama. The slaughter of the Jacobites by the redcoats at Culloden cannot be changed despite efforts. First two seasons (set in Scotland and Paris) are especially gripping and addictive. It slows down a bit as they escape the redcoats to North Carolina and the New World, but it picks up again. Now in the middle of Season five. Sixty-one episodes.

There are also short stand-alone pieces like *A Very English Scandal*. Just three episodes. Hugh Grant as MP Jeremy Thorpe. To say much more would be to reveal spoilers. A terrific one evening three-hour binge perhaps.

European Offerings

Once you get deeply into British offerings, it is a short hop to get to Scotland, Ireland, and Europe, especially northern Europe and Scandinavia. Here are a few good ones. Skip if you cannot handle foreign languages or subtitles. Your loss though.

From Germany *Babylon Berlin*, fourth season just now released. Neo noir. The entire series takes place in Berlin during the Weimar Republic starting in 1929. The lead character is a WWI veteran suffering from shellshock (PTSD). He is a police inspector from Cologne on a secret mission to dismantle an extortion ring thought to have compromising pornographic material implicating senior government leaders. Everything about the program is just about pitch perfect. *Cabaret* combined with tense police procedural with Nazis on the rise. Also, from Germany comes *Deutschland 83* about a young East German military officer sent to West Germany as an undercover spy for the East German intelligence service. The first season has eight episodes. The second was retitled *Deutschland 86,* and the third season, *Deutschland 89,* will be released this year. Slight resemblance to *The Americans*, but very slight.

From Norway, we like *Occupied* (political thriller 2015–2016, original idea by Jo Nesbø, third season just released. Now twenty-four episodes) and *The Heavy Water War,* a six-episode series about the effort to disable the Norwegian plant that produced heavy water, to deny it to the German effort to develop a nuclear weapon. The story is said to be historically accurate although some historians quibble. Very good.

Canada

Bad Blood, two seasons, fourteen episodes. Canadian organized crime in Quebec and Montreal. Loved it.

Also, *Flashpoint* about a SWAT team in Toronto. Tense shooting scenes balanced by fascinating character development in the ensemble cast. Contrasts with US shows in attitudes toward firearms. Five seasons, forty episodes.

France

Engrenage (Spiral). French police, lawyers, judges. Darker than *The Wire*, and not as addictive. But addictive still. Seven seasons, seventy episodes. Ongoing.

Mixed Productions

Chernobyl, 2019 five-episode series. British/US collaboration. No excuse not to watch this splendid (and somewhat chilling) series.

Scotland

Hamish Macbeth (1995–1997, twenty episodes). Slightly dated but still charming police procedural. Light escape. Unlike many of these, suitable for children. And again thanks to WDM, *Shetland,* following Detective Inspector Henshall, who has returned to the Shetland Islands after his wife's death to raise his daughter. In the beginning, he takes on local crimes but then increasingly bad criminals as the series moves forward. You may need subtitles to master the Scottish accents, happily a feature that most Smart TVs or portals offer (even for programs in English). Five seasons, twenty-six episodes.

Spain

High Seas. Two seasons so far, sixteen episodes. Soap opera on a ship. Period piece. Entertaining. Not "riveting" but nice to watch.

Israel

Fauda. This translates to "chaos" from the Hebrew. It deals with frontline issues in the Israeli/Palestinian conflict. Compelling and tense. Third season just released. Thirty-six episodes so far. Quite intense.

Spy, six-episode miniseries about an Israeli Mossad Arab agent sent into Syria via Buenos Aires to spy in the time leading up to the 1967 Six-Day War. He is uncovered in the end by the Russians and executed. This is not a spoiler as we learn this in the first few minutes. The tension is in how it all unfolds.

Ireland

Dublin Murders. We are just now almost through this. This eight-episode miniseries is complex, riveting, and very engaging. A murder in the woods in 2006 is related to a murder in 1985 in the same woods, and the detective inspector in charge of the 2006 investigation was with the children when they disappeared in 1985; his female partner has a mysterious past as an undercover police officer, revealed in bits and flashbacks. There is constant tension from many angles throughout each episode. We shall finish it before this is published.

Books.

More than a decade ago, I started listening to books using the audible.com software. Commuting for several years back and forth every weekday from Easton to Washington (nearly four hours per day in the car) was a perfect way to get through one or two books each week, which became about eighty-plus books per year. Over time, our "audible books listened-to list" came to number in the hundreds. Now the technology has advanced. I can and do buy a Kindle edition and then also get the audible version. I can read the Kindle and then pick up in the last spot listening and then pick up where I stopped listening on the Kindle. Talk about the best of all worlds. Also, a smartphone can be placed under the pillow, a timer set, and the reader will either keep you awake or read you to sleep, depending on the book and the point in the book. But I also still buy actual books whenever I find a local independent locally owned bookstore, which at the moment seems to be only in St. Michaels now that the News Center closed, an unpleasant surprise from which I may never recover.

Anyway, the following selections are subjective, sometimes organized around writers, sometimes organized according to readers, and sometimes barely organized at all. But I will start with Albert Camus's *La Peste* (*The Plague*), written in 1947. In a commercial port in Algeria, a disease appears as if from nowhere. It begins inconspicuously, with the appearance of a few disordered rats and then works its way virulently through the human population, aided by indifference, hypocrisy, laziness. Shops close, streets empty. But the infection picks up steam, spreading according to a geometric progression, producing a steeply rising "death graph." *En masse,* the city is quarantined, but inside its walls there is a shortage of medical staff and lifesaving equipment and a controversy over whether masks are useless. And much more. It's relevance to COVID-19 "lashes you across the face." The perfect companion to the times; unless you seek a total escape from the times.

Now, I move to readers because there are some readers who are so outstanding to my ear that I will "read" (that is, listen to) anything they do. At the top of this list for me is Patrick Tull. He is dead now (2006) but he was my introduction to great books through listening. Here is the best of what he has done that I have listened to.

1. The entire *Master and Commander* series, comprising twenty-and-a-half books, each about ten to twelve hours. This is the series by Patrick O'Brian that captivates nearly all men who read the books (and a few women, too). They are set around the Napoleonic wars and center on Captain Jack Aubrey of the Royal Navy and his ship's surgeon, Stephen Maturin. Readers come away with broad and deep knowledge of much of the history of that era, not to mention vast knowledge of the many details of sailing vessels of the era. Many people who have actually read the books choose then to listen to them once they discover Patrick Tull.
2. Many Dickens novels, most notably *Great Expectations, The Pickwick Papers, and David Copperfield.* These books come alive under his command. Incidentally, *The Pickwick Papers,* Dickens's first book is not well known. As read by Tull it is beyond hilarious. A true treasure.
3. *Rumpole of the Bailey Series.* Tull does not read all of these, but those he does read are not to be missed. Each story is maybe forty minutes,

so they are quickly digestible one at a time (there are dozens, too). The constant humor is understated British droll to a T (or a bottle of Chateau Thames). Excellent material, especially for lawyers. Their author is John Mortimer, a brilliant British lawyer and writer. His autobiography, *Clinging to the Wreckage,* is read by Tull and should be heard.

4. The *Brother Cadfael Chronicles.* This is a series of some twenty-odd books featuring Brother Cadfael, a Benedictine Monk. The books are set in a monastery in twelfth-century England and can be described as a kind of crime drama. Nearly all are narrated by Tull, and those are well worth the time.

There are other readers who pair well with writers. John le Carré reads a lot of his own books, and most of those he does not read are read by Michael Jayston, whose voice seems almost the same. There is not a le Carré book I would hesitate to recommend, whether by reading or by listening. For the spy/international dramatic story, there is no better writer. He is a writers' writer. But even other great writers consider him to be the master, and not just of one genre, but simply as a writer of great novels involving complicated stories and nuanced characters.

Another writer whom I find strong and engaging is Robert Harris, also British. Four of his books in particular I found unusually good. *An Officer and a Spy* is a spellbinding dramatic historical novel about the Dreyfus affair in France in the late nineteenth century. Just as good, in fact even better in a way, is the Cicero trilogy: *Imperium, Conspirata, and Dictator.* Taken together, these are heavily researched dramatizations of the life of Marcus Aurelius Cicero and the transformation of Rome from republic to dictatorship. The books, narrated by his slave/secretary, are set in the period from 80 to 45 BC, a time when Caesar, Pompey the Great, Mark Antony, Cicero, and Cato all vied for influence within the increasingly fractious dissolving Roman republic. These are a great way to learn more than you might have thought possible about this era while turning pages (or listening) with full attention. Harris's *The Ghost Writer,* while not a "great book" per se, is a wonderful and cleverly developed espionage story.

A few years ago, we stumbled across a small but extraordinary collection of books about China. Three of the best of these are written or coauthored by Jung Chang, who survived the Cultural Revolution and ended up at Yale and then London. Her masterpiece is *Mao: The Unknown Story* (2005). The sweep and extraordinarily researched detail of this book are beyond astonishing. It is the most detailed biography of Mao ever written, and it puts almost everything else ever written about him to shame. Its only critic, so far as I can tell, is Henry Kissinger, who evidently was thoroughly misled by Mao and his cadres and has his credibility to defend. He loses. This is a long book that proceeds slowly and chronologically with great patience and detail. Anyone wanting to know about China in general and Mao must read or listen to it. Once it has been read or heard, the reader will never think about China or Mao in the same way ever again. Mao was one of the worst mass murderers in history. Probably worse than Hitler or Stalin. Until now, the details of all that were simply not known outside China.

Jung Chang has written two other superb books: *Wild Swans* (1991) and *Empress Dowager Cixi* (2013). The former is the story of her grandmother and mother (and her young self eventually) and their survival under the Japanese, the Nationalists (Chiang Kai-shek) and eventually Mao and the Communists. It is a harrowing tale, presented in such a way that it cannot be put down for long. The latter is an engaging biography of the regent and Chinese Empress Dowager Cixi, who effectively controlled the Chinese government in the late Qing Dynasty[31] for forty-seven years, from 1861 until her death in 1908.

Still on China, here are more titles in rough order of my preference: *The Beautiful Country and The Middle Kingdom*, John Pomfret (detailing the history of the complex and shifting relationship between China and America from 1776 to now); *The Hundred Year Marathon*, Michael Pillsbury (the struggle between China and the United States for dominance; criticized as factually unreliable and too political, but still very readable); *Midnight in Peking*, Paul French (true crime genre, chronicling the aftermath of the brutal killing of a British schoolgirl in January 1937); *Fifth Chinese Daughter,* Jade Snow Wong (autobiography detailing the challenges to an American born Chinese girl); *The China Mission,* Daniel Kurtz-Phelan (George Marshall's unfinished war, 1945–1947 is the subtitle). Compare this to *Mao*. Marshall was likely duped by Mao even more than Kissinger.

I must mention two books that shed serious light into the Hermit Kingdom, North Korea. The first is fiction: *The Orphan Master's Son* by a Stanford professor of writing (Adam Johnson) who made more than a dozen trips to North Korea. So, while a novel, it is masterful in providing information about life in that totalitarian country. It won the 2012 Pulitzer Prize for fiction. The other is autobiographical and equally fascinating although in a wholly different way. The book is *The Girl with Seven Names,* by Lee Hyeon-seo, a defector who escaped and later guided her family out through China and Laos. Surprisingly, her mother disliked the West and wanted to go back. This alone should tease you into wanting to read the book.

General knowledge books of great merit are *Sapiens, by* Yuval Noah Harari is likley at the top. From opening sentence to last paragraph, this is one of the best nonfiction books I have read. Stupefyingly good. I also ripped through Bill Bryson's *A Short History of Nearly Everything* and *The Body, A Guide for Occupants.* I dedicate a separate paragraph to Bill Bryson. I read all his stuff and love much of it.

One can get captured by history books about London during the Second World War. My two favorites are both by Lynn Olsen: *Citizens of London* and *Last Hope Island.* Read them and you will never think of WWII in the same way again. The former provides insights into Churchill not elsewhere unearthed. His abuse at the hands of Roosevelt in the presence of Stalin and his failure to attend Roosevelt's funeral have been airbrushed out of American history but fully explained here.

I thought myself knowledgeable about the background of World War I. I had after all, read Barbara Tuschman's *The Guns of August* while in college. Well, I was quite wrong. Three years ago, I went deeper and read Margaret McMillan's two masterpieces: *The War that Ended Peace* and *Paris 1919.* These are brilliant histories and once you read them you thirst for more detail. Such is provided in *The Sleepwalkers,* by Christopher Clark and *The End of Tsarist Russia* by Dominic Lievens. These all provide a keen sense of the inexorable pull to world war starting in 1870 with the Franco-Prussian war and many other events, including the Russo-Japanese War, the Serbian regicide, the two Balkan wars, and much more. This period from 1870 to 1919 was perhaps among the most consequential of any fifty years in history. Of many books covering the period, these may be among the very best (although I have not read all those others, so who knows).

These books led, sort of by free association, to a strong interest in the Ottoman Empire. I have not gone as deep here as I intend but am starting to do so. I started with *Istanbul: City of Majesty at the Crossroads of the World,* by Thomas McFadden, detailing the founding of the city by the Greeks in about 660 BC and its development into the twenty-first century. Spellbinding for a historical novel focused on a single city or area. Then came *The Fall of the Ottomans*, by Eugene Rogan, a detailed and complex revelation for most Western readers under the age of a hundred. As the *Times Book Review* in 2015 put it:

> In November 1914, the world's only great Muslim empire was drawn into a life-or-death struggle against three historically Christian powers—Britain, France and Russia. All parties made frantic calculations about the likely intertwining of religion and strategy. The playing out, and surprise overturning, of these calculations informs every page of Eugene Rogan's intricately worked but very readable account of the Ottoman theocracy's demise.

It is a good starting point for further reading, which is where I am on this subject. There is much to read, and scratching the surface, as I have done, is hardly enough. But these books do intersect in a lot of helpful ways with several of the WWI books mentioned above.

World War II period novels. I happen to have been seduced a few years ago by the Alan Furst books from first to last. The first was *Night Soldiers* (1988), the most recent is *Under Occupation* (2019). These are pure fiction, but in the context of mostly real prewar and wartime (for Europeans) events. They are generally set in the period 1937–1941. Many are set in Poland and Paris or Paris and elsewhere in Eastern Europe. The books capture a certain mood of prewar and early WWII Europe and frequently or almost always involve some flavor of espionage. But they are storytelling "mood" novels not action novels. Still, they are taut and, in my view, excellent (although some are of course better than others). If you do not like the first one or two you won't like the rest, so stop. If you do like the first one or two, you will be addicted. They are best read in order, at least the first few, but all can stand alone, too.

For American history and biography, Ron Chernow's *Washington* and *Hamilton* are the new gold standard. They are page turners. David McCullough's *John Adams* is one of some four hundred biographies of Adams, none of which I have read other than McCullough's. People far more well-read than me say it is the best. Jon Meacham's *Thomas Jefferson: The Art of Power* is superb, although the recent onset of spasmodic cancellation culture has put Jefferson's reputation at risk, as has the fact that his slave mistress Sally Hemings (with whom he had six[!] children) turns out to have been his wife's half-sister. Say what?

Mayflower, by Nathaniel Philbrick. As a *Mayflower* descendant through multiple passengers, this book was a distressing revelation. Americans are taught about the pilgrims and the First Thanksgiving. What they next learn about American history leaps forward 150 years to the battles of Concord and Lexington. This cartoon version of history is a canard. This book sheds uncomfortable light on the viciousness of the pilgrims during the roughly five decades after the Plymouth settlement: 1622–1675, the period covered by this book. By the middle of the book, one gets the feeling that these Puritans were more like an American Taliban than a people seeking to escape persecution. They come across as persecutors. One example: having been saved by the Indian Squanto at the time of the First Thanksgiving (in whose honor there stands a huge statue in Plymouth, Massachusetts), they later sold his children into slavery in Haiti. This is an unsettling and myth-busting book insofar as it sheds light on a post–Plymouth Rock historical period about which even educated Americans seem to know almost nothing. It was news to me.

Finally, in this area of focused American history, is Russell Shorto's *The Island at the Center of the World,* based on newly discovered archives in Dutch at the New York Public Library. They were hiding in plain sight. The result is a masterful book about the fifty years of New York (then New Amsterdam, the capital of New Netherlands) under the Dutch (1624 and after), whose imprint on New York was probably far greater than that of the British. This is fully explained in the brilliant page-turner book.

This has gotten way too long, but I cannot let it pass without mentioning my strong recommendation that readers read or listen to anything by Graham Greene, who was "forced" on me by Steve and Joan Calkins during a visit to Dublin a few years ago. *The Quiet American,* written in 1955 and set in Vietnam in 1954 is my favorite. It anticipates precisely what happened after the Americans took over from the French in their opposition to Ho Chi Min. *Our Man in Havana* and *The Power and the Glory* are also on my "top of Graham Greene" list. But frankly there is nothing by him not worth reading. His serious books involve his Catholic religion. But what he called his "entertainments," are no less worthy as novels.

Other writers I recommend are Cormac McCarthy (especially *No Country for Old Men*, *All the Pretty Horses*, and *The Road*); Ian McEwen (especially *Atonement*, *The Comfort of Strangers*, *The Innocent*, and *Solar*); Margaret Atwood (especially *The Blind Assassin*, *Alias Grace*, and the *Oryx and Crake* trilogy*)*; Khaled Hosseini (*The Kite Runner* and *A Thousand Splendid Suns*); and Daniel Silva (*The English Spy* and *The Black Widow*).

There are several writers who have written many fine books, but I have only read one of them. A short list of these is *Innocent Traitor* by Alison Weir; *Christine Falls* by Benjamin Black; *The Story of Edgar Sawtelle* by David Wroblewski; *Serena* by Ron Rash; *Restless* by William Boyd; *Labyrinth*, by Kate Mosse; *Middlesex*, by Jeffrey Eugenides; *Stones Fall* by Ian Pears; *A Gentleman in Moscow* by Amor Towles; *Cutting for Stone* by Abraham Verghese; and *The Good Soldier* by Ford Madox Ford. All very worthy of attention. I recommend listening, as readers are outstanding in all cases.

Special mention for a new translation by Julie Rose of Victor Hugo's 1862 *Les Misérables*. The reader brings this truly massive book and its memorable characters (the hunted man Jean Valjean, his relentless pursuer Javert, Cossette, Mario, and many others) alive and lets its greatness shine through. Also, best heard.

Lastly, I have lived in Europe and briefly in London. The bookstores in London are full of books with titles like *Who Lost America?* and so forth. A relatively new blockbuster is out by an American named Jackson O'Shaughnessy. The book is *The Men Who Lost America*. It is an extraordinary read. The war was unpopular in England. The French and the Spanish were far more threatening. Parliament was against the war. Much of the government was against the war. The generals were against the war on the grounds it could never be "won." In this book, the war comes across much like the Vietnam War was viewed in America during the 1960s and 1970s. Everybody hated it, but senior government officials, especially George III, wanted to see it through. However, the supply lines were too long, horses and troops were hard to move across the ocean (plus the ships were needed to confront the French and the Spanish in the Caribbean and elsewhere), and George Washington's army kept retreating, thus avoiding any major confrontation until the British army blundered into Yorktown, a peninsula that could be shut off relatively easily. And the French Navy led by Admiral Rochambeau happened to be at the other end of the peninsula. Game over. A truly fascinating book. Heavily researched with much reliance on primary source documents from the period. The British never had a chance. This is somewhat different from the heroic mythology of my very American education.

Reader, if you have gotten this far, bless you. I apologize for the length of this, which began as a short blurb. But we are all mostly housebound and so we have time to find, and maybe interest in finding, things to watch and read. I hope this might help you pick and choose.

7

The Next New Normal

April 28, 2020

Having been under house arrest for many weeks now, I have in recent days been thinking about what it might actually mean for all of us, as a practical matter, when the governors of the various states decide to "open up" things. But I get ahead of myself.

The stock market, while down by some indices more than 15% (having come back from being down plenty more than that), seems to have to a significant extent shrugged off the reality that economic activity in this country has substantially declined and in some segments disappeared. Aerial photographs of highways show few cars and no trucks. The skies are eerily silent, almost reminiscent of the time after 9/11; restaurants are closed. While some stores are open, JC Penney and other big-box department stores all seem headed for Chapter 11 bankruptcy. Amazon beat them up, and the quarantine seems to be pushing them off the cliff. Layoffs are everywhere. A lot of the jobs will not come back anytime soon. Maybe millions.

And then there is oil. In a flash, oil prices are near zero. There is no place left in the United States to store oil or other petroleum products. Just a week or so ago oil had a negative value. People would pay you to take millions of gallons of oil if you could. It reminds one of. Saudi Arabia declared oil war on Russia and the two of them declared oil war on the entire U.S. oil industry. The glut of oil is unprecedented at a moment when there is little demand. The owners of the assets used to produce oil from small wells and fracking operations may be in bankruptcy before summer. Just the situation in the oil industry alone is astonishing; it is *The Sorcerer's Apprentice* in more dimensions than I can process. Strangely, the left seems to applaud the assault on if not the demise of this business segment, perhaps being unaware that the industry employs more than two million people and indirectly employs many times that.

Meanwhile, so far as I can tell there really does not seem to be any news on the news anymore except that Kim Jong-un seems to have disappeared. Everything else on news programs makes my eyes glaze over and for me boils down to one of three things: (1) constant blabbering and data about COVID-19, which have become mind-numbingly irrelevant to people who are quarantined at home; (2) vicious attacks on the administration for its handling of the crisis by people who would be viciously criticizing the administration for other reasons in the absence of this crisis; and (3) efforts by various camps to blame each other, prior administrations, or China for the lack of adequate testing or masks in this country. It is all quite baffling. At least in the mainstream press and media, and on social media, too (in other words basically everywhere) vast amounts of time and energy are being spent by educated adults with bylines or a microphone trying to fix the blame rather than fix the problem. This aspect of the current "normal" is just like the old "normal" in other words.

One thing, however, has come through the Coronavirus cacophony with a mild degree of clarity. You may remember that just a few weeks ago we were told it was a matter of life and death that we "flatten the curve." One had to read reliable sources of information to appreciate *why* this was so important, but it was. The point was to avoid overwhelming the medical community with a tsunami of infected patients who could not be handled all at once. Well, if one looks deep enough, one finds that throughout most of the United States the curve *has* been flattened! This should be a stunning victory, right? Not so fast. Flattening the curve, it turns out, does not mean the problem is over. It just means it goes on longer but without overloading the capacity of the healthcare system to deal with infected individuals. The same number of people (or maybe more) will become infected but under the blanket of a nicely "flattened curve." How much longer? Nobody, and I mean nobody, knows. What does this mean? I am not sure, but I think it means that the economy will stay weak and endangered for much longer and that when the dust settles, a lot of our old favorite places might not be in business any longer.

When our governors say it is safe now to go "back to normal," will people travel on airplanes? Will they go to crowded restaurants? Will they go to sporting events? Concerts? Any place where there are lots of other people in close contact? I do not know, but I kind of doubt it. Maybe social closeness versus strong remnants of social distancing will become a highly visible differentiator between generations. Older people (either because they are smarter or more vulnerable) may continue living under a looser version of today's social distancing rules—making exceptions for socialization with a small circle of friends or acquaintances who, by all appearances, are certifiably virus free. The younger generations, naturally perceiving themselves immortal, might return to conduct somewhat resembling the old normal. This is what college students did during spring break before Florida finally closed the beaches. The younger generations will probably behave this way again. Immortality is, after all, very cool. But that may not last after some of them end up becoming infected and dropping dead from the blood clots, which now appear to be the real silent danger of COVID-19, not lung problems.

There are also some weird data buried in the economic picture. The medical health professionals have become the faces and the heroes of the crisis, just as the fireman and first responders were the heroes of 9/11. But here's the thing: many hospitals are on the edge of financial danger, and some will fail. This is at first not intuitive but is on second glance obvious. Elective surgeries are not happening. Routine doctor visits are not happening. People who used to rely on the emergency rooms as their primary care source are not going to the emergency rooms. Hospital capacity (beds) is greatly and uncharacteristically underutilized almost everywhere. Health professionals are being laid off in some fairly substantial numbers my relatives in the field tell me (this does not seem to have made it much to the news delivery systems, so maybe it is not true, but I think it is).

So, why has the stock market *not* gone into a much larger collapse? Nobody, and I mean nobody, seems to understand why. Experts like Bill Gates and Warren Buffett do not seem to understand what is keeping the market afloat given the bloodbath going on in the real economy on the ground. Since much of my life savings is bound up in the equity markets I am not complaining yet. But I feel as if I have to pinch myself every now and again. After all, unemployment seems to be approaching Depression-era levels, and more than one in five Americans have recently become unemployed. The government's multitrillion-dollar bailout is not much more than a really expensive Band-Aid, but it cannot keep enterprises afloat where they are not even open for business or where there is no demand for their products or services. The trillions of dollars shoveled into the system presumed a reasonably fast return to "normal."

So, to return to where I started, what will our community and our business environment look like when we come out of our quarantine into the warmth of spring? The "old normal" has been around for decades. Social activity was the norm. Today's normal is quarantine and social distancing. Antisocial. Not normal. Life post-COVID-19 will be different. Companies will operate differently. Offices will become less essential. Interesting sidelight: I learned recently that it is harder to buy an affordable webcam to use with Zoom, BlueJeans, Skype, or other audio-visual social or business events than it has been to buy good toilet paper! This is surely an indicator of one aspect of the next normal. It will involve more connections by way of audio-visual technology and fewer connections by way of actual physical presence.

This will not just be a personal change but a change in the way enterprises do business. My doctor now has a fully equipped audiovisual capability for appointments via Zoom or some such platform. My financial advisor has the same capability. My lawyer has the capability. I am on a nonprofit board. We have been meeting via Zoom video conferences and it seems to work very well. This does not bode well for the commercial real estate business, which might find itself under stress from technology-facilitated conference spaces. My liquor store and my grocery store accept telephone or internet orders and payment by credit card without any personal contact; they leave the goods in a box or bag for pickup near the parking lot. Believe it or not, even CVS now delivers in Easton, just like the family-owned drugstore did when I was growing up in the 1950s! But when things finally do "open up," attendance at sporting events, concerts, plays, political rallies, the nominating conventions, and a host of other such events will signal the direction of the next new normal. I have a pretty strong belief and expectation that it will be really different from the old normal. I hope it is better than today's normal.

8

Lockstep Lockdowns and L'Affair Flynn

May 26, 2020

I have been thinking in the last couple of weeks about two particular subjects, not as unrelated as at first glance they might appear.

Lockstep Lockdowns

The first has to do with the unusual demands, mostly on the left, for the continued lockdown of the economy and the quarantine of the citizenry based on public health concerns and the advice of elements of the medical profession. This view is being contested, more or less on the right, by various groups who decry the increasing economic wreckage being caused by the lockdowns; the disregard of First Amendment religious rights; and more broadly the loss of individual liberties that have resulted (putting to one side the fact that nonviolent inmates are being released from crowded prisons in the name of social distancing—so there is that increase in liberty for some fortunate felons).

What first got me thinking about this in a more than ordinary way was a fascinating article in the *Wall Street Journal* about "Freedom and Sweden's Constitution."[32] As many will know, there has been virtually no lockdown in Sweden, and social life there proceeds largely under the prepandemic rules. (The reasons for this are set forth in the article at note 32.) At the risk of oversimplification, the Swedish people trust each other; they trust their elected officials; and most importantly they trust their public institutions. Certain vital public institutions are not subject to political oversight and therefore do not have to respond to political pressure. Their public health institutions have a broader vision than, for example, the CDC. Those trusted Swedish institutions take into account secondary and tertiary order impacts of decisions made to protect health and safety. The noninterference of the government in these types of public institutions (what some might call a "deep state") is embedded in the Swedish Constitution itself. The cornerstone of the Swedish response to the coronavirus is its constitution's most important part, the Regeringsform. Chapter 2, Article 8 states:

> Everyone shall be protected in their relations with the public institutions against deprivations of personal liberty. All Swedish citizens shall also in other respects be guaranteed freedom of movement within the Realm and freedom to depart the Realm.

The Public Health Agency of Sweden—like other public bodies, such as the world's oldest central bank, the Riksbank—operates with an incomparably high degree of independence from the government. Chapter 12, Article 2 of the Regeringsform spells this out:

No public authority, including the Riksdag [Parliament] or decision-making body of any local authority, may determine how an administrative authority shall decide in a particular case relating to the exercise of public authority vis-à-vis an individual or a local authority, or relating to the application of law.

This Swedish model is not readily characterized as "left" or "right." But it represents an extraordinary pact that seems to bind Swedes to each other, their agencies, and their elected representatives. It is hard to imagine such consensus and trust in these United States. We have always been a fractious polity other than for short periods (during World War II perhaps). I was exchanging thoughts and emails with a beloved niece who married a Turkish man some twenty-five years ago and has raised her family in Istanbul, one of the most wonderful cities in the world I have never visited. She was a journalist until her newspaper was shut down by Erdogan in the wake of the failed revolution. She is a keen observer from afar, with a unique perspective on events in America. She sent me a fascinating article from a publication ("Consent Factory") that I had never heard of. The article, entitled "Virus of Mass Destruction," is here. [33] The opening paragraph reads as follows:

> There comes a point in the introduction of every new official narrative when people no longer remember how it started. Or, rather, they remember how it started, but not the propaganda that started it. Or, rather, they remember all that (or are able to, if you press them on it), but it doesn't make any difference anymore, because the official narrative has supplanted reality.

After discussing some examples of this, the author moves along to the general thought that

> … it is the goal of every official narrative to generate this type of herd mentality, not in order to deceive or dupe the public, but, rather, to confuse and terrorize them to the point where they revert to their primal instincts, and are being driven purely by existential fear, and facts and truth no longer matter. Once an official narrative reaches this point, it is unassailable by facts and reason. It no longer needs facts to justify it. It justifies itself with its own existence. Reason cannot penetrate it. Arguing with its adherents is pointless. They know it is irrational. They simply do not care.

This entire thesis is then presented in terms of the current coronavirus narrative, or at least the narrative put forth by much of the left. We thus see threatening signs: police and judicial actions against citizens for social contact, including religious participation; millions of people downloading contact tracing applications; hairdressers and barbers put in jail; the bleaching of beaches in Europe and other such irritatingly authoritarian actions. These incremental steps—toward a little more authoritarianism here and a tad more there—are all justified on the grounds that the virus is a deadly threat to humanity as we know it. It is all for our own good. Thus, we are bombarded by frightening statistics, albeit not usually in any fully comprehensible context. The shrieking headlines are indeed a bit scary. And many of the authoritarians are doubtless acting with a measure of good faith. These incremental steps indeed may be for our own good—provided we have the resources to avoid the economic impact of the lockdown. Provided we are part of the 1% or the 5% maybe.

Anyway, whether the problem is the virus or the economic wreckage, blame is cast at the administration, China, various large state governors, MSNBC, Fox News, the rest of the media and anyone else who might be a handy blame target for various target audiences. Indeed, the search for someone or something upon which to fix the blame seems to be more energetic than the search to fix the problem, a subject on which there is no consensus. Multiple narratives twist and turn all interconnected with the main narrative of a health crisis so serious that it is worth wrecking the world economy and eliminating some thirty to forty million jobs in the United States, not to mention increasing the national debt by unimaginable amounts.

I do not mean by these remarks to be dismissive of the dangers of COVID-19. It can be dangerous and deadly to many people. It can also be harmless to many people. It is not understood. It is justly feared. Most likely there is not any altogether "right" or "wrong" on how to deal with the pandemic. But our public policy approach to the problem ought at least be capable of taking into account rational and obvious trade-offs. However, after so many weeks of economic catastrophe (see reports here about The Death of a City (NY)[34] and restaurant failures *en masse* across America[35]) I am beginning to get the feeling that some of the lockdown decisions are being made and have been made by the same people who say, about almost anything, "If this saves one human life, it is of course worth the cost." It is sad that we do not have public administrations as in Sweden that can avoid tunnel vision and can seek to balance multiple risk and reward factors in a multifaceted and multidimensional way. In so doing, they seem to bring about outcomes that balance short-term health and economic issues against long-term health and economic issues. Here, the debate never seems to get very much further than sloganeering.

My niece and I exchanged emails about much of this and about the oddity that it is not the "fascist right" in this country but rather "the liberal left" that seems the most committed to the narrative that prescribes a form of near-totalitarian lockstep lockdown. But it was her summation that took my breath away. She found it at once pathetic and sad that the liberals in the United States, and their actions with regard to the coronavirus, brought to her mind the last lines from George Orwell's *1984*[36] after the protagonist Winston Smith had finally given in to the totalitarian regime. The last sentences of the book are these: "But it was all right, everything was all right, the struggle was finished. He had won the victory over himself. He loved Big Brother."

The Flynn Affair

The second thing on my mind recently has been the puzzling, indeed bizarre, public discourse in the media and by the judiciary itself over the decision of the Justice Department to move to dismiss the prosecution of General Michael Flynn. The Justice Department's motion and subsequent events are something of a spear in the heart of the long-accepted herd narrative about the general. Indeed, it threatens to create a new narrative altogether about extraordinary misconduct from the inception by the FBI and Department of Justice in all aspects of their handling of the Flynn affair.

The guilty plea, the prosecution, the decision to dismiss the prosecution, and the judicial attacks on the general and the Justice Department by the presiding judge present an unprecedented and improbable spectacle. The entirety of the matter calls to mind a Frankenstein stitching together of *The Bonfire of the Vanities*,[37] the Dreyfus affair,[38] and the 1793–94 Reign of Terror,[39] with the media playing the role of the Committee of Public Safety,[40] Judge Sullivan playing the role of the Jacobin leader Maximillian Robespierre,[41] and William Barr playing the role of Émile Zola, the writer who laid bare (in his famous "J'Accuse" open letter [42]) the corrupt motives within the French Army and the French government that underpinned the baseless prosecution of Colonel Dreyfus. Readers may well recall that Zola was actually imprisoned for a year for exposing the crimes (a phony libel charge), much as today's media mob would imprison Attorney General Barr for such conduct. In each case, the real offense seems to have been the disruption of the herd narrative.

The Justice Department's decision has unleashed a tsunami of criticism of the attorney general for doing what responsible prosecutors are routinely applauded for doing: dropping a case that has been laced with layer upon layer of prosecutorial misconduct within the FBI and the Justice Department. It has been routine in this country for decades that the sins of the prosecution relieve the defendant of criminal responsibility for that with which he was accused. This is not an approach to law and justice intended to reward the conduct of the defendant but rather an approach to maintain an undoubted integrity within the criminal justice system itself.

Those who condemn Attorney General Barr, and they are many, seem to do so on at least two unrelated grounds, neither of which has any pertinence to the matter at hand. *First,* he is treated in much of the media as a handmaiden of President Trump with a long history as a believer in the constitutional defensibility of strong executive power. Right or wrong, these might be reasonable political attacks if Mr. Barr was running for political office, but they have nothing to do with whether the misconduct by the prosecutors in the matter of General Flynn was itself grossly improper or even criminal. *Second,* the critics of the Justice Department's motion to dismiss the prosecution, and this appears to include the presiding judge Emmet G. Sullivan, [43] focus on the fact that General Flynn has done some very bad things over the last few years. And it seems beyond dispute that this is true. See for example this article from the conservative American Enterprise Institute about General Flynn's bad judgment [44] and this more mainstream op-ed piece from the *Washington Post* headlining that Flynn is not a martyr but instead a crook and a crackpot [45] whose embrace by the right is intended to distract the public from what the writer, Paul Waldman, describes as the administration's "spectacular failure on the coronavirus pandemic."

Mr. Waldman's article posits that the brouhaha surrounding the misconduct of the prosecutors is just part of an "attempt to create a new fake 'scandal' that will send us all down an endless rabbit hole chasing absurd lies and conspiracy theories." Meanwhile, in the background and without modern precedent, Judge Sullivan has appointed a retired judge friend of his *to oppose* the Justice Department's motion to dismiss General Flynn's prosecution, and he has also invited "the public" (a "public mob" one is tempted to say) to file *amicus curiae* (friend of the court) briefs expressing views as to what he should do with the government's motion to dismiss the Flynn prosecution. It all has the feel of gladiator combat in the coliseum. What sayeth the public mob about General Flynn: thumbs up or thumbs down? People's reactions seem to depend not on any facts but on their political views.

The majority of the commentators seem to hold several simultaneous and somewhat conflicting views more or less along these lines: General Flynn is a bad person; his prosecution was sullied by massive misconduct; because

General Flynn is a bad person, he should be sentenced to jail; the prosecutorial misconduct is just a shiny object being used to distract you from the reality that William Barr is a bad person and that President Trump is worse. Like Schrödinger's Cat,[46] General Flynn can be thought of as simultaneously alive and dead. Does the conduct of the prosecutor matter anymore? If the majority agrees that a person is or has been "bad," should that be the end of it? Wither the rule of law?

What in the world is one to make of this strange cognitive dissonance?[47] This confusing state of affairs led me to mistrust much of what I was seeing or hearing in the media. And so last week I was determined to find and read the actual May 19 mandamus petition[48] filed by General Flynn's new lawyers and limit myself more to primary source materials. A mandamus petition is a petition filed by a litigant in a higher court under the All Writs Act of 1789,[49] which authorizes federal courts to issue writs "in the aid of their respective jurisdictions and agreeable to the usages and principles of law." In this case the higher federal court is the United States Court of Appeals for the District of Columbia Circuit. A mandamus petition is for all practical purposes a lawsuit against the judge by a litigant filed with the appellate court. The mandamus petition in this case is frankly far more interesting than any of the press reports about it. It is twenty-nine pages long (double spaced) and lays out a tale of prosecutorial misconduct and judicial irregularity that seems to warrant all of the relief asked for, including the replacement of Judge Sullivan with another judge should any further proceedings be required.

What makes the mandamus petition in this case especially unusual is that the party opposing General Flynn, the Justice Department, will not defend the judge's conduct: so he is in a very real sense on his own. For a sitting federal judge, this is threatening and awkward. I believe judges tend to take this sort of thing quite personally. So, Judge Sullivan has had to do what other accused people have to do. He has hired his own personal lawyer[50] (interestingly, the same lawyer who represented Justice Brett Kavanaugh before the Senate Judiciary Committee) to defend his judicial conduct in front of the appellate court that sits over him. Moreover, the appellate court has taken the extraordinary step of *sua sponte* (on its own without being asked to do so) ordering Judge Sullivan to file his answer to the mandamus petition within ten days (from Thursday, May 21), while at the same time inviting the Justice Department to comment on the mandamus petition. Judge Sullivan might be displeased that the only case the appellate court mentioned in its one-page order is a 2016 ruling by the same court *granting* a writ of mandamus against a district judge who refused to dismiss a prosecution because the judge thought the Justice Department was letting the defendant off too easily.

The Flynn mandamus petition is an extraordinary document, fitting for the extraordinary set of circumstances giving rise to it and appropriate to the extraordinarily contentious times in which we live. For some years now we have lived in a media and political world where opinions are ubiquitous, the truth is a matter of opinion, and actual facts are simply background noise no less malleable than opinions. I, for one, am hoping that the judiciary will prove to be the one place in our pantheon of government institutions where the facts still matter and where judicial outcomes expressed in opinions are based on the application of objective law to objective or at least observable facts.

9

The Ecstasy of the Mob. Virtue Signaling, Moral Clarity, and a Letter from Istanbul

June 20, 2020

The Ecstasy of the Mob

The murder of George Floyd by a handful of Minneapolis police officers and the reactions and counter-reactions to this event around the country and around the world have provided more to think about than can be thought about in days, weeks, or months. See links to photos here.[51] Nonetheless, one can observe some objective realities and reach some tentative conclusions. I cannot escape the persistent notion that these events, occurring in the context of a medical and economic catastrophe of unprecedented proportions, represent a historical hinge. That hinge is turning and leading us in the United States and elsewhere down a different path than otherwise would have been followed. At the moment, it is unclear where that path might lead. However, at least in the short term, it is hard to imagine the new path leading to a better place than the old one. And there are troubling signs the new path could lead to an even more dangerous place. Nonetheless, as I have said in many previous columns, hope springs eternal.

The George Floyd protests began with a clear and objectively legitimate focus: the militarization of the police and the seemingly routine mistreatment or murder of black men at the hands of white policemen and, to some degree, the legal system itself. But within days, perhaps even hours, the protests expanded exponentially, geographically, numerically, racially, and otherwise. To some extent due to social media, this was and is nothing at all like the Watts riots of 1965,[52] the Detroit riots of 1967,[53] the 1968 riots[54] in the wake of the murder of Martin Luther King, the Orangeburg Massacre and other events of that tumultuous year, or the 1992 Los Angeles riots[55] after the acquittal by a Los Angeles jury of the officers videotaped beating Rodney King. For the first time in my lifetime (i.e., since 1943) large segments of major cities were given over to the ecstasy of the mob. Six blocks in central Seattle seceded from the United States and remain apart. The Paris Commune[56] (the event that turned Karl Marx into a major international figure) writ small came to Seattle, and the authorities continue to encourage the revolutionaries in their secession. How this will end in unclear, but well is not high on the list of probabilities.

At the same time, and all around the country and the world, statues of major historical figures have been torn down or defaced. Abraham Lincoln has been treated no better in this respect than Robert E. Lee or Jefferson Davis. Many statues of Christopher Columbus have been torn down. Mobs have defaced statutes of abolitionists like Mathias Baldwin and Union war heroes like Admiral David Farragut and General George Thomas. The tomb of the unknown soldier of the American Revolution in Philadelphia was vandalized last weekend with the words "committed genocide." A mob of college students toppled statues of American pioneers on the University of Oregon campus. The images are jarring and unsettling. The perpetrators appear to be young men and women mostly not of color.

The gleeful mob pulling down these monuments, defacing statues, and demanding that US military bases be renamed do not operate within any limiting principle. They do not distinguish between those who fought for freedom against the British Empire and those who fought for Union against the slave states of the South. To them, the union itself was a crime against humanity long before the South seceded.

As the political editor of *The Federalist* wrote [57] this week: "This is the 1619 Project come to life. If the American Revolution was fought to protect and preserve slavery, then the entire history of American colonization and westward expansion is a litany of crimes that nobody should celebrate. The founding fathers are no less guilty than the leaders of the confederacy—*not* just because they own slaves but because they founded the United States as a nation conceived not in liberty but in white supremacy." New York, under the slippery hands of Mayor Bill DeBlasio and District Attorney Cyrus Vance, Jr., has decided *not* to prosecute the rioters who vandalized St. John's Cathedral and other notable places in Manhattan, but instead to return the City to the policing policies of David Dinkins, which could hardly have been more destructive. As Vance put it:

> The decision not to prosecute seems to stem from a new policy toward protest-related transgressions. The prosecution of protestors charged with these low-level offenses undermines critical bonds between law enforcement and the communities we serve. Days after the killing of George Floyd, our nation and our city are at a crossroads in our continuing endeavor to confront racism and systemic injustice wherever it exists. Our office has a moral imperative to enact public policies which assure all New Yorkers that in our justice system and our society, black lives matter and police violence is a crime.[58]

Vandalism against houses, cathedrals, small businesses, cars—anything at all in fact, does not count anymore. Today's virtue signaling gives a strong nod to anarchy over any semblance of public order. And so, New York has pledged to go back to the future of the 1970s, when property values cratered and the city enjoyed the highest murder and crime rate in the nation, mostly in neighborhoods of color.

The Press, Virtue Signaling, and Moral Clarity

A recent movie review by Mark Judge had much to say about the ecstasy of the mob and the movies he reviews on the subject are worth reading about.[59] But his closing paragraph is much broader and has a special poignancy today:

> While both *Panique* and *Richard Jewell* are commentaries on particular cultures and particular times, they share a message that is archetypal and timeless: Without due process, without law, without the presumption of innocence, people submerged in an environment of hysteria quickly devolve

into wolves. Members of the press are usually the worst offenders, taking sides and fueling the carnival atmosphere rather than searching for the truth—which usually comes out long after it is too late.

Ah, the press. The fifth estate. The object of such special constitutional protection under the First Amendment. In a few short years most of the press—indeed the media more broadly—in the United States has lost all standing to any claim of independence or objectivity. Several articles recently have probed the capitulation of major elements of the media to the fascist intelligentsia. Two such articles are worthy of special mention: "The American Press Is Destroying Itself" by Matt Taibbi,[60] and "Is There Still Room for Debate?" by Andrew Sullivan.[61] These are chilling articles.

Taibbi's piece focuses on the ouster of editors of *Bon Appetit, Refinery29, Variety, the Philadelphia Inquirer*, and even the *New York Times* amid accusations of political incorrectness, insensitivity to certain identity groups, toxic workplace culture, and the like. The editor of *Variety*, Claudia Eller, was placed on leave[62] after calling a South Asian freelance writer "bitter" in a Twitter exchange about minority hiring at her company. The self-abasing apology ("I have tried to diversify our newsroom over the past seven years, but I HAVE NOT DONE ENOUGH") was insufficient. The *Philadelphia Inquirer*'s editor was forced out after approving a headline, written in the context of considerable property damage caused by rioters and looters in Philadelphia, "Buildings Matter, Too." Once one accepts the entirety of the dogma behind Black Lives Matter (and failing to accept all of that dogma is grounds for shunning and shaming), it is capital offense to suggest that anything else might also "matter."

In the most publicly significant incident, the *Times* editorial page editor was ousted for greenlighting an editorial by Arkansas Republican Senator Tom Cotton entitled, "Send in the Troops."[63] As Cotton points out in the piece, he was advancing a view arguably held by a majority of the country. A *Morning Consult* poll showed 58% of Americans [64] either strongly or somewhat supported the idea of "calling in the U.S. military to supplement city police forces." That survey included 40% of self-described "liberals" and 37% of African Americans. To declare a point of view held by that many people not only not worthy of discussion but so toxic that publication of it without even necessarily agreeing requires dismissal of the editor, is a dramatic reversal for a newspaper that long cast itself as the national paper of record.

In the case of Cotton, Times staffers" protested on the grounds that "running this puts Black @NYTimes staff in danger."[65] In other words, according to the apparatchiks on the staff of the *Times*, the ousted editor's decision was not merely ill-considered but literally life threatening. The Times first attempted to rectify the situation by apologizing, adding a long editor's note[66] to Cotton's piece that read, as so many such apologias do, like a note written by a hostage.

Then, editors begged forgiveness for not being more involved, for not thinking to urge Cotton to sound less like Cotton ("editors should have offered suggestions"), and for allowing rhetoric that was "needlessly harsh and falls short of the thoughtful approach that advances useful debate." That last line is sadly funny in the context of an episode in which reporters were seeking to preempt a debate rather than have one at all. Obviously, no one got the joke since a primary characteristic of the current political climate is the total absence of a sense of humor in any direction.

The Sullivan article is especially trenchant, focusing as it does on the dilemma of living in a country where adherence to a particular ideology becomes mandatory. If the United States has not yet arrived at that point, it is within sight. Sullivan, a journalist of enormous talent demonstrated over many decades, considers the difference between the Communist orthodoxies of Eastern Europe during the Cold War and the uniquely American ways of enforcing uniformity of thought. He goes back to the Puritans with their skill at "shaming and stigmatizing" (for example, see *The Scarlet Letter*), Prohibition, the Hollywood Blacklist, and more.

He then proceeds to discuss "the new orthodoxy," referred to by some writers as the "successor ideology" to liberalism. This "new orthodoxy" is rooted in what journalist Wesley Lowery calls "moral clarity." He told *Times* media columnist Ben Smith last week:

> …that journalism needs to be rebuilt around that moral clarity, which means ending its attempt to see all sides of a story, when there is only one, and dropping even an attempt at objectivity (however unattainable that ideal might be).

And what is the foundational belief of such moral clarity? That America is systemically racist, and a white-supremacist project from the start that, as Lowery put it in *The Atlantic*,[67] "the justice system—in fact, the entire

American experiment—was from its inception designed to perpetuate racial inequality."

Sullivan makes the point that this argument deserves to be aired openly in a liberal society, especially one with such racial terror and darkness in its past and inequality in the present. But it is an argument that equally deserves to be engaged, challenged, questioned, and interrogated. The new orthodoxy, however, does not wish to have this debate. The fascism of today's intelligentsia, bred in the country's most esteemed universities over decades, will not allow this debate. *This is because there is nothing to debate.* The intelligentsia teach us, and with considerable confidence and condescension, that America has never been about freedom or liberty but has always been and still is about oppression. The ideals about individual liberty, religious freedom, limited government, and the equality of all human beings were always a falsehood to cover for, justify, and entrench the enslavement of human beings under the fiction of race.

There is no room for discussion that these values competed with the poison of slavery and eventually overcame it in an epic civil war whose nearly one million casualties were overwhelmingly white. Indeed, more white men died *in captivity* during the Civil War than were killed during the entirety of the Vietnam War.

The "new orthodoxy" view of the world may have simplistic "moral clarity," but it is bereft of any hint of "moral complexity." To quote Sullivan:

> The crudeness and certainty of this analysis is quite something. It's an obvious rebuke to Barack Obama's story of America as an imperfect but inspiring work-in-progress, gradually including everyone in opportunity, and binding races together, rather than polarizing them ... Question any significant part of this, and your moral integrity as a human being is called into question.

There is little or no liberal space in this revolutionary movement for genuine, respectful disagreement, regardless of one's identity, or even open-minded exploration. In fact, there is an increasingly ferocious campaign to quell dissent, to chill debate, to purge those who ask questions, and to ruin people for their refusal to swallow this reductionist ideology whole.

Letter from Istanbul

Regular readers may remember that I have from time to time brought my niece from Turkey into these columns. As I have mentioned, she has lived in Istanbul for some decades now, raised a family there, and was, until the government shut down her newspaper, an esteemed journalist. She is accomplished, intelligent, and opinionated; we do not always agree. Yet living halfway around the world, raising a family educated outside of the United States (all while still having some connection to the United States), she provides the unique and informed perspective of an expat with a more global perspective than we are accustomed to getting here. I sent her the Matt Taibbi article (referenced at the beginning) with a bit of commentary. Her slightly edited response was this:

> I have been waiting, almost inexplicably, to respond to this for a few days, not even knowing where to begin, so deeply do I agree with it. I could "almost" (but maybe not quite) even trace my move to this area of the world to a reaction to the stifling groupthink embodied by that strange wing of American liberalism. It was terrible when I was a student at the University of California, but it seems to be even worse and more virulent now.
>
> The endless "wokery." The nonstop virtue-signaling. Virtue-signaling being that totally useless form of activism that amounts to nonaction actions, like publishing lists of books that you're planning on "educating" yourself with on social media, I guess in the hope that others will see that you've done this, and then do the same. Round and round it goes, achieving nothing, or almost nothing at best.
>
> The stifling of the press is the worst. This article hit close to home, as I've loved The Intercept (though mostly for Glenn Greenwald) and Lee Fang's stuff for a while, and I had NO idea he had come under such ridiculous attack. The NYT hypocrisy is why I've refused to read it for at least 5 years now; they drive me crazy with their two-faced neo-liberal corporate Democrat upper West Side fakery. Such extreme

wokery, all the while championing useless and destructive wars in the Middle East, trying to play both sides with their straight-up Zionism combined with faked human-interest stories about faraway lands and peoples. Give me a break.

Needless to say, all of this has come to a head during the Corona times, since the mask has finally fallen on so much. This includes the relentless driving of the fear narrative over Corona, combined with the ruthless backing of the total shutdown which has led to the loss of jobs and livelihoods so great that it will change the face of the US and the world for years to come. The intolerance to hear other sides of THAT story—like why a complete shut-down might not be such a great idea after all–walks hand in hand with the intolerance to even the mere mention of different political or ideological viewpoints. All in all, a distressing landscape.

Personally, it's why I'm grateful for the ocean of information available from other sources now, though in general I tend these days to read non-American online sources anyway, from Turkish writers (on Twitter; they're insane and wonderful!) to the Japanese owned FT, and The Guardian and others. And in doing so, I reduce my chances of being trapped in that hideous world of virtue-signaling wokery that I imagine would drive a person crazy.

There are many problems in this country. It is hard to see whether there are many, or any, real solutions. Our leaders despise each other, and their hatred of each other justifies their departure from previous political norms. Society, too, is also deeply divided. Civil political discourse has almost ceased. The failure to signal your virtue in approved ways (whether superficial or just disingenuous) leads to various forms of shaming. And social media performs the role of the old East German Stasi at no cost to the government. Post war Eastern Europe, present day China and increasingly Turkey and Russia achieved Orwellian goals through government measures. In this country we have the media doing the job, and quite well, too. The ironies, as they might say in England, beggar belief.

10

A [New England] Republican's View of Policies for a Unified Way Forward

July 4, 2020

So, here we are at last: on the verge of class warfare, racial warfare, gender and other identity warfare, political warfare, a war on police (crime having won the war on crime), the erasure of Western and American history, and the predominance of mob- and groupthink. And that just describes the last week or two. There does not seem to be any consensus about anything. It is hard to imagine the speed with which all of this has gelled, although the elements have been building for years. COVID-19 seems to be making a resurgence, and the economy seems ready to respond with further decline.

Independence Day is upon us, and July 4 no longer feels patriotic. One even wonders if the great American Experiment has actually failed. If so, where did it go wrong? Well, I don't know. But I do feel that everything I read now is mired in analysis paralysis. Everybody has reasons to think other people are wrong. I have read virtually nothing recently about a possible path forward. Accordingly, this column is devoted to thinking about policies from a New England Republican's conservative point of view, which might serve as a foundation for the future: policy approaches that could be embraced, and I think should be embraced, by a wide swath of the population no matter their politics. Hope springs eternal. The policies I propose have not in all cases been deeply researched; nor am I prepared to defend each down to the last detail. They are relatively high- or mid-level and notional. Some will be controversial, others less so; others not at all.

Health Care. The ability of American citizens to obtain affordable health care did not have to become a political football. In the end, we are either going to have a single-payer health-care system paid for by taxpayers or we are going to have a market-based system supplemented by the existing single-payer system (e.g., Medicare and Medicaid). A market-based system would be far more efficient, and it would be supported by hospitals, physicians, and nurses, all of whom are going to get the short end of the stick under a single-payer system, as they now do under Medicare and Medicaid. Patients also, of course, will get the short end of the stick under a single-payer system, with health care being to a meaningful degree rationed.

There is an enormous irony in all of this. The core idea of so-called Romneycare, which evolved (or transmogrified you might say) into Obamacare, was that everybody should be required to purchase health insurance in much the same way that everybody is required to purchase liability insurance for their automobiles. This was not some radical left-wing socialist idea. It was an idea that came from the conservative Heritage Foundation at the outset of the Reagan administration. It was a market-based conservative idea. It still is. Properly implemented, it would also take health care off the backs of employers, thus reducing the cost of products and services and making them more competitive with products and services produced outside this country. The supreme irony of recent years is that supposedly conservative groups opposed the law in the Supreme Court on the grounds that it was unconstitutional to force people to buy health insurance ("eat their spinach" was the catchy metaphor that gained traction). The Republican administration turned against market-based principles in its legal argumentation, and legislatively it crippled those features of Romneycare (er, Obamacare) that might have made it more successful. The administration talked of "repeal and replace," but the "replace" piece of it was always, and is today, a ghostly mirage.

Anyway, one way or another, we are going to have health care in this country that does not exclude people with preexisting conditions and that is available to at least all citizens and maybe even some noncitizens. But for the moment, and to avoid controversy over noncitizens in America, of whom there are many millions, I am focusing just on citizens. Whether one is a hard-right conservative, a moderate conservative, a centrist Democrat, or a hard-left Democrat, universal health care is coming to America, and anyone with some remaining faith in capitalism or free markets should be rooting for a market-based health-care system that provides universal coverage, including for preexisting conditions, and against a single-payer system. This means everybody must be required to purchase coverage. Those who genuinely cannot afford to do so will end up on Medicaid. Those over sixty-five can choose Medicare (which is not "free," which grossly underpays providers but is subsidized by the private market).

Education and Student Debt. There has been for some time now much clamoring babble about a federal bailout for federally funded student debt. Such student debt stands at roughly $1.7 trillion today.[68] This is nearly twice the amount of total credit card debt (about $900 billion) currently outstanding in the United States. This is a staggering number. There is no reason for people who paid for their education to be responsible for those who didn't. There is no reason for people who chose to forgo an education to pay for those who did not forebear. And so on. This is not to say, however, that the student debt problem should be ignored or left unresolved. It should not be ignored, and it can be resolved through straightforward market mechanisms.

As I have written before in these pages, federally guaranteed student debt, like an IRS obligation, is not dischargeable in bankruptcy. There is little reason to keep this policy; student debt should be dischargeable in bankruptcy. Beyond that, the universities and colleges who take the money that students borrow should be required to pay back half of the debt in the event the student becomes obliged to discharge the obligation in bankruptcy. This would provide colleges and universities with some real incentives to have a stake in the future success of their students. This in turn might cause them to think about their curricula and its relevance to the real world. That would be refreshing. It would also be refreshing to require all high school graduates to be able to pass the same tests that immigrants have to pass in order to obtain citizenship. This might assure some minimal knowledge of American history, which today seems to be largely lacking.

Education and Political Bias. Most colleges and universities accept federal monies for a variety of research and other purposes. A condition of accepting such funds ought to be a commitment to evenhandedness in faculty hiring and something approaching balance in tenured faculty and curricula. I appreciate that this is potentially quite a slippery slope. I doubt we want the government too involved in our educational curricula. However, the universities can no longer be trusted to supply anything approaching balance in their own curricula, so somebody with a stake in the balanced education of our population needs to step in. The details of this issue would need to be worked out. But the federal money ought to have some strings attached that tether the universities to the national interest to some extent. Many developed democracies (Japan, France) and autocracies, too (China) have a core curriculum requirement, and this works to their advantage in labor and management markets. It could do so here.

Education and National Service. There is a strong consensus in this country that education is important. I do not necessarily mean higher education in the sense of a four-year college or graduate school but education sufficient to provide schooling that can sustain a comfortable middle-class life for a married couple with children. Many people cannot pay for even a junior college education, much less a four-year college education or graduate school.

One way of facilitating an educated population is through national service. I believe that we lost something valuable in this country when military service became wholly voluntary and the population divided into those who would never dream of serving their country in the military and those who, for economic or other reasons, chose to serve their country (or who had no practical economic choice). Thus, during the Vietnam War, half of the country came to hate the military and perhaps even hate the country itself, while the other half developed a subtle contempt for the former. Things have gone further downhill to date. It is time to consider a national service program. At its simplest, a program might work something like this: a person giving two years of national service (military or civilian) would be entitled to two years of college education at any public or private institution. This would be geared toward trade schools or junior colleges. A person giving four years of national service (military or civilian) would be entitled to four years of collegiate education at any public or private institution. A person giving seven years of national service (military or civilian) would be entitled to additional years of education (e.g., medical school, law school, business school, etc.).

The essential idea is that people would do low-paid national service work and thereby earn a worthwhile education. The system might not have to be year for year; perhaps certain types of military service (e.g., combat-related) might be worth more; and there are certainly circumstances where the education might precede the national service (medical, for example), but the basic bargain or contract would be national service for education.

Income Taxes. Few topics in America are more controversial or less well understood than taxes. Who pays what percentage of what taxes involves nothing more than a collection of objectively determinable facts. I provided a variety of objective facts on this topic in my very first article for this publication last fall.[69] The pandemic changed the circumstances. The national debt is now much larger, the economy has shrunk, and tax receipts have gotten smaller. Taxing the rich out of existence might be satisfying to some, but it would impoverish the country even in the short term and dramatically so in the longer term.

It seems beyond obvious that we are not going to spend less on Social Security, Medicare, Medicaid, and the military, which together account for roughly half of our entire federal budget of $6.15 trillion. Defense spending, by the way, which many people seem to think is a source of unlimited money to spend on other things, is about half of the Medicaid/Medicare budget. The actual federal budget deficit now stands at $3.4 trillion and national debt at $26.5 trillion. The human mind is barely able to comprehend how large a number that is, but it puts national debt at 133% of the nation's gross domestic product. During WWII it was comparably huge as a percentage of GDP. In times of economic prosperity, countries should run budget surpluses. But until the onset of COVID-19, we were enjoying an economic boom, and yet the national debt kept rising. This is not sustainable, and yet politicians on both sides of the aisle seem content to ignore this elephant in the room. This is probably because interest rates have been at unprecedentedly low levels for so long that politicians cannot imagine the consequences of interest rates rising from about 2% to 6–8%. Should that happen, the interest on the national debt ($386 billion) would triple (to $1.2 trillion) or quadruple (to $1.5 trillion almost overnight). In these circumstances it is hardly surprising that younger generations heap contempt upon the boomers who have superintended all of this.

So, what to do? Whether we are talking about the top 1% or the top 5%, there is not enough money there to make a serious dent in this problem. To address this massive deficit, we would have to increase taxes on the middle class and perhaps even tax the 49% of the population that pays no federal income tax at all. But there is neither the political will nor the political courage to do that in this country now or in the foreseeable future. We are no longer a serious enough country to do such things. Therefore, it seems almost certain that we will have little or no choice but to do what nearly every country in the world has done: institute some kind of a value-added tax (VAT)—essentially a national sales tax. Such a tax would be introduced as a "very small" and perhaps "temporary" tax, a minor annoyance. But over time, just a few years really, it would probably grow to something between 10% and 15% or more as it has elsewhere. Cynicism aside, a party concerned with fiscal rectitude should consider embracing this solution now, while there still might be time to rein in the recklessness of the current tax and budget policies. Eventually, politicians of all stripes might well embrace this solution because of its relative political costlessness. In other words, this is a call or plea for political cowardice, not political courage, but sometimes the outcome can be the same. We need to pay for all the services our representatives voted to provide. A VAT could do the job. Not pretty, somewhat regressive, but likely effective. Also a necessary counterweight to the tax-the-rich-and-their- heirs [70] attitude beginning to seep into mainstream democratic thinking if the *New York Times* is still a measure of anything.

Finally, there is the matter of optics and equity. I believe there is much to be said for feathering in somewhat higher tax rates for couples making more than $500,000 or individuals making more than $250,000. While the actual amount of money raised might not be significant, there is an optics issue with taxing individuals making $250 million a year at the same rate as an individual making $250,000 per year. I see no rational reason for not adding a percentage point of marginal tax rate for those making $1 to $2 million or more; and an additional percentage of marginal tax for each $5 million above that. For example, at $2 million of ordinary income, the marginal tax rate might be, say, 40%; it would become 41% at $7 million; 42% at $12 million; 43% at $17 million and so forth. It could be capped at between 50% and 60% or perhaps even more. This extra tax would largely be felt by highly paid corporate executives, investment bankers, hedge fund managers, rock stars, and highly paid athletes. This would have the salutary impact in many cases of letting people put their money where their mouth is.

Capital Gains Taxes. The history of capital gains taxation in this country has been one of change and inconsistency.[71] Taxation of corporations and shareholders is also nuanced and subtle, although all of that is lost when public debate and political discussion is involved. Today's mantra is that the capital gains tax rate should be the same as ordinary income. This would be terrible economic policy since it would encourage consumption over savings or investment. But terrible economic policy does not often get in the way of political ambition.

On the other hand, the spread between ordinary income taxes and capital gains taxes has rarely been more than it is today, and this creates legitimate optical issues of inequality and unfairness. There is good reason to decrease the spread between ordinary income taxes and capital gains taxes. Some of the underlying detail can be found here.[72] Let us begin with some simple propositions. Let's say you invest risk capital in a stock and invest $10,000, money on which you have of course already paid taxes. Now, after more than a year, you decide to sell that stock. Let us say you sell it for $20,000. Let us say further that your marginal federal income tax rate is 37%, and your state rate is 13%, for a total of 50%. What is the "proper" amount of capital gains tax that you should pay on the $10,000 profit? There is no perfectly right or perfectly wrong answer. This is a policy question. The answer supplied by those whose animating political principles involve the phrases "tax the corporations" and "tax the rich" will say that you should pay $5,000 of tax on that $10,000 profit because there should be no difference between capital gains and ordinary income.

But a policy designed to encourage investment of capital, which is both risky as well as necessary to encourage business expansion and job creation, would likely observe that taxing capital gains at a somewhat lower rate than ordinary income would provide investors an incentive to invest this risk capital. This would be a key benefit to society at large. Today, the capital gains rate is almost half the ordinary income tax rate. For political reasons, perhaps apart from economic policy reasons, this spread seems unnecessarily large. A spread of fifteen percentage points seems generally adequate and consistent with the average spread over many decades past. It might also be possible to have tax brackets within capital gains that would tax modest capital gains at a lower rate than massive capital gains. The main point for now is simple: encourage investment, the creation of factories and jobs; the creation of prosperity. In short, a sensible and maybe bi-partisan approach would be to tax capital gains in such a way that the total federal and state take would be about 15 percentage points less that the federal and state rate on ordinary income.

There are obviously some very important details that would have to be worked out, but in terms of a high-level approach, slightly higher taxes on the very rich does not seem especially burdensome and might do much to bring a sense of unity to the country. Could a left-leaning government restrain itself from putting into place confiscatory taxes? Perhaps not, but maybe. Could a right-leaning government resist lowering taxes on the upper brackets and thereby doubling the national debt? We have seen the answer to this, and it seems to be mostly "no."

Immigration. The immigration problem in this country only seems insoluble because it has become so hopelessly politicized. It is in fact solvable. If there were any political will, it would be relatively simple to harden the border and eliminate most of the illegal immigration that goes on every day. If the border were secure, it would then be possible, one hopes, for a political process to deal with those now millions of people who were brought to this country as children illegally and who are now adults but who have no obvious path to citizenship. These are the so-called Dreamers, and they number about 3.6 million out of a total illegal immigrant population of 11.3 million (although there are different categories of Dreamers; only about half of these—1.8 million—entered the United States before their sixteenth birthday. Only eight hundred thousand of these have qualified for DACA protections over the five years of the program[73]). They need to be given a path to citizenship, but they also need to demonstrate that they have earned citizenship. It could in some cases be a path to deportation. The absence of a serious criminal record might be one important criterion; the regular payment of taxes might be another. Military or other national service might provide special consideration as well. This should not be as big a problem as it has turned out to be. The illegal immigrants who overstated their visas now exceed those who entered illegally, as reported by NPR.[74] Their absolute numbers are unclear, but they simply should be deported. To the extent there is a path to citizenship for the majority of the illegal/undocumented immigrants, it should involve going to the back of the queue along with other aspirants. Again, our unseriousness in problem solving is revealing itself with stubborn persistence.

Vocabulary. Relatively recently, vocabulary in America has become full of prohibited words, some of them normal everyday words that have been now declared objectionable as microaggressions. This has created a massive generation divide. One dares not use certain words. The works of famous authors are being burned and destroyed because of their use of certain words. The First Amendment notwithstanding, I cannot even use them here without undue risk of retribution of various kinds. Freedoms get lost in small bits until one day they have gone underground.

But there is one ubiquitous insult that can be freely applied today to essentially anybody in America: "racist." That word, which was not even published in any dictionary prior to 1902, once had a relatively specific and narrow meaning: "a belief that race[75] is the primary determinant[76] of human traits and capacities and that racial differences produce an inherent superiority of a particular race." Today, some 150 years after the end of slavery in America, there are without doubt many traces of vestigial racism. A close observer would take note that this was and is meaningfully true with respect to earlier groups of immigrants who were subjected to discrimination: Italians, the Irish, the Chinese, and others. But the legacy of slavery has made this charge of racism against blacks much easier to hurl; more likely to stick; and indeed, more likely to be a valid charge in certain cases. But in many cases, it is not a valid charge, and the making of the charge creates its own dangerous and maybe silent but angry backlash. Or maybe it creates an atmosphere among the targets of the charge of uncaring indifference—a tuning out of the "conversation." It was just such a silent backlash against identity politics that elected President Trump.

In the circumstances, I believe it would be helpful if we could come up with a new word to describe the perceptions that whites have of blacks and browns and that blacks and browns have of whites (and of each other, too). I am not sure what that word should be, and I am not going to try to invent one today. But the more the word *racism* is tossed about at all whites, all blacks, all browns, or others, the greater its negative impact. The ninety-four-year-old woman from New York City who was filmed while being punched in the face by a thirty-three-year-old black youth with 103 arrests (and who fell down and smacked her head on a fire hydrant while the man looked back and casually walked away) is now very afraid of young black men. That does not make her a racist. Asian or other business owners whose stores in New York; Minneapolis; Atlanta; Walnut Creek, California;

and elsewhere were completely looted by marauding gangs of young black men and women with guns and sledgehammers while the police stood by and watched may have developed an understandable fear of young black men and women, particularly in large groups, not to mention a similar fear of law enforcement. I doubt this makes them "racists," although in some cases it might.

Young black men who experience regular traffic stops by white policemen may have a justifiable fear for their lives. This does not make them racists, but it does make them understandably fearful of even routine traffic stops by white police officers. Police enforcement of laws against blacks and browns does not make the police officers racists. In New York, more than half of the police *are* blacks and browns. People who have suffered at the hands of Islamic terrorists may be fearful of Islamicists. This may make them Islamophobic. This is in many circumstances no more shameful than being arachnophobic—afraid of spiders. The point is that rational and reasonable fears based on actual events have become so stigmatized that they are considered more heinous than the events that caused the reaction. This is evidence of an unserious and increasingly purposeless society eating itself.

I would welcome the introduction of a new word or vocabulary to describe this fearful wariness that groups of people may have with respect to other groups of people. To lump all such wariness under the words *racist* and *racism* seems about as smart has throwing gasoline at a small fire: it surely assures a larger fire or explosion. Sadly, it is the media and the politicians who hurl these charges about in hopes of gaining votes or ratings. In this way they have become more part of the problem rather than part of the solution.

Police and Taxpayer-Funded Unions. Whether the entire police force in New York City should be defunded because of the actions of several police officers in Minneapolis is a question that, one would think, answers itself in the negative. But the war between the police and the rest of society seems to have captured the media and is spreading all over the country. This is sad, particularly since it is happening at a time when dashboard cameras and body cameras are becoming ubiquitous, and the accountability of police departments is becoming more apparent. But police departments are being defunded, in most cases quickly and mindlessly. The results are available on YouTube. The YouTube clips of looting on a grand scale, literally superintended by local authorities. Examples at this footnote[77] represent the truly frightening side of anarchy.

To be fair, and to provide some perspective, there is also *The Onion*'s trenchant headline and story about the outrage of protesters looting without first creating a private equity firm.[78] The droll humor of *The Onion* aside, does anyone wonder why federal background checks associated with gun sales during the month of June were at the highest levels since such statistics began being recorded in 1998? Indeed, according to yesterday's *Wall Street Journal*, 40% of these 3.2 million June background checks were associated with first-time gun buyers. See *The Guns of June*.[79] This will continue through July and August, one suspects.

It is not possible in a paragraph or two to do justice to this entire topic. But it is possible to note as a placeholder that taxpayer-funded unions tend to gather extraordinary political power, especially in large cities. It is not much of an overstatement to say that publicly funded unions effectively enter into bargains with urban administrations, virtually always democratic, and those bargains involve trading votes for economic benefits, including particularly (a) early retirement benefits and (b) union benefits that limit and often virtually eliminate individual accountability. Local administrations literally delegate to the unions the hiring, firing, and disciplinary problems. This problem has been decades in the making and may never be solved unless the political subdivisions involved wind up in bankruptcy, which is happening slowly but steadily around the country. For the most part, it is only through bankruptcy that the administrations that entered into the budget-busting contracts are able to abrogate those contracts. They do not seem to have the political will to do so otherwise. If they did have the will, the defunding or elimination of many public employee unions could be a good starting point since it only benefits some especially powerful unions and the career politicians who buy their support.

In any case, and to end up near where I started: things are a mess and getting worse. Anyone who thinks otherwise has probably not been paying attention, which would be understandable. There is a need for some unity going forward. I am hopeful that the bulk of the propositions set forth here can form the core of a unified view as to how this country might most justly and sensibly move forward without constant hostility and rancor and how the country might recapture a sense of purpose beyond individual and generational self-indulgence.

11

A Positive Path Forward

August 18, 2020

We live in a perilous political time. Everywhere we look, most especially in the media, we are confronted with conflict between and among identity groups, political groups, and especially these days ambiguous groups defined by words that obscure their purpose or intent. Words have lost much of their obvious meaning. Social justice combines two words, each of which has a clear meaning, to create a phrase that with each passing year has become increasingly Orwellian. Nobody really knows what the words now mean, and what they mean depends on who is saying them, and in what context.

The seeming breakdown of civil society and the growing dysfunction of our political system are all amplified by a pandemic that has no end in sight. Yet in the midst of this most depressing set of circumstances in the middle of this most depressing year, I have just read a book that spends its first half presenting the darkest imaginable picture of our country and our political system and yet ends with a sense of powerful optimism: a message that we can put ourselves back together with some relatively simple solutions that could re-create the political system to which our founders aspired.

The book is *The Politics Industry* by Katherine M. Gehl and Michael E. Porter. It is of very special interest to me because for nearly five decades I have been an antitrust lawyer focused on antitrust law and competition policy. This is a field that examines industries and markets, usually in a framework involving mergers, consolidations, other potentially anticompetitive corporate combinations (such as cartels), price discrimination and still other forms of anticompetitive conduct such as monopolies, attempts to monopolize, or monopsonies (which are buying-side monopolies), and the problems of market structure, duopolies and the failure of market performance. There are thousands of antitrust lawyers and economists who study markets and their structures, trying to understand their strengths and weaknesses or seeking to attack (or defend) their participants in governmental or private litigation.

The received wisdom regarding markets is that monopolies are bad for many reasons (lack of customer choice, innovation, price constraints, and so on). Duopolies (meaning two rivals in a business or market) can also be dangerously anticompetitive (by fostering collusion, facilitating oligopolistic interdependency, stifling innovation, dampening price competition and so on). Consumer choice is the source of considerable innovation in markets and is generally thought to fuel market efficiency. Markets blockaded to new entry by high-entry barriers may tend to be anticompetitive, especially to the extent that there are a limited and small number of rivals operating in the blockaded market (higher than competitive prices and lower than competitive innovation more likely). Markets that are "concentrated" (meaning a small number of rivals account for a very large percentage of the entire market) can foster oligopolistic/anticompetitive outcomes.

Michael Porter, one of the two authors of the book, is a competition economist. He has spent his life studying companies, industries, and even nations from the perspective of competition, competitive advantages, and so forth. His coauthor, Katherine M. Gehl, was president and CEO of Gehl Foods, a high-tech food manufacturer. She hired Michael Porter as a consultant some years ago, thus beginning the relationship and subsequent collaboration that produced this extraordinary book, *The Politics Industry*.

The authors examine the "politics industry" as if it were a commercial market. Viewing what they come to call "the political-industrial complex" as a market with its own ecosystem, incentives, rewards, and structure is brilliantly original. They start by analyzing this industry as they would analyze any commercial market, beginning with the participants and the structure. First, there is the rivalry between existing competitors: Democrats and Republicans. This is the dominant duopoly. The only real substitute is Independents. A third party is a theoretical new entrant, but the barriers to new entry are formidable and virtually impossible to overcome. This industry has *suppliers*: candidates, campaign talent, think tanks, lobbyists, and so on. The industry also has *buyers*. These buyers are customers (voters) and include donors, primary voters, special interests, and average citizens. These voter buyers are served through various *distribution channels*, including paid advertising, direct voter engagement, social media, and other media.

Looking at this entire ecosystem through that prism, the authors uncover blinding (and, once recognized, obvious) insights and come up with surprisingly simple solutions. It is, in short, perhaps, the most important book on American politics of the past century and one which every voter in every state who cares about political dysfunction would do well to read. And happily, not only is it a short book (fewer than two hundred pages), one can read a 2017 Harvard Business School paper that laid out many of the main points in the book. And for nonreaders, one can link to two or three separate YouTube videos where the authors discuss most of their main points. So here are some of the basics.

First, politics is a private industry dominated by two competitors, the Republicans and the Democrats. It is a duopoly. It is a private industry with high barriers to entry. The ecosystem surrounding this industry is a $20 billion/year industry comprising elected officials, their staffs, lobbyists, advertising agencies, PACs, consultants, and so on. This is just at the federal level. This number would balloon if comparable elements of the ecosystem from the state level were added. And if we include the revenues of all these political organizations, the politics industry inflates to over $100 billion per election cycle.

Second, it is the conventional wisdom that our system is broken and needs to be fixed. But to put it more accurately, the system is not broken at all. It functions to achieve exactly those goals for which it is carefully designed by the duopolists. The primary goal for which the system is designed is the reelection of individual candidates and the preservation of the duopoly.

Unlike commercial markets that operate under governmental rules and regulations, and enforcement mechanisms such as the antitrust laws, the politics industry makes its own rules and enforces them when it pleases, primarily to exclude potential rivals. This is why third-party candidates almost never get on a debate stage—the rules require candidates to achieve impossibly high approval ratings before they can get on stage, but they cannot get those ratings without being on stage. This is obviously a form of Catch-22. You get the idea.

In a competitive commercial market, rivals compete to serve customers, which is to say consumers. In the political-industrial complex, customers are not served by the duopoly. Customers, which is to say voters, can be divided into five segments depending on how they engage with the duopoly. Thus, there are partisan primary voters, special interest voters, donors, average voters, and nonvoters. The parties prioritize their attention to the voters who can most advance their interests through the two currencies of politics: votes and money (or both). The most powerful customers are therefore partisan primary voters, special interests, and donors. These groups represent a fraction of the fewer than 20% of registered voters who vote in primaries. Princeton and Northwestern University studies from 2014 examining congressional action on nearly two thousand policy issues find that "when the preferences of economic elites and the strands of organized interest groups are controlled for, the preferences of the average American appear to have only a minuscule, near-zero, statistically non-significant impact upon public policy."

Third, the single most important proposition demonstrated by the authors is probably this: there is virtually, and more often than not literally, no overlap between the legislator's incentive to be elected and his or her incentive to achieve goals desired by a majority of the voters or goals that are in the national interest. Stated slightly differently, there is simply no intersection between acting in the public interest and the likelihood of getting reelected. Indeed, if acting in the public interest means acting against the interests of your party's "base," then acting in the public interest runs a high risk of being "primaried." For politicians, this is a relatively new and terrifying verb.

Duopolies are not inherently good or bad, but as politics is currently structured, the same two rivals are guaranteed to remain empowered no matter how poorly they serve the public interest. This would be a catastrophic problem for customers in any commercial industry. The authors describe it as a "nightmare" for a democracy.

Fourth, it is important to grasp the "rules" and their impact. How do we decide who gets placed on the ballot? How do we decide who wins? The rules that govern these questions are the industry's *elections machinery*. And once a candidate is sent to Washington as an elected official, how is the legislator permitted, or constrained, to draft legislation and turn bills into laws? What rules and practices determine how Congress works? These rules are the industry's *legislative machinery*, which is like software humming in the background of an operating system. One is barely aware of this machinery's presence, yet it has a powerful impact on everything.

Elections Machinery. Two key features of today's elections machinery cement unhealthy competition: party primaries and plurality voting. Party primaries are mostly a rigged game. This is partly because of gerrymandering and partly because of the committed voters and donors who vote in party primaries, largely to the exclusion of others. This is also partly because of ballot access rules and "sore loser" rules prevalent in many states by which the parties prevent: (a) ballot access to those who have not yet demonstrated strong electoral support and (b) primary losers from competing in the general election under any label at all. The Delaware sore loser law gave Senator Coons a seat in Delaware over the loser of the Republican primary, who, according to polls, would have defeated Senator Coons by more than twenty points. Forty-four states have "sore loser" rules that prevent a primary loser from running in the general election. There is of course nothing in the US Constitution about gerrymandering, sore loser rules, or any of the other features that permit the parties to control the primary system. These rules are written and enforced by the parties themselves to limit new entry and to maintain their duopoly. And they function exactly as intended.

It is not an overstatement to observe that party primaries are the centerpiece of elections machinery. They ensure, almost as if by design, that the public interest and a person's electability do not intersect.

Plurality voting is the other feature that tends to corrupt the system. Many might be surprised to learn that our elections are not designed to ensure the election of the candidate with the broadest appeal to the most voters. In a three-way race, a candidate can win with as little as 34% of the vote—indicating that two-thirds of voters preferred someone else. This is precisely what happened in Maine in 2010 when Paul LePage won his party's gubernatorial primary with only 37.4% of the vote and then won the governorship with only 37.6%. So, nearly two-thirds of voters—Democrats and Republicans—did not select the candidate who would now be their governor. This plurality system of voting incentivizes candidates not to speak to a broad cross-section of the electorate but rather to target a just-big-enough base of partisans who can push them slightly ahead of their opponents.

Plurality voting also creates "the spoiler effect." How did Mr. LePage secure the governorship of Maine (despite substantial unpopularity)? An Independent entered the race and won more than 8% of the vote. Had the Independent not run, most of those votes would have gone to LePage's rival, who would have then won the election. Both parties do everything in their power to avoid allowing potential spoilers into the race, and for the most part they are successful. In commercially competitive markets, it is a bedrock article of faith that more choice is better for the consumer for many reasons. Politics may be the only industry where we are regularly told (by the rivals) that less competition is better for the customer.

Legislative Machinery. An in-depth discussion of the arcane *legislative machinery* rules is beyond the scope of this modest description of this fascinating book. But a couple of examples will suffice. First, there is something known as the "Hastert Rule." This is something that is relatively recent, and probably not very well understood outside of Congress. It is also not a written rule. The Hastert Rule dictates that the Speaker of the House will not allow a floor vote on a bill unless a majority of the majority party—the Speaker's party—supports the bill *even if a majority of the full House would vote to pass it.* This is a particularly egregious example of today's partisan legislative machinery in action, now the standard practice of Speakers of both parties. This rule, not found in the Constitution, not codified, not written down anywhere, cements hyperpartisan control over the legislature. This rule cost the country $24 billion for sixteen days of shutdown in 2013, which 90% of Americans did not want.

It is important to appreciate how normal—how very "water to the fish"—this type of partisan machinery has become to most of us, including journalists and editorial boards. Little or nothing was written at the time of the 2013 shutdown that illuminated the lunacy of a single person's ability (a single person elected by a small number of one party's primary voters in one district in one state) to stop a democratically elected legislature from solving a problem practically everyone in the country wanted solved. As the authors put it: it is partisan oligarchy.

From the end of World War II until the mid-to-late 1970s, congressional committees were the heart and lungs of Congress. And they were in a great many ways nonpartisan. Bills did not go to committees to die as they do now: they went to committees to be hammered out by legislators (and professional staffs) seeking to serve both constituents and country. As the book explains, ground zero for the partisan takeover of Congress was the House of Representatives during the 1970s, when the Democratic majority (which had been in place for more than forty years) became fed up with conservatives using committees to hold up liberal bills. The takeover of the *legislative machinery* (the committees) by the parties started small, first by reviving the Democratic Caucus. While most legislators previously had little contact with party leaders once in office, this changed in 1969, when Democrats began holding monthly meetings in which they set agendas, devised legislative strategies, and coordinated so that all members spoke in one unified voice.

The second front was an attack on committees. The Democrats mitigated the power of committee chairs, limiting the leaders' control over the committee agenda, and transferring to party leadership the authority to appoint subcommittee heads. To have a chance at securing a committee chair, members would need to demonstrate loyalty to the party leaders responsible for putting them in their positions. Going forward, any chair who ignored party directives did so at his or her own risk.

After co-opting the committee chairs, the leadership then turned to its rank-and-file members. In 1975, the job of making committee assignments was transferred from the Ways and Means Committee to a newly formed Steering and Policy Committee, chaired by the Speaker and dominated by party leadership. Career trajectories for members now hinged on preserving good standing with party leaders.

Then, even with control over committee members, the Democrats were unhappy that bipartisan committees could still make key decisions. So, beginning in the 1970s, the Democrats started bypassing committees altogether, employing partisan task forces to manage important policies. These task forces were staffed with Democrats selected by the Speaker to carry out the party's agenda.

Finally, to complete the creation of fully partisan legislative machinery, the party commandeered the Rules Committee, which had traditionally prided itself as a neutral referee, making impartial decisions on which bills would move to the floor, in what order, and under which rules of debate. Under the new regime, nothing could come to the floor without the Speaker's approval. When writing legislation, committees no longer had to think about what the best policy would be or what would be favored by a majority in the House. Instead, a critical step was to put forward policies that could get by a cadre of partisans appointed by a party leader and in complete control of the congressional calendar.

In 1994, when the Republicans took over the House of Representatives for the first time in more than a generation, there was no deconstruction of this partisan legislative machinery. Instead, it was embraced, expanded, and amplified. Speaker Gingrich put freshmen acolytes on some of the most prestigious committees based on loyalty not seniority. He also worked to dismantle the nonpartisan structures that had supported the day-to-day legislative work of Congress. This meant cutting the professional staff by a third—most especially the economists, lawyers, and investigators who worked for committees, not for individual members.

No single one of these events drew much attention. The media did not seem to think anything was particularly amiss. The long, slow, but steady slide into hyperpartisanship happened almost completely out of sight. Today, most bills die in committee and Conference Committee negotiations, which are nearly extinct but were once commonplace. In the 114th Congress, there were just eight conference reports, down from sixty-seven in the 104th Congress a decade earlier. Now, when one party controls both chambers, majority leadership meets behind closed doors and then simply announces the outcome of its internal negotiation to the other side.

As the book puts it:

> The consequences of a political-industrial complex overrun by unhealthy competition are horrifying—and, even scarier, utterly normalized. It is accepted as normal when the Mitch McConnell's and Nancy Pelosi's of America—currently our most powerful members of Congress—announce publicly and proudly that their top priorities are either resisting the current President or electing more members of their own party. It is normal that bipartisan bills are killed despite majority support. It is normal that a "lobbying index" of companies that derive big earnings from lobbying outperformed the S&P 500 over the last decade. And it is normal that the richest country in the world … has its credit downgraded as a result of partisan political gamesmanship. What could be more irresponsible?

General Consequences

The book posits that unhealthy competition in the politics industry has resulted in five horrifying consequences for our democracy.

1. ***Lack of Problem Solving.*** In our current political system, legislators acting as elected officials according to public need actually increases the chance that they will lose their jobs. Keeping a problem or a divisive issue alive and festering is a proven method to attract and motivate partisan voters, special interests, and committed donors to each side, delivering both key currencies (votes and money) in return. There was a time when landmark legislation would pass with strong bipartisan support. In this century, important legislation is passed only along partisan lines (see, for example, the Affordable Care Act, Dodd-Frank, the Tax Cut and Jobs Act). This is a stupendously wrongheaded design flaw.

2. ***No Action Without a Time-Sensitive Crisis and National Debt.*** When a national security crisis occurs, a natural disaster hits, or a government shutdown or debt downgrade looms, Congress does take action, sometimes even strict action. But the trade-off is that the action is virtually never paid for with current funding. Instead, Congress uses deficit financing, which passes the cost of the bill on to future generations by adding the spending to the national debt. There is no party standing strongly for fiscal responsibility anymore; both Republicans and Democrats have realized that in the absence of a serious competitor raising the issue (as Ross Perot did in 1992), there is no political benefit to fiscal responsibility.

3. ***A Country and Society More Divided.*** Competition is personal. It involves not only politicians but also citizens. While party rivalry is intense, it is nonetheless constrained because head-to-head competition for the middle is mutually destructive. Instead, the rivals increasingly seek to compete in ways that reinforce their differentiation and separation from one another. The political-industrial complex increasingly plays the identity-politics game, painting fellow citizens on the other side as "enemies." One sees this clearly on social and other media, within communities, and even in families.

4. ***Political Disillusionment.*** The American public has never been more dissatisfied with the political system. Public trust in the federal government is hovering at a near sixty-year low. In 1958, three out of four Americans trusted the government. By 2017, just one in five did. The percentage of self-identifying Independents is as a near all-time high — 41% versus 30% for Democrats and 28% for Republicans. Worryingly, millions of Americans

have begun to lose faith in democracy as a system of government. Only a third of those born between 1980 and 1996 (millennials) believe it is essential to live in a country that is governed democratically. Support for authoritarianism is on the rise.

5. *Lack of Accountability.* In any other large (and thriving) industry with this much dissatisfaction with the only two players, some entrepreneurs would see it as a phenomenal business opportunity and create a new competitor responding to what the customers want. This will not happen in the political-industrial complex because the duopoly works extremely well together in one particular way: to rig the rules of the game to protect themselves from new competition. In many spheres this problem has some very specific consequences.

Specific Consequences

1. Immigration. As a nation, we have chosen to make immigration a partisan issue rather than solving the problem. The problem has been on the edge of a solution many times, but the solution was strangled for partisan political reasons, frequently by distinguished elements of both parties, including then junior Senator Obama, who felt obliged to torpedo the McCain-Kennedy bill for fear it would provide a tactical victory for his upcoming presidential opponent.

2. Economic competitiveness. Competitiveness is central to the welfare of every nation. The nation is competitive if it creates the conditions for two things to occur simultaneously: businesses operating in the nation that (1) compete successfully in global markets while (2) lifting the wages and living conditions of the average citizen. Today, the United States is fulfilling only half the definition of competitiveness. Large and midsize companies here are thriving and creating prosperity for those who found, run, and invest in them. But middle- and working-class Americans are struggling, as are many small businesses.

Since the beginning of the new century, productivity growth has fallen, leading to a significant drop-off in economic output and a smaller pie to divide among the population. Established firms are investing less, and our economy is becoming less dynamic as the rate of new business formation has slowed. The American Dream is under threat. What used to be a guarantee that American children would earn more than their parents did is now just a coin toss. The era of shared prosperity has ended. Regions surrounding cities like San Francisco, Boston, New York, and Washington are booming with vibrant, knowledge-based clusters. But within these oceans of affluence sit islands of hardship, and outside these oceans of affluence sit other oceans of economic decline and inequity.

Signs of competitive decline are plentiful, and most of them can be traced to government action or inaction—but in either case partisanship is still an issue. Indeed, our strengths are concentrated in areas driven by the private sector, while our weaknesses tend to be in areas driven by state and federal policy. Thus,

> we face in astronomically expensive and inequitable health care system; onerous and costly regulatory and legal systems; a convoluted, loophole-filled tax code; a public education system that fails to equip children with the skills needed in the new economy; crumbling highways, railroads, and airports that are a national embarrassment. And things are only getting worse.

The authors observe that it is not that we do not know which areas we need to address to unlock American competitiveness. Nearly everyone inside and outside of Washington agrees that we must improve our infrastructure, streamline regulations, address abuses in the international trading system, and balance the federal budget. There is a surprising amount of consensus. The problem is that consensus does not produce solutions. We do not have a policy problem. We have a politics problem.

A Quality-of-Life Recession

Some worldwide statistics tell a chilling story. The United States has fallen into twenty-sixth place overall in social progress compared to other OECD countries, far behind countries such as Portugal and Slovenia. The United States ranks near the bottom among the thirty-six countries of the OECD on a specific group of indicators, including education, environment, health, personal safety, inclusiveness, rights and freedoms (including particularly freedom of expression, access to justice, and freedom of religion), and property rights. The United States is 35th in maternal mortality and 33rd in child mortality. Beyond the OECD, overall health outcomes are comparable to Jordan or Panama. In secondary school enrollment, a springboard for citizen opportunity, we are 22nd out of 36 in the OECD. Beyond the OECD we are on a par with Serbia. Our homicide rate is 35th out of 36 within the OECD. We rank 31st on access to basic drinking water. With respect to personal safety, we have fallen behind countries like Indonesia, Ghana, and Sierra Leone.

Our society is fracturing; quality of life is declining for many, Our government used to be able to solve problems; now we cannot. We are no longer the country we have always liked to think of ourselves as. Meanwhile, the political-industrial complex continues to grow and prosper.

A Way Forward to Solutions

The book spends thirty-five or so pages talking about the Gilded Age and the political dysfunction that plagued the country during the latter part of the nineteenth century and the early part of the twentieth. The parallels between then and now are striking. The solutions to the problem of political dysfunction during the Gilded Age involved the success of the Progressives of the time (who bear no ideological relationship or resemblance to the progressives of today). But the reaction to that political dysfunction did involve ballot reform, direct primaries, the introduction in many states of "direct democracy" (ballot initiatives), the direct election of Senators, changes in the legislative machinery that resulted in stripping away the power of the Speaker (the then-powerful Joe Cannon) over the Rules Committee and the decentralized control of committees made independent by the then new seniority system, and the regulation of money in politics.

The solutions to the political dysfunction problems of the Gilded Age worked for many decades. The country came to global and political maturity in the wake of World War I, depended on a strong and largely respected government during the Great Depression, contributed to the annihilation of Hitler's Germany and Imperial Japan in World War II, and emerged as the strongest economy in the world and a world leader in manufacturing, medicine, the building of postwar Europe, the building of the modern American infrastructure, and the building of world's first large and relatively affluent middle class. But slowly, and in hindsight inexorably, the political-industrial complex duopoly returned to its the Gilded Age form. But today there is no effective "muckraking" journalism, no Theodore Roosevelt, and no credible movement to bring about the needed systemic change. Other than, that is, a motivated citizenry. *The Politics Industry* should be seen as the first credible blueprint for systemic reform. The systemic reform outlined is beguilingly simple, requires no constitutional amendment, and can be implemented state by state relatively quickly. Indeed, some states are already moving in that suggested direction.

New Rules for the Electoral Machinery

The Final Five Voting System. This is simple. It consists of two parts: (1) open, single-ballot, nonpartisan primaries in which the top five candidates qualify for the general elections and (2) ranked-choice voting (RCV) in general elections. Successful change requires the adoption of both these elements, not just one.

Top-Five Primaries. One would no longer vote in a Democratic primary or a Republican primary. Every candidate from any party, as well as Independents, would appear on a single ballot (with a partisan affiliation next to their name if they desire). All voters would be eligible to vote in the primary. There would be no gatekeepers deciding on who goes on the ballot. The top five finishers would all go on to the general election. They could all be Republicans; they could all be Democrats; they could all be Independents; or some combination of these or something else. While the top-five proposal has not yet been implemented, some single-ballot, nonpartisan primary pioneers are paving the way, including California, Washington, Maine, and soon Massachusetts and maybe our own Maryland.

Uncompetitive general elections preceded by highly partisan primaries had serious adverse effects on California politics. The introduction of top-two primaries changed the calculus significantly in the number of competitive races across the state doubled immediately. Landslide victories decreased, and the number of incumbents who lost in the general election increased greatly. To win a general election, candidates have to appeal to a broader cross-section of the electorate. And when elections change, governing changes. California's notorious gridlock began to loosen as voters began electing more politicians committed to solving problems. By 2016, the approval rating for California's legislature hit 50%, up from 10% in 2010.

The pushback came from California's partisan political leaders—the duopoly's gatekeepers. Leading up to California's primary elections in 2018, US House of Representatives majority leader Kevin McCarthy, a California Republican, said, "I hate the top-two." The then House minority leader Nancy Pelosi, a California Democrat, said California's top to system "is not a reform. It is terrible." The fact that the leaders of the duo making up the duopoly hated the change speaks volumes about the wisdom behind it.

But the book urges that the top-two open primaries system does not go far enough in infusing our elections with some healthy competition. Recognizing that there is no perfect number, the authors believe top five is optimal for three reasons. *First,* the additional slots in the general election make it highly unlikely that a single party will capture all five spots. *Second,* top five ensures that more voters are likely to have a choice they support come November. And *third*, more choice means more competition for candidates and ideas, and more competition means more elected officials who are more accountable to citizens—and more accountability in an industry means better results. The authors make a convincing argument for a top-five primary yielding optimal results.

Ranked-Choice Voting General Elections. This is also simple. Whereas plurality voting can elect candidates without majority support, RCV does the opposite. For candidates to win, they *must* pass the 50% threshold. Here is how it would work. When you arrive at the polling station on Election Day, you receive a ballot with the names of the five nonpartisan primary winners. The ballot would invite you to pick your first, second, third, fourth, and fifth choices. The book assumes that the candidates in the hypothetical are Thomas Jefferson, Alexander Hamilton, George Washington, John Adams, and Abigail Adams.

After the polls close, the first-place votes are counted. If one candidate receives more than 50% of the first-place votes (a true majority), then the election is over. But if no candidate gets a true majority, the candidate in last place is eliminated. In this case, let's say that Hamilton, Abigail Adams, George Washington came in first, second, and third. respectively. Thomas Jefferson came in fifth. But votes cast for Jefferson would not be wasted because voters who selected him as their first choice have their ballots automatically transferred to their second choices. Let us say now that most of Jefferson's supporters have George Washington as their second choice. When the ballots for Jefferson are redistributed to his voters' second choices, George Washington is pushed over the 50% threshold, and he wins the election.

While most Americans may not have heard of RCV, it is far from a new idea. In 2002, Senator John McCain recorded a robocall urging voters to support a ballot measure to adopt RCV, stating that it would "lead to good government because voters will elect leaders who have the support of the majority." That same year, McCain's future opponent, Illinois State Senator Barack Obama, sponsored Illinois Senate Bill 17894 to establish RCV in-state and congressional primaries. Both proposals were ahead of their time; neither of them passed. But in 2018 Maine became the first state to adopt RCV, and Massachusetts will vote on RCV in November 2020. The benefits of this approach are not just theoretical. It has been utilized in several municipalities to elect various city officials. In these places, voters report that candidates focused on the issues of the campaign rather than denigrating their opponents. If candidates need to win second place (or even third place) votes to make it over the 50% threshold, campaigning by simply attacking opponents will have limited utility. RCV ensures that the winner will always have support from the broadest possible portion of the electorate. And importantly, RCV eliminates the enormous barrier to entry that plurality voting creates. Combined with nonpartisan top-five primaries to create final-five voting, the authors are convinced that it would be transformational.

Reengineering Legislative Machinery

To some extent, most of the energy of the book is expended in describing the problems, and in prescribing solutions to the *electoral machinery*. One suspects that the authors believe that the *legislative machinery* would tend to repair itself through the influence of those selected by the new *electoral machinery*.

Nonetheless, their first prescription is to use a proven management practice to reimagine the legislative machinery from scratch: zero-based budgeting. With this method of budgeting, used by many organizations across the private sector, all expenses must be justified and approved according to anticipated value, not history. They suggest putting aside most of the rules of the House and the Senate, the rules of the Committee on Rules, the volumes of rules upon rules optimized and weaponized over the decades. They suggest putting aside the informal rules and practices as well as customs that create separate podiums, separate cloakrooms, and separate dining rooms for Democrats and Republicans, and that seat the chamber according to party. They suggest putting it all aside and then reimagining zero-based budgeting from a clear, white space. Some of the old customs or rules, like old furniture, might prove useful, but most of these, they suggest, can be left aside.

Obviously, if the *electoral machinery* is not changed in a way that eliminates hyperpartisanship, there is no hope at all that the *legislative machinery* could be motivated into useful action. This is not a chicken/egg problem. The *electoral machinery* must be changed first. Procedural and substantive legislative reform can, and surely would, follow.

Our circumstances in the United States are bad and getting worse. The ideas put forth in this book are original, well thought out, and indeed brilliant. This is precisely the sort of change that people deeply concerned about political dysfunction and national decline should applaud and seek to bring about as soon as possible.

12

The Politicization of the American Judiciary

September 28, 2020

The death of a Supreme Court justice has once again unleashed the forces of hypocrisy and bloviation. It is almost entertaining to see each side excoriating the other for doing precisely what they would be doing if the shoe were on the other foot. Yet beneath it all, there is a legitimate political reason for all of this hyperactivity: the American judiciary has become more powerful than many legislatures, and even a single judge with lifetime tenure and no political accountability can stop presidential action or legislative enactment in its tracks. This problem has been brewing for a long time and it will not go away anytime soon.

In a different context, I wrote about this back on March 3, just before the Great Lockdown began. The context then was a discussion about an extraordinary book by Jonathan Sumption, a retired British Supreme Court Judge: *Trials of the State and the Decline of Politics*.[80] The context now is a vacant Supreme Court swing seat on the cusp of one of the most contentious presidential elections in American history. There are many depressing things to note about the current state of the American judiciary, and I will note but a few of them here. But there are also some relatively straightforward solutions to some of the problems, and I will note them as well.

Problems. As I noted last March (Chapter 5 of this book), the expansion of law is one of the most significant phenomena of our time. The law touches nearly everything. The law has more power than the family regarding the well-being of children, more power over social behavior than most churches, and increasing power over commercial interests large and small. The expansion of individual and group constitutional rights has placed matters before courts that, in virtually every other developed country in the world, are handled by legislatures and therefore have the power of real political legitimacy. Judicial power is power against which the electorate has only limited and indirect political recourse. Worse yet, however, increasingly politicians in general, and the 2016 and 2020 presidential candidates in particular, promise if elected to deliver judges of a certain ideology—and indeed youthful judges who can be expected to serve for many decades. We see this at the state level in gubernatorial elections as well: politicians running for office on the promise of a truly biased and nonneutral judiciary.

On the left, we have promises to appoint minorities of every kind and character: minorities who will interpret state or federal constitutions to expand group rights over individual rights whenever the opportunity presents itself. On the right, this is seen as illegitimate, antidemocratic, and a grave threat to personal and religious liberties. Candidates of the right promise judges who will "enforce the law" and not "make it up." We also hear promises to free society from the yoke of the left and from the tyranny of politically correct groupthink, to protect individual and religious liberties, and to remain faithful insofar as is practicable to the provisions underpinning our founding documents. On the left, this is seen is the continuation of structural racism and the perpetuation of social injustice: terms that have become as inflammatory as they are bereft of agreed meaning.

These tend to be big issues. They often affect the day-to-day lives of citizens. Yet, it was not until the Supreme Court's 1973 decision legalizing abortion during the first trimester (*Roe v. Wade)* that the issue of judicial politicization became fully "nationalized." I do not mean to ignore the Court's 1954 decision in *Brown v. Board of Education* declaring "separate but equal" educational systems for blacks and whites to be unconstitutional. However, that decision had deep constitutional roots and did not present serious constitutional controversy inside or outside the legal community. Certainly, the bussing remedies later imposed by the judiciary were controversial, no less so in Boston, Massachusetts, than in the Deep South. But there was never sharp national division over the core question of whether segregated schooling was constitutionally permissible or proper. One does not have to peer into the dark penumbral shadows of the US Constitution to discover the constitutional right that *Brown* enforced.

But the expansion of individual rights post-*Roe* has often been controversial and has not infrequently relied on a relatively elastic view of one or more constitutional provisions. Below is a sampling of important Supreme Court decisions finding certain things constitutional or unconstitutional. My point here is not to criticize any particular decision as right or wrong but rather to take note of the outsized role of the judiciary, ultimately the Supreme Court, in being the arbiter of long dormant or newly discovered individual "rights." Not included in this list are Supreme Court decisions confirming the constitutionality of rights established by legislative action, of which there are many. But legislative declarations of rights are of a totally different character than judicial declarations of rights, given that the former have the imprimatur of democratic legislative legitimacy.

The Equal Protection clause of the Constitution has underpinned a great many of the landmark cases in this area, the most well-known of which were part and parcel of the unwinding of the nation's segregation laws. These cases have gradually expanded over the last several decades to prohibit decisions by government agencies or private instrumentalities based in whole or in part on race, sex, or religion. Thus, affirmative action by schools and colleges became largely prohibited, although some of these cases are being modified to allow consideration of race and gender in the name of diversity in view of the developing judicial consensus that "a diverse student body is beneficial to all students."

1. Beginning in the early 1970s, statutes and business practices designed to "protect" women (and children) were found to be discriminatory (at least toward women) and hence constitutionally impermissible under the Equal Protection Clause of the Fourteenth Amendment.
2. In 1986, Supreme Court found that a Georgia law that criminalized certain acts of private sexual conduct between homosexual persons did not violate the Fourteenth Amendment. From and after 1996, the Supreme Court cases turned and went the other way, constitutionally protecting homosexual, bisexual, and transsexual activity. By 2003, the Supreme Court had declared consensual same-sex conduct to be a constitutionally protected privacy right, and as a result all of the sodomy laws of the United States were invalidated.

3. The right of same-sex couples to marry was first declared by the Supreme Court of Massachusetts in 2003. By 2015, the Supreme Court had declared that the Fourteenth Amendment required states to license the marriage between the same- sex couple and to recognize a marriage between two people of the same sex when their marriage was lawfully licensed and performed out of state.
4. State statutes requiring abortion providers to have admitting privileges at a hospital proximate to their location violated the Constitution because it placed a substantial obstacle in the path of a woman seeking a previability abortion.
5. Beginning in 1990, the Court heard a handful of decisions on "end of life" issues concluding that (a) the State may constitutionally oppose the request of family members to terminate life-sustaining treatments in the absence of evidence of a clear earlier wish by the vegetative relative; (b) the Controlled Substances Act does not prevent physicians from being able to prescribe drugs needed to perform assisted suicides under state law; and (c) a state law prohibition on assisted suicide does not violate the Equal Protection Clause.
6. Teaching creationism in public schools is unconstitutional (1987).
7. A university cannot use student dues to fund secular groups while excluding religious groups (1995).
8. Prayer in public schools even when initiated and led by students violates the Establishment Clause (2000).
9. A government program that provides tuition vouchers for students to attend a private or religious school of their parents' choosing is constitutional because the vouchers are neutral toward religion and therefore do not violate the Establishment Clause (2022).
10. A state's "no aid" constitutional provision prohibiting state aid to religious schools violates the Free Exercise clause by explicitly discriminating against institutions on the basis of religion (2022).

A much longer list of similar cases establishing or modifying individual constitutional rights can be found at Wikipedia here.[81]

The judiciary has not always sought out this power, but it has rarely shrunk from exercising it either. The judiciary cannot necessarily be faulted for entertaining cases that are brought before it; however, the judiciary *can* be faulted for taking away from legislatures the business of establishing "rights" where the Constitution itself is genuinely silent. Indeed, most of the individual rights that have been declared or discovered in the Constitution by our Supreme Court have been enacted by legislation through a democratic, legislative process in other countries. Still, in a number of cases the judiciary's opportunity to exercise its awesome power is the product of the abandonment of power by legislatures. With regard to contentious social issues, Congress, preoccupied as its members always are with reelection, too often has declined to enter the fray for fear of taking a position that will offend some voting bloc.

I expect that had the Supreme Court not decided *Roe v. Wade* in 1973, abortion rights in most states would have been established through a democratic legislative process in much the same way that end-of-life law is developing (see above). Imagine if that chapter of the culture wars had never been written? It surely would have meant that the Supreme Court never would have become perceived by so many as the most important branch of government and in its own way the root source of so much political dysfunction in this country.

In addition, and often for similar decision-avoidance reelection-related reasons, legislatures have engaged in unsupervised delegation of authority to administrative agencies that perform largely legislative functions both at the federal and state level. Individuals and enterprises aggrieved by these administrative agencies must therefore go to the courts for recourse, thus putting into the hands of the courts a seemingly endless variety of large and small administrative law issues that should be essentially legislative matters. As these administrative issues find their way to the courts (and they always do), we have the courts faced with accepting the administrative state or substituting themselves for the agencies, which have become de facto substitutes for the legislatures. And while the agencies are typically part of an executive branch of government, courts these days rarely defer to executive branches when seeking to manage or micromanage administrative agencies. We therefore see courts performing (or even sometimes usurping) legislative functions, administrative functions, *and* executive functions.

We see this particularly in "hot button" issues such as those involving immigration, agricultural and other land use, oil and gas production and distribution, and micromanagement of certain state election rules (polling hours and deadlines for mail-in ballots are among the current issues that have drawn in the judiciary). To quote from Jonathan Sumption: "To adapt the famous dictum of the German military theorist Clausewitz about war, law is now the continuation of politics by other means." This situation has created what is known generally as "the Administrative State" or, more ominously, "the Deep State."

Another facet of the judicial tyranny problem is that a single federal district judge (out of roughly seven hundred to eight hundred such judges) can enjoin indefinitely the implementation of executive directives, whether presidential or administrative. Still further, a single sitting federal district judge can declare an act of Congress unconstitutional. These individual judicial actions are, of course, subject to appeal. Yet we have seen over the last several years that the appellate process can be frustratingly cumbersome and hardly less "political" than the decisions of individual district court judges. Swift executive action on controversial matters has become virtually impossible. Interested groups, left or right, file their lawsuits before judges whose biases are well known and in circuits whose political tendencies are equally well known. Political litigants, in other words, often get to pick their judges and do so with some skill. This is not lost on the media, which spends real time lionizing favored judges and demonizing disfavored ones. Judicial careers and reputations can be shined and buffed by the press (or tarnished). There is even a term for this: it is called the "Greenhouse Effect," [82] named after *New York Times* reporter Linda Greenhouse, who covered the Supreme Court from 1978 to 2008. Arguably, the judicial desire for media respectability has pulled more than one conservative justice or judge noticeably to the left.

In the circumstances, it is hardly surprising that candidates for executive offices wish to reshape the judiciary so as to make it reasonably compliant with their political agenda. Yet, over time, the judiciary becomes perceived, as it largely is now, not as a source of disinterested independent judgment but rather as "just another bunch of politicians." And not only are they unelected, they serve for life, which these days may mean into their late eighties or beyond.

The credibility of the judiciary itself is at risk. In fact, it is past that point. The judiciary in certain areas already lacks credibility. When Chief Justice Roberts says there are no Obama judges and no Trump judges and so forth, he is not taken seriously. He is not believed. This is because such a statement is simply not true.

We are about to be subjected to several weeks of horse feathers and hypocrisy in connection with the nomination of a Catholic woman with many children who has rocketed through an extraordinary career. There will be hour after hour of mock outrage, faux shock, and real Kabuki theater. The left is and forever will be apoplectic that a liberal Jewish justice could have "her" seat "taken" by a conservative Catholic justice. The right will do everything it can to fill the vacancy before the end of the president's current term, it being rightly fearful that the current administration will not have another term. Indeed, the 2020 election, in one respect, is beginning to have the feel of the 2016 election insofar as both campaigns put enormous stress on the nature of the judges that would be appointed by the winning side. Candidates run on the explicit promise that they will deliver reliably biased and ideological judges who will share the political ideology of the candidates' supporters.

This is an appalling situation about which thoughtful judges should feel nervous if not embarrassed. Yet judges, like everyone else these days, have a point of view about the proper role of government, the rights and responsibilities of citizens, and indeed the rights of noncitizens—illegal aliens. Increasingly the views of the judges from the left and the right are as incompatible and hostile to each other as are the views of the citizenry at large.

Indulging the perhaps heroic assumption that norm-breaking approaches will not be taken, there are some solutions, which must start at the margin with incremental change.

Potential Solutions. There are some solutions to some aspects of the problems. But first of all, "packing" the court with more justices would exacerbate the problem, delegitimize the court, and turn our judicial system into something of a laughingstock. However, should the Democrats win the presidency and the Senate in five weeks, this might well happen. And DC and Puerto Rico might be rocketed into statehood to assure four more Democrat senators, too. Things are that bad. But the politicization of the judiciary could be mitigated. Here are four modest proposals, three of which could be simple.

Proposal #1: Term limits. There are at least two obvious ways to impose some flavor of term limit. First of all, retirement could be compulsory at a certain age, say seventy or seventy-five. Or an individual justice's term could be limited to twenty or twenty-five years. This kind of proposal might not contravene the Constitution because Supreme Court justices whose terms expire could continue to serve as trial judges or appellate judges on a circuit court. This would keep intact their "lifetime" appointment, but it would not be a lifetime on the Supreme Court itself. There are respectable views that thus is constitutional[83] and also that it is not.[84] It seems to me worth a shot.

Proposal #2: Impose a statutory requirement that no single judge can declare an Act of Congress unconstitutional. All challenges to an Act of Congress should be heard by a three-judge panel, with three sitting judges from three separate circuits (appellate judges should be included in the pool from which random judges would be selected). The decision of this three-judge panel would be immediately appealable to the entire Supreme Court, which would be directed by statute to expedite the appellate process.

Proposal #3: Similarly, impose a statutory requirement that no single judge can enjoin any presidential executive order. All challenges to any such executive order should be heard by a three-judge panel, with three sitting judges from three separate circuits (appellate judges should be included in the pool from which random judges would be selected). The decision of this three-judge panel would be immediately appealable to the entire Supreme Court, which would be directed by statute to expedite the appellate process.

Proposal #4: We are in urgent need of an adult and functioning Senate that reasonably protects the rights of the minority party. On November 21, 2013, Senator Reid (D. Nev.) led the Senate Democrats to use the so-called nuclear option to eliminate the use of the filibuster on executive branch nominees and judicial nominees except for the Supreme Court. When the Republicans took control of the Senate in 2015, they kept the 2013 rules in place and on April 6, 2017, Senate Republicans eliminated the remaining exception by invoking the nuclear option for Supreme Court nominees. This was done in order to allow a simple majority to confirm Neil Gorsuch to the Supreme Court.

The filibuster has had a long and somewhat undistinguished and even dishonorable history. It has been used in bad faith by both parties: first by the Democrats to support the suppression of blacks in the South for many decades and then by the Republicans in their regimented opposition to everything Obama. It is an imperfect tool. And perhaps it should not or cannot be brought back for presidential appointments in the current political environment. In fact, it could disappear altogether.

But it ought to be possible before too long for special legislation to come into place that would require some type of "super majority" approval for Supreme Court nominees if not for other appointees. This would require agreement by significant elements of each party for any judge to be confirmed.

I appreciate that I might be accused of extreme naïveté in thinking that any of these proposals are realistic. Indeed, just a few weeks ago at the funeral of John Lewis, the former President Obama raised the prospect of eliminating the filibuster altogether, characterizing it as a "Jim Crow relic." See *The Atlantic:* "Why the Filibuster Could Be Gone."[85] Maybe so, but if the Senate is no less fractious or partisan than the House, then it is nearly pointless to have a Senate at all. Better perhaps to switch to a parliamentary system where the legislature has literally all the power and appoints a prime minister to act as head of government—and can be held fully accountable for its use or misuse on short notice. But I digress. The beauty of a well-functioning parliamentary system is a topic for another day. However, I will say this: the recent "cancellation" of the Founding Fathers and their works in many quarters may open the door a crack for the institution of a brand-new political system. A constitutional monarchy might look pretty good compared to what we have become. Would it not be nice to have a beloved nonpartisan head of state who is not the head of any government. I am trying to remember why we fought a revolution against that in 1775.

13

The Biden Family Business, Ethics, and the Rule of Law

November 3, 2020

While I have no special insight (or maybe no insight at all) into the outcome of tonight's election, recent revelations about the Biden family (the apparent selling of Chinese and other nations' access to Joe Biden by his son, his brother, and others for millions of dollars, some of which allegedly went at least indirectly to Joe Biden) brings to my mind several thoughts. But first a few sentences of essential background. The first line of defense against the initial revelations by the *New York Post* was that this was Russian disinformation. The second line of defense seemed to be that this could not be true because none of the media were reporting it, and if it were true, the media would of course be reporting it. After Mr. Bobulinski's firsthand eyewitness account of events, supported by contemporaneous emails and documents,[86] was broadcast on national television, a soft third line of defense developed: that this was "old news" unworthy of comment. An equally soft fourth line of defense was that this was just a political smear and that Joe Biden did nothing illegal.

One does not need to dislike Mr. Biden or like Mr. Trump to recognize that something quite troubling happened and is now being ignored: sort of like the "crazy uncle in the attic" whose rantings are ignored by dinner party guests. It is not as if peddling influence to foreign governments is new. The Clinton Foundation raised hundreds of millions of dollars from Middle Eastern potentates based on the presumption that Mrs. Clinton would become president. A week after the 2016 election, the foundation was effectively finished. President Bill Clinton sold nights in the Lincoln bedroom to large donors, mostly domestic, but perhaps foreign, too. Powerful politicians have spouses and children who seem to end up making gobs of money, sometimes even right out of college. Chelsea Clinton had a starting salary of $650,000 or so. Hunter Biden has lots of company selling access, perhaps indeed from both parties. But the Biden family business is troubling not only because Joe Biden was vice president at the time but also because he is on the verge of becoming the actual president-elect tonight or this week.

It has always been clear that the Biden story is not the product of Russian disinformation. The facts, after all, come from Hunter Biden's own laptop. The role of Mr. Giuliani did give the early disclosures an odor of political mischief though. And indeed, one could imagine that a foreign power, even Russia, might have pushed the story; however, that would not make it "disinformation," it would just make it Russians peddling the truth. This might be a bit concerning to some but in no way an exoneration of the Biden family's conduct.

The fact that the original story was banned from social media and not carried in the major newspapers of the United States (these two circumstances are still going on to some extent) is, to me, in many ways more concerning than the apparent corruption of the Biden family business. If the real possibility of serious corruption by senior elected officials is not newsworthy, then we have truly entered the twilight zone of soft totalitarianism that we have written about previously in these pages. I don't think we ever thought that our Constitution, which protects the press from the government, would see a situation in which the press shackled itself to a particular political party in such a way as to deny itself the very freedom guaranteed by the Constitution. Media staff can and do get editors fired for stories they allow.[87] Things have only gotten worse recently. A story in RealClearPolitics from a couple of days ago reports about the move afoot by staffers at the *Wall Street Journal* to defang the editorial page writers. Almost as alarming is the bizarre handling of the story by NBC News, detailed here by George Washington Universotuy law professor Jonathan Turley last weekend.[88] As he put it:

> There is something incredibly insidious in this story. The media has allowed itself to be boxed in by the Biden campaign. Reporters willingly bought into the narrative that

there is no real story to pursue over the laptop. The longer they have ignored the story; the more difficult it is to admit that there are real issues raised by these disclosures. Reporters simply cannot walk back from the dismissal of a story even as it grows daily with new disclosures. The only recourse is to discredit another story and another source.

The regularity of influence peddling in Washington is one of the reasons it was referred to as "the swamp" that needed to be "drained." This was an animating feature underpinning the election of Donald Trump in 2016. Many years ago, Michael Kinsley, a soft-spoken, extremely articulate liberal columnist coined the notion that what was scandalous in Washington were not politicians' illegal acts but rather things they did that were technically legal. Most politicians (and others) caught up in some kind of scandal usually claim victory if what they did was not a crime (or at least if they were not convicted of the crime). This is an extremely low bar for respectability. So here we are on election day (and perhaps on the verge of a sweeping Biden victory) confronting a somewhat unique situation, although it may have its parallels with 2016.

In my view, the attorney general should appoint a Special Counsel to investigate the matter, and this should be done within weeks of the election. The legislative criteria for appointing a Special Counsel are as follows:

> The Attorney General will appoint a Special Counsel when he or she determines that criminal investigation of a person or matter is warranted and:
>
> 1. that investigation or prosecution of that person or matter by a United States Attorney's Office or litigating division of the Department of Justice would present a conflict of interest for the Department or other extraordinary circumstances; and
> 2. that under the circumstances, it would be in the public interest to appoint an outside Special Counsel to assume responsibility for the matter.

It seems clear beyond peradventure that the monies received from the Chinese, and perhaps others, by the Biden family warrant at least an investigation. If Mr. Biden wins the election, there is zero chance that his attorney general would have the courage or the sense of ethical duty to follow the lead of President Trump's then-attorney general and appoint a Special Counsel whose investigation could touch the president. It also seems clear that should Trump prevail in the election, his Justice Department would be deeply criticized even more than now if it undertook an investigation of the Biden family business.

The most neutral and responsible approach to the whole matter would be for Attorney General Barr to appoint a nonpartisan, disinterested Special Counsel and let that person proceed unhindered by political considerations left or right. It has been Democrats who have often demanded the appointment of Special Counsel and tended to lecture us about their appropriateness in a variety of different circumstances. Many Democrats, troubled by the recent revelations, might welcome an independent Special Counsel. Indeed, the progressives within the Democratic Party might see the appointment of the Special Counsel as a unique opportunity to accelerate the "incapacitation" of the new president so as to be able to install Vice President Harris as president. This would have the further incidental benefit of allowing now President Harris to appoint a vice president under the Twenty-Fifth Amendment, which is subject to the approval of a simple majority of both houses of Congress.

But many of the elected Democrats most likely would be aghast at a Special Counsel prospect as it would put them in a Hobson's Choice of embracing, however grudgingly, the Special Counsel, or urging the president or the attorney general to fire that person, with whatever political consequences might ensue. Given the quiescence of the media and its collaboration with institutional Democrats, there is a good chance that the firing of the Special Counsel would be treated yawningly as perfectly appropriate. The bulk of the media might simply embrace the narrative that the appointment of the Special Counsel was illegitimate, politically motivated, and never appropriate to begin with and hence should be undone immediately. No matter how the Democratic Party might react institutionally, we would find out whether they are interested in the rule of law or the rule of the Democratic Party. Those are not the same things by a long shot. I also have to confess that I would find it amusing to watch certain familiar Democrat politicians, well known for bloviation, react to a potentially wide-ranging investigation of one of their own. But more importantly, we have heard nearly every elected official in Washington say that "nobody is above the law." Is it going to be true in the case of the Biden family business or not? In the world of a Biden victory, the answer to that question will rest in the hands of the Democrats.

14

Winners, Losers, and Survivors

November 10, 2020

Well, I am glad the election is finally over. I also think that we will all survive quite nicely, at least in the short term. But what a weird ride. Donald Trump was not even the biggest loser. The pollsters and the media seem to me to have lost more. To be sure, President Trump was personally repudiated, but the pollsters and the media had virtually every major prognostication dead wrong. There was no "blue wave." The Democrats lost a half dozen or more seats in the House of Representatives and, at least for the moment, Republicans seem to have maintained control of the Senate, subject to the Georgia runoff elections. Even if the Democrats capture the Senate and the vice president is poised to break a tie vote, that will mean the party can go no further to the left than its most conservative senator will abide. Further down ballot, the Republicans maintained control of all of the state legislatures and governorships that they previously had and flipped a number of state legislatures as well, significant in a decennial redistricting year.

Much to the dismay of the Democratic Party, even the despised Mr. Trump gained substantial ground among black men and Latinos, as well as other voters of color. He actually lost support among white men compared to 2016. As *The Economist* magazine pointed out, exit polls suggest that Mr. Trump increased his share of support from every group except white men. If that is right, Democrats won the election chiefly through their improved turnout effort, not by wooing voters from Mr. Trump. This may not bode well for unity going forward.

On the other hand, it is not clear that "Trumpism" will survive the absence of Mr. Trump. It is not even clear what "Trumpism" really is. For the last four years, as *The Economist* points out, Trumpism has been whatever Mr. Trump said it was. Yet there are some influential Republicans, such as Senator Cotton from Arkansas and Senator Rubio from Florida, who have attempted to turn the party into an actual vehicle for the working-class concerns Mr. Trump raised. But in a way, Mr. Trump himself emerged as the main obstacle to the conservative movement he inspired. His low approval rating along with the election results suggest that he was again backed by Republicans who dislike him but could not bear to vote for the alternative. Hence, as pointed out in *The Atlantic*, "Never Trumpers" may have been among the big winners, especially if Republicans maintain control of the Senate after the Georgia runoff elections. They will have gotten rid of Mr. Trump himself but recaptured the semblance of a political party that has expanded its constituency beyond any of their hopes or expectations.

The Week magazine headlined that "The Left Just Got Crushed." So much for the Democratic fantasy—the one that seemingly never dies—of unobstructed rule. Democrats didn't just want to win and govern in the name of a deeply divided nation's fractured sense of the common good. No, they wanted to lead a moral revolution, to transform the country—not only enacting a long list of new policies but making a series of institutional changes that would entrench their power far into the future. Pack the Supreme Court. Add left-leaning states. Break up others to give the left huge margins in the Senate. Get rid of the Electoral College. Abolish the police. Rewrite the nation's history, with white supremacy and racism placed "at the very center." Ensure "equity" not just in opportunity but in outcomes.

Yet the toxicity of Mr. Trump himself generated a historically huge opposition. One gets the feeling that most of the vote for Mr. Biden was an anti-Trump vote, not a pro-Joe vote. As Mr. Biden himself has said, he will be a transitional figure. Where the party will go after his tenure is not clear, nor is it clear that Ms. Harris will be the future of the Democratic Party, although the press seems to have already anointed her as such. Yet it is difficult to imagine her as one who could appeal to any meaningful segment of the seventy million who voted for Mr. Trump.

Other points to ponder:

1. The South is open to the right Democratic candidate, whether Georgia, North Carolina, South Carolina. All of those states could turn as blue as Virginia. This is a bright spot for Democrats and a

danger area for Republicans, who are broadening their base but must do more or lose ground.

2. The entire business of polling must change. This will take time. It might not even be possible to get reliable poll numbers anymore.
3. The media (press and social) needs to return to fact gathering and reporting. The media can do far more mischief than any foreign power. Social media in particular seem to have earned the loss of their Section 230 immunity, and their loss of it should be swift and bipartisan.
4. The conflict inside the Democratic Party is just beginning—again. It is unclear how much of the Democratic Party is aligned with the whole "woke" mob (or with the historical middle-roadism of Mr. Biden), but it does not seem likely that Mr. Biden will embrace them, although he must not appear to reject them either. He must walk a tightrope. Should the Democrats capture the Senate in January, Mr. Biden might prove unable to resist the woke progressives. I have a suspicion that he might even be hoping for Republican control of the Senate to as to avoid the intraparty warfare, but that is probably not so.
5. Mr. Biden ran on pandemic management and unity. The pandemic will run its course and it seems unlikely a Biden administration will make an ounce of difference inasmuch as state policies dictate living habits. As for Mr. Biden's professed quest for unity, it might be hard to establish in a world where the constant and consistent message from the Democrats—all of them—for the last four years has been: resist, overturn, boycott, surveil, investigate, sue, leak, and impeach. Only a real Truth and Reconciliation Commission, managed by someone of the stature and grace of a Nelson Mandela, seems capable of overcoming all of that.

I wonder about the Middle East. Do the Democrats truly wish to ditch oil production and become, once again, dependent on Saudi Arabia and other Gulf States oil? Secretary Pompeo seemed to have a strategy, although not one that was clearly articulated, to use American worldwide oil dominance to pressure the Gulf States into alliances with Israel and to create a Middle East largely aligned against Iran, as well as China. One can only speculate regarding what a Biden administration's Middle East policy might look like.

But it is reasonable to speculate that basic policies could turn into a John Kerry/Susan Rice reprise, but greener and less focused on geopolitical issues or interests.

But as I have ended several of these ruminations over the last year, hope springs eternal.

15

Ruminations on the Biden Justice Department

December 8, 2020

We have a greater opportunity than usual to engage in rank speculation and congenial rumination about what various facets of the Biden administration might look like. My remit for the moment is the Justice Department and some of its constituent pieces.

Bearing in mind the hysterical way in which Mr. Barr has been treated by most of the media, I am going to begin by thinking a bit in historical terms about the Justice Department. Full disclosure, I have known Bill Barr for a long time and consider him to be a man of integrity and honor who has long put country before politics. Of course, like you and me dear reader, he is a human being, capable of making mistakes. Whatever his mistakes, I believe he has demonstrated his value and loyalty to country in a variety of ways and under different presidents. He has not been a lap dog or a lackey of President Trump, although he has done the assigned job of the attorney general of the United States to defend the constitutionality or legality of the administration's rules, regulations, and legislation.

So, caveat stated, a short rumination on my adult memories of the attorney general. For political purposes, I shall consider my adulthood to have begun with the 1960 election of John F. Kennedy. He appointed his brother Robert F. Kennedy as the sixty-fourth attorney general of the United States. The appointment was criticized, most notably by the *New York Times*: "It is simply not good enough to name a bright young political manager no matter how bright or how young or how personally loyal, to a major posting government." Other reporters or opinion writers felt much the same.[89] Nobody loathed Robert Kennedy more than Lyndon Johnson, who reportedly took great pleasure in signing into law a 1967 nepotism statute that, among other things, appeared to make it impossible for a president to appoint immediate family members to the cabinet or, some argued, even to the White House staff. President Kennedy himself told people, maybe in jest, that he "just wanted to give [Bobby] a little legal practice before he becomes a lawyer." Bobby was not amused.

President Johnson appointed Nicholas Katzenbach and then later his old Texas friend Ramsey Clark. President Nixon brought us attorneys general sixty-seven through seventy. John Mitchell was above all a loyalist; his career as attorney general was cut short by his conviction of multiple crimes committed during the Watergate affair. His successors were in certain ways controversial but not for their loyalty to the president.

President Ford appointed Edward Levi, who was best known for his reform of the then-common cowboy tactics of the FBI. He was not a servant of the president in the manner of Bobby Kennedy or John Mitchell. The same was doubtless true of Jimmy Carter's two attorneys general, Griffin Bell and Benjamin Civiletti. President Reagan's attorneys general (seventy-four through seventy-six) were William Smith, Edwin Meese, and Dick Thornburgh. Mr. Meese was quite controversial and attacked for past ethical lapses; the others were highly regarded even by the opposition.

President George H. W. Bush appointed William Barr as attorney general number seventy-seven. Mr. Barr was not considered a Bush loyalist in the sense I have been describing, but he had long been a strong defender of presidential power. Nonetheless, his confirmation for the post in 1991 involved "unusually placid" hearings, and it was said he enjoyed a "sterling reputation" on both sides of the political aisle. [90]

President Clinton appointed Janet Reno as his attorney general (number seventy-eight), and she served for nearly eight full years in the position. Somewhat remarkably, she managed to avoid being drawn into the various legal, ethical, and sexual controversies swirling around President Clinton during much of that time.

The George W. Bush administration accounted for three different attorneys general, all of whom were experienced men with no particular personal ties to the president. This is a slight contrast to the Obama attorneys general, Eric Holder and Loretta Lynch (eighty-two and eighty-three). Holder was a confidant and close ally of the president; he was unabashedly loyal and presented himself to the public as the president's "wingman," not a term designed to suggest independence of judgment but rather as one there to defend the president personally. The *Miami Herald* took him to task last January for his criticism of William Barr and accused him of considerable hypocrisy.

Then, for nearly two years, there was Loretta Lynch, whose reputation seems unlikely to recover from her unfortunate secret meeting with Bill Clinton on a private plane on the tarmac of an airport during the presidential campaign of 2016. This, coupled with her inability to control her subordinate James Comey and her confused quasi-recusal from the Hillary Clinton email brouhaha, have left her with a sullied reputation.

This glance at the past is intended to provide a degree of perspective so that we can view the present and the future through a clearer lens. For starters, one would not normally expect Joe Biden to appoint as his attorney general someone whose main job he perceived to be the protection of the Biden family. On the other hand, the appointment by William Barr of John Durham as a special counsel with a broader warrant to continue his investigation into the 2016 Russiagate controversy is doubtless going to have a material impact on who gets the job of attorney general (or maybe more to the point, on who does *not* get the job). Sally Yates has been on various short lists, but with John Durham as special counsel, and given that she is a potential target of that investigation, it seems unlikely that she would be appointed.

That said, an early decision of President Biden will be whether to terminate John Durham as special counsel. Attention-seeking congressmen like Gerald Nadler and Adam Schiff have already called for Durham's termination: Nadler on the grounds that he is not eligible[91] and Schiff on the grounds that "Barr is using the special counsel law for a purpose it was not intended: to continue a politically motivated investigation long after Barr leaves office." [92] Jonathan Turley, on the other hand, wrote: "The move confirmed that, in a chaotic and spinning political galaxy, Bill Barr remains the one fixed and immovable object." Importantly, the appointment makes a public report more likely. Prosecutors do not normally prepare reports. Special counsels do. As Turley wrote over the weekend, President Trump himself was irate at the appointment and claimed that it was a "smokescreen" to delay the release of the report. Trump seems to have missed both the legal and political significance of the action. In Turley's words: "From a political perspective, the move is so elegantly lethal that it would make Machiavelli Green with entry." [93].

The Durham investigation, while not as directly focused upon the Biden administration in the same way that the Muller investigation was focused on the Trump administration, nonetheless touches Biden and could bleed into matters related to the Hunter Biden affair.

It is with some of this in mind that the media apparatchiks have come up with a list of names that supposedly are in serious consideration for the attorney general position. The diverse list is full of heavy hitters, political veterans, and new faces. It is also doubtless incomplete. But to me the most notable things about the people mentioned thus far are that: (1) none seem to be particularly progressive; all seem to be Obama centrists; and none seem to have any obvious political axe to grind (with potential exceptions noted below); and (2) none seem to fit into the "loyalty to the President *uber alles*" mold. Here are those most mentioned.

1. **Merrick Garland**. Highly qualified by any standard. Had Hillary Clinton won the 2016 election, the Republicans would still be kicking themselves for denying him a seat on the Supreme Court. He served as deputy assistant attorney general in the criminal division of the Justice Department during the early years of the Clinton administration and then as the principal associate deputy attorney general. He supervised the investigation of the 1995 Oklahoma City bombing and oversaw the prosecution of Timothy McVeigh.
2. **Jeh Johnson.** Is a well-qualified African American who served as secretary of the Department of Homeland Security from 2013 to 2017. Before that he served as general counsel of the Department of Defense. Under President Clinton, he served as general counsel of the Department of the Air Force.
3. **Doug Jones**. He has served briefly as a senator from Alabama, having defeated Jeff Sessions but then been defeated by Republican Tommy Tuberville. He also served as US Attorney for the Northern District of Alabama.
4. **Deval Patrick.** Patrick was the governor of Massachusetts and quite close to President Obama. He was a candidate for the 2020

Democratic nomination but dropped out after just a few weeks. He headed the Civil Rights Divisions of the US Department of Justice. He also served as a managing director of Bain Capital, executive vice president and general counsel of Coca-Cola, and vice president and general counsel of Texaco.
5. **Lisa Monaco**. She is a former federal prosecutor who served as White House homeland security advisor during President Obama's second term. She has been an advisor to the Biden campaign.
6. **Sally Yates**. Acting attorney general in the early days of the Trump administration, until the president fired her for ordering Justice Department lawyers to not make legal arguments defending President Trump's executive order on immigration and refugees.

By the time this gets into print, other names may have been mentioned. Xavier Becerra was on the list but was appointed today to another cabinet position (HHS). As seems to be reasonably well understood, many of the rumors about who will get what job will turn out to be untrue, and often this misdirection is intentional. This is because the transitional process is a perfect opportunity for: (a) reporters to flatter sources by suggesting those sources should be considered for major jobs; (b) team Biden to float someone's name to flatter him or her; (c) a person who wants to be considered for a key job to float his or her own name; (d) other constituencies in the Democratic Party to push their preferred choices; and so on.[94]

Still, if "the press" is to be believed, Biden wants to "restore the Independence" of the Justice Department and refocus it more on civil rights. Having chosen Janet Yellen (white female) for treasury, Anthony Blinken (white male) for state and having three defense choices (Jeh Johnson, Michele Flournoy, and Lloyd Austin) somewhat hanging out there for several days, the justice position is not getting as much attention as might be thought normal. But to my eye, one of the most remarkable things about *all* of his cabinet appointees thus far is how centrist they are. It would be hard to imagine any of them being appointed by Bernie Sanders or Elizabeth Warren, for example. To use a phrase that is highly derogatory when used by members of antifa, all of the candidates for the job of attorney general can be thought of as "Globocaps," or global capitalists. And this is true of most of those already appointed to senior positions and most of those reportedly under consideration for other senior positions.

So, while Team Biden is making headlines for appointing a record number of individuals who are LGTBQ, most people do not seem to be overtly "progressive" or "radical" when it comes to most economic or other core policy issues. To be sure, they all despise Trump, and do not care for Trump supporters either.

No matter who Biden selects, it would be surprising to me if the Justice Department's mission became the continuation of the past vendetta against the Trump administration. One suspects that competition policy will be high on the agenda of the Justice Department, as it has been under the Trump administration, but probably more aggressive on the merger front against big tech. The powers that be who enforce competition policy around the world seem all equally fed up with big tech, and therefore considerable investigative activity is likely to take place in that space.

The Civil Rights division of the Department of Justice will have to contend with the BLM movement and associated demands for reparations of one sort or another. This is a field in which Biden must tread carefully since it could end up pitting him against what he has always liked to think of as "his people—Joe Sixpack." Somewhat similarly, the focus on LGBTQ, and the stated goal of making the Justice Department more "independent" (of what I wonder), does suggest the stirrings of an agenda to advance and protect the LGBTQ community, which certainly broke heavily for Biden and whose vocal influence is in inverse proportion to its size. It is a group that punches well above its weight. Justice Department actions in this area would almost certainly bring the Biden administration into conflict with various religious groups and could be a source of considerable disunity. And should the Civil Rights division efforts be blocked at the Supreme Court, as is quite imaginable, this could help to create a particularly noisy community within the Democratic Party for packing the Supreme Court to eliminate the influence of the current majority. No matter what happens in Georgia next month, there are going to be a lot of issues to mediate within the Democratic Party. It could be quite a messy thing to watch and possibly give the media a fresh look at the real world after four years of being mesmerized by Trump land.

16

What Will They Do without Trump to Bash?

January 5, 2021

First of all, good riddance to 2020 and welcome 2021! Second, no year is off to a proper start without a look back at the prior year through the memorable eyes and hilarious brain of Dave Barry. However bad 2020 was, his review of it is enough to bring laughing tears to the eyes of left and right alike. Indeed, he is one of the few people left in the world who can skewer everyone with a light touch and not seem generally, well, hateful - without that special malice that seems to so afflict the left. His column is sadly behind the *Washington Post* paywall for some.[95]

Third, I have been wondering what all those reporters, their staffs, the editors, op-ed writers, late-night comedians, big-tech moguls, the universities and their academic apparatchiks, sonorous and not-so-sonorous voices on public and private radio, and the rest of the center-left will do once the curtain finally falls on the remnants of the Trump administration. Certainly, the *New York Times* writers seem as energetic as ever—even just yesterday exclaiming about the "lack of decency" in the country, especially that part of it that might have supported any aspect of the Trump administration, describing Republicans as: "Traitors to Democracy and Profiles in Cowardice."[96] So much for healing and unity. The Grey Lady seems bent on vengeance, like Madame Defarge but without the knitting.

I am reminded, in a way, of Richard Nixon's first farewell speech in 1962. Those of you under a certain age may not remember that after losing a close election to John F. Kennedy in 1960, reportedly thanks to then Mayor Daley and the cemeteries of Cook County, Illinois, Nixon ran for governor of California but got badly trounced by Pat Brown. In the wake of that he gave what, at the time, was a "famous" press conference during which he announced to the national press corps that they "would no longer have Dick Nixon to kick around anymore." The national media generally disliked Richard Nixon, and Nixon disliked the media. But compared to the relationship between the media and Donald Trump, it was all light-hearted child's play.

Yet after the assassination of President Kennedy in 1963, and indeed even before then, the national press turned on the Democratic administration and its handling of the Vietnam War, the slow pace of civil rights progress, women's rights, the environment, and more. One wonders whether that can happen today. Huge segments of the print, cable, and broadcast media; Congress; Hollywood; and big tech have spent four years in an all-out no-holds-barred battle against President Trump, everything associated with his administration and, more shockingly, all of his more than seventy million supporters. In the process, inch by inch and step by step, any semblance of objectivity was set aside. Late-night comedy reportedly never hosted non-woke celebrities, politicians, news makers, or just plain folks. By the time of the 2020 Long Hot Summer and BLM, the media was bringing us nothing but Orwellian stories, headlines, and onscreen runners about "mostly peacefully looting," "mostly peaceful arson," "mostly peaceful car bombings," "mostly peaceful shootings" and so forth. We were asked to believe these voices of authority and certainly not our "lying eyes."

So, I wonder, what topics will occupy producers, directors, scribblers, editors, and their staffs? And as the emotional toll of hating Trumpism wears out, will anybody listen to what they say anymore? Will they pay attention to the frailty of the president, the mediocrity of many of his cabinet appointments, the developing and serious battle for supremacy between the Democratic progressives and the old-line Democrats like President-Elect Biden? Even today, two months after the election, the editorial pages, the op-ed pages, MSNBC, CNN, and the broadcast networks still manage to find the energy to attack Trump and any congressperson who engages in the same conduct that congresspersons engaged in when challenging the Trump victory in 2016 or the Bush victory in 2000. See the article "Treason is a Matter of Dates."[97]

One worries that we have reached a level of hypocrisy so extreme that it cannot realistically be walked back. And beyond hypocrisy, the renaming of classrooms, buildings, statues, parks, and anything else that might have a suspect name moves forward apace. This is the creeping toward the mainstream of critical race theory. As an op-ed piece in the *Wall Street Journal* put it on Christmas Day, no one has noticed, or at any rate pointed out, the basic contradictoriness of exposing, emphasizing, and displaying our national sins on the one hand, while on the other trying to obliterate every trace of them from historical record. See "The Woke See No Evil—and Nothing but Evil."[98]

In California, they have established a "Renaming Committee" (as Dave Barry would say, "I am not making this up") that has flagged forty-two separate San Francisco schools whose names the committee has declared must be removed because of associations was slaveholding, colonizing, oppression, or some other crime against critical race theory. We thus say goodbye to schools named after Abraham Lincoln, Francis Scott Key, California Missionary Father Junipero Serra, the writer James Russell Lowell and many others, including surprisingly that conservative Democrat stalwart Senator Diane Feinstein. Stranger still, proposed House rules for the next session of Congress would eliminate gender-specific family terms like uncle, aunt, niece, and nephew and replace them with "parents' sibling," "siblings' child" and the like.

Thus far, the signs of pushback are modest, although one suspects that there is much silent pushback going on in the country. Nonetheless, there appeared a few months ago quite an interesting article in a publication I have never heard of (*New Discourses*) taking up the question of "The Woke Breaking Point."[99] The article is a fascinating guide to having conversations with friends or acquaintances who have not yet reached *their* woke "breaking point" and interrogating them as to whether there is anything that could *ever* cause them to reach that point, referred to as *peak woke*.

Anyway, we are about to be launched into the Biden administration, and we have no idea about the policy inclinations of the new administration, whether with respect to taxes, immigration, packing the Supreme Court, making Puerto Rico a state (so as to add two Democratic senators); foreign policy in general; US policy toward China, Russia, Iran, North Korea, Iraq, and Afghanistan in particular; or much of anything else. The electorate voted by a healthy margin (based on the popular vote anyway) for "not

Donald Trump." One senses that the election outcome was based more on a severe case of "Trump Fatigue" than based on opposition to a number of his policies, although to be sure those policies tended to be presented in ways that were, shall we say, suboptimal. Almost everybody who thinks about immigration policy agrees that we need a mechanism to citizenship for many of the so-called Dreamers, although they are surprisingly small in number. People seem to agree in general that we need to have secure borders, although nobody was willing to agree with Mr. Trump's articulation of the solution, which seemed at bottom insulting to Mexicans and those from Latin American countries.

The leadership of the Democratic Party generally agrees that we have a serious problem with China, both economically and militarily. Russia, with a GDP roughly the size of Italy, is an altogether different sort of problem than China, which has a navy approaching the size of our shrinking navy and may soon have a larger economy. It certainly has more influence in the world: influence not maintained, one might note, through alliances along the lines of NATO or otherwise but by unilateral strength. China's foreign policy is very much a "China First" policy writ large. China does not engage in bilateral or multilateral activity in any meaningful way.

So, we are entering interesting but perhaps, at least momentarily, calmer times. Perhaps a time of American decline in the world, much like Britain in the 1950s after Suez. Or perhaps a time of economic renewal. In any case, deep in the bowels of the new administration, we may find that the thought-police tyrants will organize themselves in the shadows more so than in the open. A fascinating article, again from this new-to-me publication called *New Discourses*, along those lines can be found here. [100] But as this issue goes to press, we are about to begin the runoff elections in Georgia, certainly one of the more consequential state runoff elections in living memory for most of us.

Let us hope that the rage of recent years has not become addictive. As Jonathan Turley mentioned in a post yesterday, this sort of rage "becomes a license to hate. While few will admit it, the Trump years were a release from decency and civility. We have become a nation of conflict junkies." My hope, however, runs the other way. I am trusting that the unserious journalists, editors, news directors and other influence peddlers will have to stop focusing on the center-right "despicables" (f//k/a/ deplorables) and actually get back to informing the general public of newsworthy events within the new administration. This may not require courage so much as just a return to the good old days when they could look good and attract eyeballs by making those in power look bad. It seems to me a strange hope that the press will cherish and use its freedoms in a rough approximation of nonpartisanship but, as ever, hope springs eternal.

17

On American Diversity and Its Origins

April 13, 2021

Author's note. This article turned out to be quite different from what I expected to write when I started. I intended to write a rumination about diversity in America and whether it has evolved from a good thing to an arguably bad thing. But in researching the topic I read the book that is the subject of this review, and the more I thought about it, the more I wanted to bring to this readership a review of the book, with some amount of commentary so that all readers will, should they have the pleasure of buying and reading the book, have a common baseline understanding of the fascinating impacts of American diversity over the last four hundred years. With such a common understanding, any discussion of diversity should be much more knowledgeable and certainly more interesting. The book is American Nations: A History of the Eleven Rival Regional Cultures of North America *by Colin Woodard.*

This is not a new book (it was published in 2011) but it was new to me. Along the way, I got more than I bargained for and came away surprised that so little of what I learned had been part of any academic curriculum I had ever been exposed to. One event in particular of considerable influence in America during the seventeenth century was the English Civil War, which I do not recall learning much about during my own education. Another aspect of the American experience, derived from the Dutch in New Amsterdam in the early seventeenth century, was the extraordinary *tolerance* for diversity, which gave at least commercial New York and parts of the new country such strengths. But that tolerance for diversity strikes me as having transmogrified grotesquely into a multiplicity of legal requirements for diversity in many dimensions but not these days including thought or expression.

The book begins early on by bursting a bubble. Americans have been taught for centuries to think of the European settlement of the continent as having progressed from east to west, expanding from the English beachheads of Massachusetts and Virginia to the shores of the Pacific. Generations of frontiersmen pushed into the wilderness to achieve their destiny as God's chosen people: a unified republic stretching from sea to shining sea inhabited by virtuous, freedom-loving people. Like so much of our oversimplified American history, this is quite wrong. *American Nations* describes the development of separate North American "nations," from southern Canada to much of northern Mexico. The cover of the book provides a map showing the rough boundaries of the "nations," which Woodard defines, in order of their emergence: El Norte, New France, Tidewater, Yankeedom, New Netherland. the Deep South, the Midlands, Greater Appalachia, the Left Coast, and the Far West.

1. El Norte. The Americas were discovered by a Spanish expedition in 1492, and by the time the first Englishman arrived at Jamestown a little over a century later, Spanish explorers had already explored much of the heartland, including the Smoky Mountains and the Grand Canyon. They had mapped the coast of Oregon and the Canadian Maritimes, not to mention Latin America and the Caribbean. They had given names to everything from the Bay of Fundy to Tierra del Fuego. Indeed, in 1565, they founded Saint Augustine, Florida, the oldest European city in the United States.

El Norte, as envisaged by Woodard, comprises a large chunk of northern Mexico (much of the states of Tamaulipas, Nuevo León, Coahuila, Chihuahua, Sonora, and Baja California) as well as a good-sized sliver running from north of San Diego, California, across southern Arizona, New Mexico, Colorado, and Texas all the way to the Gulf of Mexico. According to Woodard, Spain's king, Philip II, used the massive riches pouring in from the Americas to build armies and an enormous naval armada with which to conquer Protestant Europe. That effort failed, but the conflict lasted for a century, exhausted the Spanish treasury, and left millions dead.

As Woodard explains it, by spearheading the effort to snuff out the Protestant Reformation, the Spanish had earned the lasting hatred of the English, Scots, and Dutch, who regarded them as the decadent, unthinking tools of the Vatican's conspiracy to enslave the world. So, the continent was divided against itself almost from the start.Moreover, by the time the Spanish reached El Norte, the empire's religious mission had become the key element of its colonial policy. The Spanish plan was to assimilate the Native Americans into Spanish culture by converting them to Catholicism and supervising their fate, work, dress, and conduct in special settlements governed by priests.

But the system had multiple flaws. Neophytes were cloistered away from the mainstream of Hispanic life; the friars made it difficult for them to assimilate; and the system was abusive, in fact not unlike the hierarchy of a plantation, with the neophytes being the slaves and often kept in chains.

In sum, as Woodard paints the picture, El Norte had no self-government, no elections, and no possibility for local people to play any significant role in politics. Ordinary people, *peons,* were expected to give their loyalty to the local *patrÓn*, who provided employment; looked after widows, orphans, and the infirm; and sponsored religious feasts. Still, we learn, the *norteños,* in fact the Franciscans, brought to Texas, California, and indeed North America most everything that today is thought of as the American cowboy culture. But by the early seventeenth century, El Norte had new Euro-American neighbors, rival cultures with advantages and manpower and resources. El Norte would be eclipsed for more than two centuries by these new forces.

2. New France. We learn from Woodard that sixteen years before the *Mayflower* landing in Plymouth, and more than a hundred years after the Spanish landed in South America. Seventy-nine Frenchmen in two ships brought with them prefabricated parts needed to assemble a chapel, a forge, a mill, barracks, and two coastal survey vessels. They reconnoitered the coasts of what would become Nova Scotia, New Brunswick, and eastern Maine looking for an ideal location for France's first American outpost. Their vision of a tolerant, utopian society in the wilds of North America would profoundly shape not only the culture, politics, and legal norms of New France but also those of twenty-first-century Canada as well. As Woodward explains, they envisioned a perfected feudal society like that of rural France based on the medieval hierarchy of counts, viscounts, and barons ruling over commoners and their servants. There would be no representative assemblies, no town governments, no freedom of speech or press.

While as in France, Catholicism would be the official religion, New France would be open to French Protestants, and commoners would be allowed to hunt and fish—rights unheard of in France. Their leader, Samuel de Champlain, hoped to bring Christianity and other aspects of French civilization to the native populations, but he wished to accomplish this by persuasion and example, not military dominance. Unlike the English and other Europeans, he regarded the Indians as every bit as intelligent and human as his own countrymen and thought cross-cultural marriage between the peoples was not only tolerable, but desirable.

We learn that the new settlement, Port Royal, would become the model for future settlements in New France, resembling a village in northwestern France, where most of the settlers had come from. Peasants cleared fields and planted wheat and orchards. Skilled laborers constructed water-powered mills and a comfortable lodge for the gentlemen, who staged plays, wrote poetry, developed epicurean delights from local resources and journeyed into the fields only for picnics.

Woodard contrasts this to the early settlers in Jamestown, who refused to sample unfamiliar foods and resorted to eating neighbors who had starved to death. And while commoners were not invited to New France's gentlemanly feasts, the local Indian chiefs were welcomed. The French gentlemen learned the various Indian languages and sent some of their children to live among the Indians to learn their customs, technology, and speech. Some Frenchmen moved into the forest to live with the Indians, a move encouraged by the critical shortage of women in Québec for much of the seventeenth century. Especially in Acadia, French and Indian culture blended into one another. And while the French had hoped to assimilate the Indians into their culture, religion, and feudal way of life, ironically they became acculturated into the lifestyle, technology, and values of the Mi'kmaqs, Passamaquoddies, and Montagnais such that new France became as much an aboriginal society as a French one—and would eventually pass some of this quality on to Canada itself.

By the mid-eighteenth century, New France had become almost entirely dependent on Native Americans to protect their shared society from invaders. Even a century and a half after the foundation of Port Royal, there were only sixty-two thousand French people living in Québec and Acadia and only a few thousand in the vast Louisiana Territory, which encompassed much of the Continental interior. To the south, however, France's longtime enemies were gaining strength and an astonishing rate, for in the Chesapeake Tidewater and New England two aggressive, vibrant, and avowedly Protestant societies had taken root, cultures with very different attitudes about race, religion, and the place of "savages." Together they numbered over 750,000, and another 300,000 inhabited the other English-controlled colonies of the Atlantic seaboard. Woodard explains all of this in mesmerizing detail and how the leaders of New France must have hoped that New England and Tidewater would remain what they had been from the outset: avowed enemies of one another with little in common beyond having come from the same European island.

3. Tidewater was the first (1607) lasting English colony in the New World. It was "a hellhole of epic proportions, successful only in the sense that it survived at all. Founded by private investors, it was poorly planned, badly lead, and foolishly located." As Woodard documents, these first Virginians had not come to the New World to farm and build a new society but rather to conquer and rule, much as the Spanish had done more than a century earlier. The Virginia Company's plan assumed that the Indians would be intimidated by English technology and submit, Aztec-like, to their rule. But the local chief, Powhatan, saw the English outpost for what it was: weak and vulnerable but a potential source of useful European technology, especially metal tools and weapons. Powhatan ruled a Confederation that spanned the lower Chesapeake, comprising 30 tribes and 24,000 people. He lived in a large lodge on the York River, attended by 40 bodyguards, 100 wives, and a small army of servants.

So, Woodard juxtaposes circumstances: while the gentlemen of New France were inviting Indian chiefs to their gastronomic indulgences, hungry Virginians were extorting corn from Powhatan's Indians by force, triggering a cycle of violence that lasted for decades. But, he explains, despite the incompetence of Jamestown's leaders, the Indians were on the losing side of a war of attrition. The Virginia Company continued to send wave after wave of colonists to the Chesapeake, particularly after it was discovered that tobacco grew very well there. And while many colonists died, the Virginia company sent two more to take the place of each who died. Indian losses from warfare, disease, and war-induced hunger could not be replaced so easily. By 1669 Tidewater's Indian population had been reduced to two thousand, 8% of its original level, while the English population had grown to forty thousand, spreading across Tidewater and clearing Indian lands to grow tobacco.

Woodard focuses on two events that he concludes changed the trajectory of Tidewater Society, setting cultural patterns that persist even to this century. The first came in 1617 when Pocahontas's husband successfully transplanted West Indian strains of tobacco to Chesapeake soil, transforming Virginia into a booming export-oriented plantation society almost overnight. The second was the English Civil War in the 1640s, the results of which prompted a mass exodus from England of the families who would come to form Tidewater's aristocracy.

Woodard goes deep into who drove the immigration from England into Tidewater. Tobacco was a labor-intensive business. Tidewater's leaders recruited their workforce from the masses of desperate, malnourished laborers who were crowding London and other English cities. They offered prospective laborers transportation to Virginia or Maryland and a fifty-acre plot of land free of charge in exchange for three years' service as a "white slave" or indentured servant. Those who responded quickly came to represent 80% to 90% of the 150,000 Europeans who emigrated to Tidewater in the seventeenth century. Few survived their period of servitude, but those who did had a reasonable chance of becoming independent farmers, and some became very rich.

He also explains how Tidewater was so very different from the Deep South. Thus, he explains that a handful of the immigrants were of African descent, starting with twenty Africans bought from Dutch traders in 1619. Unlike the Deep South, however, Woodard explains that Tidewater appears to have treated its African servants much as it did their white counterparts through the 1660s. White and black settlers were not segregated; some Africans enjoyed the few civil rights available to commoners. Some even became masters themselves like Anthony Johnson, who in the 1650s owned several African servants and 250 acres of land on Virginia's Eastern Shore. Tidewater was inequitable, but it was not yet a racially based slave society.

Maryland, for its part, was an oligarchy from the outset, the vast feudal preserve of Cecilius Calvert, second Lord Baltimore, whose coat of arms still graces the Maryland flag. Calvert was given his twelve-million-acre domain by a fellow Catholic, King Charles I, who liked the nobleman's proposal to create a nominally Catholic colony where all religions would be tolerated. As that attracted settlers from across the bay, Maryland would quickly come to resemble Tidewater, Virginia: a Protestant-dominated tobacco colony, where indentured servants worked the land and the emergent aristocracy commanded most of the profits. As Woodard explains, Tidewater and Yankee New England stood at the opposite poles of the mid-seventeenth-century English-speaking world, with diametrically opposed values, politics, and social priorities. And when civil war came to England in the 1640s, they backed opposing sides, inaugurating centuries of struggle between them over the future of America.

Woodard details how, for the new elites in both Chesapeake colonies, the overriding goal was not to build a religious Utopia (as in early Yankeedom or, as we shall see, the Midlands) or a complex network of Indian alliances (as in New France). Whether high born or self-made, the Tidewater planters had an extremely conservative vision for the future of their new country: they wished to re-create the genteel manor life of rural England in the New World. And for a time, they succeeded beyond their wildest imaginations. Yet Tidewater's gentry created a thoroughly rural society without towns or even villages. It had no need for commercial ports (and thus no need for cities) because the land was riven with navigable fingers of the Chesapeake, allowing each of the planters to build his own dock and hence engage directly in trade with London and Europe. In sharp contrast to New England, there were no public schools (the children of gentlemen had live-in tutors) or town governments. Power in Tidewater became hereditary. The leading families intermarried in both America and England creating a close-linked cousinage that dominated Tidewater in general and Virginia in particular.

Also, the Tidewater gentry embraced *classical* republicanism, meaning a republic modeled after those of ancient Greece and Rome. The Greek and Roman political philosophy embraced by Tidewater gentry assumed most were born into bondage. Liberty was something that was granted and was thus a privilege, not a right.

Woodard explains how Tidewater's semi-feudal model required a vast and permanent underclass to play the role of serfs, on whose toil the entire system depended. But from the 1670s onward, the gentry had an increasingly difficult time finding enough poor Englishman willing to take on this role. Slave traders provided a solution to the shortage, one developed on the English islands of the Caribbean and recently introduced in the settlements they had created in the Deep South. Woodard documents that this slave caste grew from 10% of Tidewater's population in 1700 to 40% in 1760.

4. **"Yankeedom,"** according to Woodard, began with the Puritans (Calvinist English settlers) in New England and spread across upper New York, the northern parts of Pennsylvania, Ohio, Indiana, Illinois, and Iowa, into the eastern Dakotas, Michigan, Wisconsin, Minnesota, and the Canadian maritime. They also had an immense influence in the founding and development of Seattle, Portland, and Vancouver in the Pacific Northwest.

Woodard tells us that the dominant colonies of New England were founded by men who stood in total opposition to nearly every value that the Tidewater gentry held dear. Hostile to landed aristocracy, noble privilege, the Anglican Church, and the royalist cause, the Pilgrims of Cape Cod and the Puritans of Massachusetts Bay had an entirely different vision for their new society: a nation of churches and schoolhouses, where each community functioned as its own self-governing republic. Yankeedom left an indelible mark on a vast swath of the continent.

As Woodard frames it, this was an area that believed it could create a better society through public spending on infrastructure and schools. From the beginning, New Englanders believed they could defend the public good from the selfish machinations of moneyed interest and could enforce morals through the prohibition or regulation of undesirable activities. He teaches us that Yankeedom gave birth to the twin political ideologies of America's imperial age: American Exceptionalism and Manifest Destiny. The Pilgrims and, to a greater extent, the Puritans came to the New World not to re-create rural English life but to build a completely new society: and applied religious utopia, a Protestant theocracy based on the teachings of John Calvin. They would found a new Zion in the New England wilderness, a "city on a hill" to serve as a model for the rest of the world. They believed they would succeed because they believed they were God's chosen people. And contrary to a central founding myth of American history, the Puritans were *not* fleeing religious persecution; they were more like an American Taliban—leaving England en masse because of their unwillingness to compromise on matters of religious policy and wishing to live apart and exclude non adherents.

Woodard also points out that the Puritan exodus also had a demographic character entirely unlike that of Tidewater, New France, and El Norte. The Yankee settlers came in families, were generally middle class, well-educated, and roughly equal in material wealth. While Tidewater was settled by young, unskilled male servants, New England's colonists were skilled craftsman, lawyers, doctors, and yeoman farmers; there were no indentured servants. Rather than having fled poverty in search of better lives, the early Yankees traded a comfortable existence at home for the uncertainties of the wilderness. This demographic advantage—and the fact that New England had relatively few epidemic diseases—enabled the population to expand rapidly from its initial settlement base. And although few immigrants entered the Tidewater region for a century after 1640, colonial New England's European population doubled every generation such that by 1660 it had reached sixty thousand inhabitants, more than twice the population of Tidewater. And Yankeedom was the most cohesive area, since nearly everyone had arrived at the same time and for much the same reason.

Woodard puts his finger on other critical distinctions, including that the New England settlement model differed from Tidewater not merely in the presence of towns but in the power vested in them. Puritans believed every community of the chosen should govern itself without interference from bishops, archbishops, or kings. Every congregation considered itself completely self-governing. Every town was a little republic unto itself. Counties had almost no power at all. New Englanders believed from the very beginning that government could defend the public good from the selfish machinations of moneyed interests. It could create a better society through public spending on infrastructure and schools. More than any other group in America, Yankees conceived of government as being run by and for themselves. Everybody was supposed to participate, and there was no greater outrage than to manipulate the political process for private gain.

Woodard also explains how education in New England came to occupy such a large space. The Puritan belief that each individual had to encounter divine revelation through reading the scriptures had far-reaching implications. If everyone was expected to read the Bible, everyone had to be literate. While the other American Nations had no school systems of any kind in the mid-seventeenth century, New England required all children to be sent to school under penalty of law. Few Englishmen could read or write in 1660, but two-thirds of Massachusetts men and more than 1/3 of women were considered literate. And while basic education was universal, those with higher education were accorded the sort of respect and deference other societies reserved for the highborn.

Woodard does a captivating job of explaining what would cause Yankeedom to become so loathed by the other nations: its desire—indeed its mission—to impose its ways on everyone else. The Puritans also feared the wilderness, "a disorderly impulsive place at the edge of their fields where Satan lurked." Unlike the settlers in New France, the Puritans regarded the Indians as savages to whom normal moral obligations did not apply. When a group of dissatisfied Puritan settlers marched into the wilderness to found a squatters' colony (Connecticut) in 1636, Massachusetts authorities engineered a genocidal war against the Pequot Indians to have a pretext to seize the region by conquest from under the squatters. In one incident they surrounded a poorly defended Pequot village and butchered every man, woman, and child they found there, mostly by burning them alive. Plymouth Governor William Bradford conceded that it had been "a fearful sight to see them thus frying in the fire in the streams of blood quenching the same" but concluded that "the victory seemed a sweet sacrifice" that God "had wrought so wonderfully for them."

Woodard teaches us that the Puritans' program of conquest was not limited to Indian peoples. During and immediately after the English Civil War, Massachusetts soldiers and preachers attempted Yankee coups in Maryland, annexed the Royalist colony of Maine, and reduced Connecticut, Plymouth, and New Hampshire to satellites of their Bible Commonwealth. For four decades, Boston ruled the region as the capital of the United Colonies of New England. Puritan courts enforced Calvinist morality against hard-living Maine fishermen and drove Anglican priests from New Hampshire. It was almost like what we think of today as Sharia law. The Puritans were, so to speak, the American Taliban.

As Woodard explains, for Tidewater gentry, New England, complicit in the treasonous rebellion and the execution of the king, was a seditious land populated by radicals committed to destroying the foundations on which society stood. For Yankees, Tidewater was a bastion of reactionary forces, its lords committed to perpetuating the enslavement of the English people begun by their Norman ancestors. Yankee fears were given new urgency after Cromwell's death in 1658 when the monarchy was restored and a "Cavalier Parliament" of Royalist sympathizers convened in Westminster. The gentlemen of Virginia and the Calverts of Maryland once again had the backing of London, and the Puritans faced a mortal threat to their young nation.

5. New Netherland. Woodard reminds us that New York began its life as New Netherland in 1624, just four years after the *Mayflower* voyage and six years ahead of the Puritans' arrival in Massachusetts Bay. Although New Amsterdam was conquered by the English in 1664, the Dutch influence has permanently defined New York City. It was established as a fur-trading post and was what Woodard characterizes as "an unabashedly commercial settlement with little concern for either social cohesion or the creation of a model society." A global corporation, the Dutch West India Company, dominated the city's affairs and formerly governed New Netherland for the first few decades. Standing between Yankeedom and Tidewater, the city emerged as a trading entrepôt for both.

Moreover, the population of New Amsterdam was as diverse as anywhere in the world. And while Jews were banned from setting foot in New France, Yankeedom, and Tidewater, dozens of Ashkenazim and Spanish-speaking Sephardim settled New Amsterdam in the 1650s, forming the nucleus of what would eventually become the largest Jewish community in the world. Indians roamed the streets, and Africans—slave, free, and half-free—already formed a fifth of the population. New Amsterdam's core characteristics—diversity, tolerance, upward mobility, and an overwhelming emphasis on private enterprise—have come to be identified with the United States, but as Woodard (and other books on this subject) makes clear they were really the legacy of the United Provinces of the Netherlands.

The Dutch had internalized the lessons of Europe's horrific and ongoing religious wars. Insistence on conformity—cultural, religious, or otherwise—was seen as self-defeating, causing strife and undermining trade and business. The Dutch trait of tolerance was just that. They did not *celebrate* diversity but *tolerated* it because they viewed the alternative as far worse. Yet New Netherland was no more moral than its English counterparts: if a commodity was profitable, it was pursued, including trade in captive humans. Indeed, according to Woodard, full-on slavery was introduced in what is now the United States not by the gentlemen Planters of Virginia or South Carolina, but by the merchants of Manhattan.

6. The Deep South. According to Woodard, the founding fathers of the Deep South arrived in what is now Charleston in 1670 and 1671. They were the Barbadian sons and grandsons of the founders of an older English colony: Barbados, "the richest and most horrifying society in the English-speaking world." The society founded in Charleston did not seek to replicate rural English manor life or to create a religious utopia in the American wilderness. Instead, it was designed as a near carbon copy of the West Indian slave state the Barbadians had left behind. This unadulterated slave society would spread rapidly across the lowlands of what is now South Carolina, overwhelming the utopian colony of Georgia and spawning the dominant culture of Mississippi, lowland Alabama, the Louisiana Delta country, eastern Texas and Arkansas, western Tennessee, north Florida, and the southeastern portion of North Carolina: "From the outset, the Deep South culture was based on radical disparities in wealth and power, with a tiny elite commanding total obedience and enforcing it with State-sponsored terror." Its expansionist ambitions would put it on a collision course with its Yankee rivals, triggering military, social, and political conflicts that continue to plague the United States well into the twenty-first century.

Unable to man their plantations with indentured servants for long, they took to kidnapping children and soon began importing shipload after shipload of enslaved Africans. Often, the slaves were literally worked to death, and so there was no replenishment of the supply through natural increase, as in the Tidewater, according to Woodard. Thus, an ongoing slave trade was required. This was the culture that spawned Charleston and, by extension, the Deep South. The planters built themselves a city where they could enjoy the finer things of life, and so Charleston quickly became the wealthiest town on the eastern seaboard. The planters spent as much time there as possible, filling the city with distractions: theaters; taverns; brothels; cockfighting rings; private clubs for smoking, dining, drinking and horseracing; and shops stocked with fashionable imports from London.

Woodard informs us that although not particularly religious, the planters embraced the Anglican church as a symbol of belonging to the establishment, and this also gave them access to London high society and the great English universities and boarding schools — societies denied to Puritans, Quakers, and other dissenters. The low country's wealth depended entirely on a massive army of enslaved blacks, who outnumbered whites nine to one in some areas. It was to keep this supermajority under control, the planters imported Barbados's brutal slave code. Of course, the Deep South was not the only part of North America practicing full-blown slavery after 1670. Every colony tolerated the practice. But, as Woodard puts it: "most of the other nations were societies with slaves, not slave societies. Only in Tidewater and the Deep

South did slavery become the central organizing principle of the economy and culture." Yet there were nontrivial differences.

Tidewater slaves made up a much smaller proportion of the population (roughly one-third versus four-fifths); lived longer and had somewhat stable families. After 1740, Tidewater's slave population naturally increased, doing away with the need to import slaves from abroad. In those circumstances, Afro-Tidewater culture became relatively homogenous and strongly influenced by the English culture it was embedded in. Many blacks whose ancestors had come to the Chesapeake region prior to 1670 had grown up in freedom, owning land, keeping servants, holding office, and taking white husbands or wives. Having African blood did not necessarily make one a slave in Tidewater. Until the end of the seventeenth century, one's position in Tidewater was defined largely by class, not race.

By contrast, the Deep South, Woodard posits, had an enormous slave mortality rate. Blacks there were more likely to live in concentrated numbers in relative isolation from whites. With newcomers arriving with every ship, the slave quarters were cosmopolitan, featuring a wide variety of languages and different African cultural practices. Within this melting pot, slaves formed a new culture, complete with its own languages, Afro-Caribbean culinary practices, and musical traditions: "From the hell of the slave quarters would come some of the Deep South's great gifts to the continent: blues, jazz, gospel, and rock 'n' roll, as well as the Caribbean-inspired food ways today enshrined in Southern-style barbecue joints."

Woodard teaches us that Deep Southern society was militarized, caste structured, deferential to authority, and also aggressively expansionist. From their cultural hearth in the South Carolina low country, the planters expanded to similar terrain up and down the coast, finding resistance only in Georgia, which had been a utopian dream area "free of liquor and lawyers." Savannah was turned into a little Charleston and low country Georgia would not be the yeoman farmers utopia intended but an extension of the West Indian slaveocracy.

7. The Midlands. So, we come to one of the last of Woodard's American Nations, the Midlands. Over the past three centuries, Midland culture has pushed westward from its hearth in and around Philadelphia, jumped over the Appalachians, and spread across a vast swath of the American heartland, all the while retaining its qualities of tolerance, multiculturalism, multilingual civilization populated by families of modest means—many of them religious—who desired mostly to be left in peace. Like Yankeedom, the Midlands were intended to be a model society, a utopia guided by the tenets of an unorthodox religion: Quakerism. Woodard (unfairly I believe) describes Quakers as "the late 17th century equivalent of crossing the hippy movement with the Church of Scientology." Quakers spurned the social conventions of the day and rejected the authority of church hierarchies. Overcome with rapture, they would fall into violent fits, or "quakes," that Woodard says, "frightened nonbelievers." By the 1690s, Quakers had developed an intense aversion to violence and war, a commitment to pacifism that was so total it would eventually doom the Quakers' control of the Midlands.

How this unpopular cult got permission from Catholic, authority-loving King Charles II, to establish its own colony is a tale not taught in most schools but told nicely by Woodard. Admiral William Penn was a self-made man who trimmed his sails to the political winds, first fighting for parliament in the English Civil War but then championing the restoration of the monarchy. Cromwell made him rich by giving him confiscated Irish Estates, but Penn later *loaned* £16,000 to Cavalier King Charles. He groomed his son William to be a respectable gentleman and sent him to Oxford. But young William was expelled for criticizing Oxford's Anglican church services and in 1667, at age twenty-six, he horrified everyone by joining the Quakers. His father tried everything to get his son on the right track, but nothing worked.

But then the father died in 1670, leaving son William Penn as one of the most famous Quakers in England, not to mention very, very rich. Quakers, he decided, needed their own country, a place where they could conduct a "holy experiment" that would serve as "an example to all nations." So, in 1680 he settled King Charles's debt to his late father in exchange for a grant of forty-five thousand square miles of real estate located between Lord Baltimore's Maryland and the Duke of York's New York. The province, as large as England itself, would be named "Pennsylvania." William Penn would have authority to do pretty much whatever he wished there, and he did.

Penn's colonization effort was well organized. Woodard provides some fascinating details. Penn offered political and religious liberty and land on cheap terms. He advertised Pennsylvania aggressively in Ireland, the Netherlands, and wide portions of what is now Germany. He presold 750,000 acres of farm lots to hundreds of investors, raising the money needed to underwrite the initial wave of colonists, establish Philadelphia, and provide the colonial government enough money for several years to avoid the need for collecting taxes. Within four years, eight thousand people were living in and around Philadelphia, a population level that took Tidewater twenty-five years to achieve and New France seventy years. Most were skilled artisans and farmers of modest means who had come as families, instantly giving the Midlands a settled and civilized tone. It was so successful it soon brought an even larger wave of settlers that would give the Midlands its pluralistic and decidedly un-British character.

Woodard describes a second immigration wave consisting of German-speaking farmers and craftsman from the Palatinate. They were people "traumatized by generations of horrific Imperial and religious conflicts that have made their south German homeland a killing field." Almost without exception, they were Protestants who arrived in large extended family groups. Some were from sects that wished to order their lives in a particular way, like the Amish, the Mennonites, or the Brethren of Christ. Thousands more were mainstream Lutherans and German Calvinists, wanting to build prosperous family farms in a peaceful setting. By the mid-eighteenth-century Pennsylvania was the only English-founded colony without an English majority.

The Germans' small-scale farming skills became legendary; they knew how to select farmland with top-quality soil, conserve it through crop rotation, and improve livestock through selective breeding. For the next two centuries, visitors invariably remarked on their tidy and prosperous farms. And they were renowned for their skills as craftsmen, having perfected log cabins and invented the Conestoga wagon, which carried generations of settlers over the Appalachians and beyond. Most of them belonged to disciplined religious sects that prized thrift and sobriety, thus solidifying their affinity with their Quaker neighbors.

As Woodard explains, the Germans and Quakers also shared a strong aversion to slavery, a stance that would set the Midlands apart from New Netherland, Tidewater, and the Deep South. The first formal protest against slavery in North America was articulated by German Quakers in Germantown, Pennsylvania. And while many wealthy Quakers, including William Penn, had come to Pennsylvania with slaves, within a decade Quakers were advising one another that slaveholding violated their "Golden Rule."

Woodard also discusses the failure of the Quakers. Thus, we learn that while Pennsylvania was an economic success in numerous proportions, its

Quaker-run government was a "complete disaster" since the Quakers' ideals were at odds with successful governance. The Quakers assumed citizens could govern themselves through self-discipline and the application of the Golden Rule. But not so, since Quakers were also by nature inclined to challenge authority and convention at every juncture. The Dutch, Swedes, and Finns of the "lower counties" became so desperate for proper governance that they broke away to form their own tiny colony of Delaware in 1704. Who knew.

The Quakers' expectation that immigrants from other cultures would embrace the worldview of the Society of Friends also proved unfounded. Beginning in about 1717, a new group of colonists began arriving on Philadelphia's docks, one whose values were in stark opposition to all the Quakers held dear. They were a warrior people from the bloody borderlands of Britain, contemptuous of the Indians, quick to turn to violence to solve problems, and committed to a Calvinist faith that held that humans were inherently wicked. As Woodard explains, these Borderlanders were fleeing their blighted homelands in Scotland and Ulster and pouring into Pennsylvania in enormous numbers: over one hundred thousand by 1775. They undermined Quaker governance, such as it was, and when the French began to move against villages and towns near Philadelphia, all semblance of Quaker governance collapsed.

By the eve of the American Revolution, large swaths of what was to have been part of William Penn's Utopia were being incorporated into other nations. In the West a new power had taken hold and was spreading southward across the Highlands. This borderlands civilization didn't control the single colonial government, but it would radically shape the future of all of the American Nations and the strange federation in which they found themselves.

8. Appalachia. This new power was what Woodard calls Appalachia, the last of the "nations" to be founded in the colonial period and also the most immediately disruptive. As Woodard tells the story, Appalachia was a clan-based warrior culture that arrived in the back country frontier of the Midlands, Tidewater, and Deep South and shattered those nations' monopoly control over colonial governments, the use of force, and relations with the Native Americans: "Proud, independent, and disturbingly violent, the Borderlanders of Greater Appalachia have remained a volatile insurgent force within North

American Society to the present day." Having no desire to give up their ways, the Borderlanders rushed to the isolation of the eighteenth-century frontier to form a society that was, for a time, literally beyond the reach of the law and modeled on the anarchical world they had left behind. They came from the war-torn borderlands of northern Britain: lowland Scotland and the Scots-Irish-controlled north of Ireland. Their ancestors had weathered eight hundred years of nearly constant warfare, fighting in (or against) the armies of William "Braveheart" Wallace or Robert the Bruce.

Woodard explains how the Borderlanders arrived in five massive immigration waves between 1717 and 1776, each a response to some disaster back in the British Isles. Midlanders were alarmed by the newcomers' rough manners and clannish loyalties. The officials did their best to get them out of town and onto the frontier, where they could serve as a buffer against French or Native American attack. Rather than trying to produce cash crops for export, the Borderlanders embraced a woodland subsistence economy, hunting, fishing, practicing slash-and-burn agriculture, and moving every few years as the soil became depleted. Life in Britain had taught them not to invest much time and wealth in fixed property, which was easily destroyed during wartime. So, they stored their wealth in mobile forms: herds of pigs, cattle, and sheep. When they did need cash, they distilled corn into a more portable, storable, and valuable product: whiskey. This would remain the de facto currency of Appalachia for the next two centuries.

Their communities began in considerable isolation from the outside world, to which they owed no loyalty. With no roads, trade was almost entirely by barter. The nearest courthouses were far away, and so justice was meted out by the aggrieved individuals and their clan by personal retaliation. From their initial stronghold in south-central Pennsylvania, the Borderlanders spread south down the mountains on an ancient eight-hundred-mile-long Indian trail that came to be known as the "Great Wagon Road." This led out of Lancaster and New York, through Hagerstown, down the length of Virginia's Shenandoah Valley, through the Highlands of North Carolina, and terminated in what is now Augusta, Georgia. The Borderlanders moved into colonies controlled by the Tidewater gentry and the great planters of the Deep South, but in cultural terms their Appalachian nation effectively cut Tidewater off from the interior and blocking somewhat the western movement of the slave trade.

As the British-controlled nations careened toward a series of conflicts with the mother country, the Borderlanders of Appalachia would play a decisive role. In some cases, they would fight in support of Britain and in others, against, but they all did so for the same reason: to resist the threats to their clansmen's freedom, be it from Midland merchants, Tidewater gentlemen, Deep Southern planters, or the British Crown itself.

★ ★ ★

Before getting back to the narrative arc of the *American Nations* it is important to pause momentarily for a high-level glance at the American Revolution. Few Americans learned of this in school, but we are reminded by Woodard that the military struggle of 1775–1882 was not fought by an "American people" seeking to create a united, continent-spanning republic where all men would be created equal and guaranteed freedom of speech, religion, and the press. Rather, it was fought by a loose military alliance of "nations," each of which was most concerned with preserving or reasserting control over its respective culture, character, and power structure. The rebelling nations did not wish to be bonded together into a single republic.

Some nations—the Midlands, New Netherland, and New France—didn't rebel at all. And, as Woodard explains, those who did were not fighting a revolution; they were fighting separate wars of colonial liberation. And the four nations that did "rebel"—Yankeedom, Tidewater, Greater Appalachia, and the Deep South—had little in common and strongly distrusted one another. They were not always fighting on the same side either: Appalachia was engaged in a struggle of liberation against the Midlands, Tidewater, and the Deep South as much as against Britain. A little known fact of interest is that Georgia even rejoined the empire during the conflict. The warring colonies allied themselves with the enemies of their enemy but had little intention of merging with one another.

Among other things, this review also skips over the important details of the Mexican-American War and the reshaping of the borders of the United States after 1848 and the Gadsden Purchase. Woodard covers this in fascinating detail. Suffice it to say that the citizens in the US portion of El Norte would suffer discrimination, disenfranchisement, and cultural challenges from their new governors but would survive a century of occupation and substantially overcome their subjugation in the twentieth century.

9. The Left Coast. What Woodard calls the "Left Coast"—the coastal zone of northern California, Oregon, and Washington—was founded by Yankees who arrived by sea in the hopes of founding a second New England on the shores of the Pacific. The mission was not altogether successful, but it left the stamp of utopian idealism that put the Left Coast on a collision course with its neighbors in El Norte and the libertarian Far West. Yet until deep into the nineteenth century, there was not much government in the Pacific Northwest other than the Hudson's Bay Company, whose local staff, interestingly, was dominated by the New French. Curiously, as Woodard informs us, until the early twentieth century, the Chinook Indians called all British people "King George Men" and referred to Americans simply as "Bostons." While the Yankees dominated the political and intellectual sphere, they were not to form a majority of the population. Within a few months of the creation of a provisional government, hundreds of newcomers arrived, mainly farmers from the Appalachian Midwest. These Borderlanders tended to settle on farms in the countryside, leaving the towns and government to the Yankees. The settlement pattern continued throughout the 1840s and 1850s, leaving New England–born Yankees outnumbered fifteen to one but still in control of most civic institutions.

In Oregon, which split from what became British Columbia in 1846, and from Washington in 1853, the Yankees dominated the scene almost completely. Salem and Portland were founded by the New Englanders, who ran most of the public schools, colleges, and seminaries and dominated debate at the Constitutional Convention of 1857, which produced a document shaping communities of independent family farmers and the very Yankee notion that individual interests must be subsumed for the common good.

The Yankee Mission in California was complicated by the fact that parts of the region had already been colonized. El Norte's culture was deeply rooted south of Monterey, and Yankee traders and travelers who decided to move to Southern California prior to the US annexation generally assimilated to *Californio* ways: they learned Spanish, converted to Catholicism, took Mexican citizenship and spouses, adopted Spanish versions of their names, and respected and participated in local politics. This El Norte influence vanished when one moved away from the coast or north of Monterey.

While California's north-south split was already apparent by the mid-nineteenth century, the 1848 discovery of gold in the American River Valley amplified the division between the Left Coast and the until-then unpopulated interior. This division was largely due to the Yankee presence around San Francisco Bay and adjacent sections of the Pacific Seaboard. Even more than their counterparts in Oregon, these Yankees were compelled by a particular mission: to save California from the barbarians, in this case the Forty-Niners, whose gold rush mentality was completely at odds with the Yankee Puritan ethos. Massive Yankee effort in establishing schools, educational curricula, religious training largely failed inland. The churches were empty on Sundays, while the saloons, brothels, gambling houses, and other such places were bursting at the seams. But while the Yankees failed in their broad mission, they had a permanent and lasting effect on coastal California from Monterey North. According to Woodward, the Left Coast blended the moral, intellectual, and utopian impulses of the Yankee elite with the self-sufficient individualism of its Appalachian and immigrant majority. The culture that formed—idealistic but individualistic—was unlike that of the gold-digging lands in the interior but similar to those in western Oregon and Washington.

10. The Far West, as Woodard calls it, was the last region of North America to be colonized. It was inhospitable for Euro-Atlantic civilizations with their emphasis on cropland agriculture, water-dependent plants and animals, and fixed settlements. The altitude was also so high that familiar crops would not grow at all. And most of the vast area's rivers were too shallow for navigation, isolating settlers from potential markets for anything they might be able to grow. Indeed, Native American tribes of the area had had two centuries to perfect mounted warfare (after the introduction of horses from El Norte), which enabled them better to keep interlopers in check. Transcontinental trails were littered with the bodies of livestock and people whose water ran out or who were overwhelmed by outlaws or Indian patrols.

According to Woodard the Far West was uniquely a nation defined not by regional cultural forces but by the demands of external institutions. The challenges of productivity required the deployment of capital-intensive technologies: hard-rock mines, railroads, telegraphs, Gatling guns, and hydroelectric dams. Yet the first settlers to the Far West were the exception to this pattern. Arriving in two geographically separate waves during 1847–1950, the earliest Euro-American colonists arrived just ahead of industrial capital. One group— the Yankee Mormons of Utah—would form a distinct subculture of independent farmers in Utah and southern Idaho. The other—the gold-hungry Forty-Niners—were highly individualistic frontiersmen in the Appalachian mold. Neither would achieve cultural dominance over the western interior.

The Mormons were followers of the Yankee-led utopian movement with its origins in Vermont and New York. They began arriving on the shores of Utah's Great Salt Lake in the late 1840s. Their leader was Vermont-born Brigham Young, the first governor of the Utah territory from and after 1850. Two years later twenty-thousand Mormons were living there. Almost all were from Yankeedom, which explains why in 2000, Utah had the highest percentage of English Americans of any State in the Union, edging out Vermont and Maine.

★   ★   ★

Woodard's book, and the many portions I have not sought to mention, contain more of interest, including the various secession efforts of the past wholly apart from the effort that led to the Civil War. But most generally, one sees in his book a never-ending tension between the American Nations he describes, a tension kept in political check by alliances that shifted in subtle and not-so-subtle ways through the complex machinery of our Constitution. And while there was much assimilation, it seems clear that the country as a whole was never a "melting pot" in the ways many of us were taught. Instead, we are living through a period of political tensions seemingly unique to the twenty-first century where group rights chew away at the national fabric, where the aspirational ideals of the founders are increasingly under attack as the hypocritical vestiges of white supremacy. It is not clear what the future has in store for a nation turning increasingly inward in ways hostile to nearly half of the population while at the same time our country is on the edge of political and economic eclipse by the stunning success of autocratic and illiberal societies in Asia and elsewhere.

I hope and expect that readers will find Woodard's view of American history eye-opening in ways that permit some rethinking about things. One curiosity is how and why Yankeedom seems to have transformed itself from its commitment to local control of all things into a champion of federal government control of so much of society, while so many of the other "nations" he describes have maintained much of their initial character.

18

With Mainstream Journalism Mostly Dead, Where Can One Find Real Journalists?

June 8, 2021

I am not sure when journalism became more about collaborating with a predetermined narrative than about uncovering actual facts. I remember in the early days of Donald Trump thinking that his constant invocation of the words "fake news" was nothing more than a wildly exaggerated and misdirected appeal to his base and their obvious animosity to "media elites." But I do know that being isolated and hunkered down for most of 2020 gave me a keen awareness that there were competing narratives on television that did not depend on actual facts. This was not a sudden revelation but a slow and iterative circumstance that developed into a crisis in much the same way that a frog can be put in water and the heat turned on. By the time the water is about to boil and kill the frog, the frog becomes aware of the change but is too late to prevent the conclusion: no escape from boiling to death. And so it was, for me at least, in being in the middle of the rising temperature of the heated news narratives.

At one extreme there was MSNBC and Rachel Maddow and at the other end of the spectrum was Fox News and Sean Hannity. Neither Maddow nor Hannity seemed influenced by facts but rather had consistent narratives that became increasingly shrill, unhinged, and offensive to common sense. Elsewhere on the media spectrum we had media enterprises chasing ratings and revenue in a similar way: CNN increasingly tilted toward the MSNBC narrative; the *New York Times*, the *Washington Post* and their acolytes in other major cities, which tilted heavily against anything Trump but in a more subtle way than MSNBC and CNN; and the *Wall Street Journal*, which stood out as a defender of many Trump policies (and William Barr), although not President Trump personally. And interestingly we saw some unexpected elements of the tabloid press, which through old-fashioned investigative journalism uncovered some astounding facts (e.g., Hunter Biden's laptop contents, the biggest non scandal of the decade) but which 95% of the mainstream media chose to ignore.

Meanwhile, nothing outside the borders of the United States was particularly newsworthy unless there was some Russian angle that could be used to tar anyone connected with the Trump administration for one or two news cycles or unless certain countries had better statistics on COVID-19 infections that could be used to criticize the administration's handling of the entire pandemic.

Living through all of these competing narratives, not to mention the monthly change of position of the administration, the CDC, Dr. Fauci, Governors Newsome, Cuomo, and others with regard to the handling of COVID-19 brought forth at some point last year a painful awareness that it was necessary to find more reliable and unbiased sources of factual information; indeed it was necessary to find new sources of actual journalism in which stories were not filtered by editors and editorial boards committed to specific biased narratives without regard to fact.

Happily, and not altogether coincidently, the opportunity presented itself in part because of the development within the media (and academia and even corporate America) of radical identitarian politics, which resulted in a number of excellent journalists being fired from newspapers such as the *New York Times*, the *Washington Post*, and others. These tended to be young journalists who failed to adhere to the religion of antiracism in the wake of the *New York Times* publication of the *Project 1619* essays and did not ignore the riots that spread through Seattle, Portland, Chicago, Los Angeles, New York, Washington, and other cities after police shootings.

The astonishing amount of violence that followed the murder of George Floyd and other police shootings was ignored by great swaths of the media, which almost uniformly described the riots as "mostly peaceful." But the media did not ignore the matter of white guilt writ large. For a few hours or so, Coca-Cola ran an advertisement featuring polar bears building a snowman in a pure white arctic environment. The snowman is finished, whereupon a baby polar bear places a Ghanaian Kente Cloth and a black BLM facemask on the snowman. At that moment up pops the tagline "Be Less White. Drink Coca-Cola."

While cities were rioting, burning, and being looted, we had a national election that took place in the context of competing media narratives that did little to persuade new voters of anything, but did much to solidify the darkly and deeply opposing views of our two major political parties and their followers. This was followed by the events of January 6 and the second impeachment of Mr. Trump, who had by then left the presidency.

Those events have spawned their own wildly differing narratives: some comparing the events at the capital to the storming of the German Reichstag by Hitler's brownshirts in 1933 and others comparing the events to the student takeover and trashing of various university administration buildings in 1968. Both of those narratives are persistent; neither is accepted by any majority, although the mainstream media tilt more toward the Reichstag metaphor. One thing that did not happen: the press did not engage in anything approaching a dispassionate look at the events, including the fact that several capitol-building police officers opened doors and escorted protesters into the building. The film clips of this show the officers saying they thought this was wrong but that they were following instructions. From whom those instructions came, we still do not know, and the press is not inquiring.

So, where can one turn to find unfiltered fact-based journalism? Well, it turns out that there is much of it, but it is no longer found in the usual places. A large contributor to the paradigm shift in journalism is Substack.[101] The *New York Times* recently did a piece called "Why We're Freaking Out about Substack,"[102] which highlights the reality that employers for journalists are shrinking, and the media filtration system that governs writers has become suffocating. Also, some very high-profile journalists, and I am talking about people who follow facts to the bitter end and do not start with a narrative into which facts are molded, have been simply canceled by their employers because of editorial pressure, advertiser pressure, or other opinion-dominated pressure.

For such people, Substack is a neutral platform that offers writers and podcasters a way to connect (for a subscription price to be sure) directly with readers and listeners. Most of the content providers also have active and useful Twitter feeds so that readers can get access to, or at least learn about, much content simply by following their chosen journalists on Twitter. There are other outlets, too, and some of the most quietly rational voices, Jonathan Turley for example, still come from older line but not mainstream media (e.g., *Politico* and *The Hill*).

So, dear reader, here are some people you might want to try out. They tend to be young, politically unpredictable both left and right, but neither woke nor imbibers of the current flavors of Kool-Aid that demand that all fact-based opinions serve the God of virtue signaling or the religion of anti-racism. They are more likely to be cogent explainers of (but still objectors to) critical race theory than defenders of it. But in all cases, they are writers and thinkers who have worthy and interesting reactions to the current crisis of journalism not just in the United States but throughout the Western world.

Jonathon Turley[103] is an increasingly prolific professor of constitutional law at the George Washington University Law School (full disclosure: I was a member of that faculty for almost a decade as an adjunct professor, several steps down the food chain from fully tenured professors such as Mr. Turley). His articles tend to be short, insightful, very much to the point, and increasingly influential. Most of his writings tend to run against the grain of the press herd, and to provide a deeper and more nuanced view of events than is found in most elements of the mainstream media. He is no defender of the radical right, but he tilts conservative on many of the issues of the day, while tilting liberal but not progressive on various social issues.

To me, Turley recalls a modern-day Walter Cronkite: he explains things simply and clearly with reference to verifiable facts and does not push any obvious narrative in disregard of known facts. He was the first serious journalist/constitutional scholar to express amazement at the unanticipated un-interest of most of the media in the Hunter Biden laptop contents story, which seems to implicate several Biden family members in taking money from various foreign governments in expectation of favors. But his reportorial writing goes well beyond the simply political. He goes especially deeply into several recent Supreme Court cases, many of which have been decided 9–0, something that no reader or watcher of the mainstream media would likely know. His point was that, at least on the Supreme Court, and more often than not, there is a strong left/right consensus on a great many issues that reach the Court. If you follow him on Twitter you will get links to his articles more or less in real time and, unlike many of the people mentioned below, you do not have to pay for access to his blog, titled *res ipsa loquitur*. A good selection of his recent articles can be found here.[104]

Then there is *Andrew Sullivan*,[105] one of the most interesting writers of the day. He is described thusly in his Wikipedia entry:

> A British-American author, editor, and blogger Sullivan is a political commentator, a former editor of *The New Republic* and the author or editor of six books. He started a political blog, *The Daily Dish*, in 2000, and eventually moved his blog to platforms, including *Time, The Atlantic, The Daily Beast*, and finally an independent subscription-based format. His newsletter *The Weekly Dish* was launched in July 2020. Sullivan says his conservatism is rooted in his Roman Catholic background and in the ideas of the British political philosopher Michael Oakeshott. Born and raised in Britain, he has lived in the United States since 1984. He is openly gay.

In his most recent article from a few days ago ("Our Politics and the English Language"[106]), Sullivan writes vividly and unforgettably about other people's writings. For example, this about Ibram X. Kendi, the current godfather of critical race theory:

> I caught a glimpse of Ibram X. Kendi's recent appearance at the Aspen Ideas Festival, the annual woke, oxygen-deprived hajj for the left-media elites. He was asked to define racism—something you'd think he'd have thought a bit about. This was his response: "Racism is a collection of racist policies that lead to racial inequity that are substantiated by racist ideas." He does this a lot. He repeats Yoda-style formulae: "There is no such thing as a nonracist or race-neutral policy … If discrimination is creating equity, then it is antiracist. If discrimination is creating inequity, then it is racist."

These maxims pepper his tomes like deep thoughts in a self-help book. Reading at least one Andrew Sullivan piece has become an essential part of my week.

Matt Taibbi has a fascinating background,[107] having begun as a freelance reporter in the former Soviet Union, including the period of time in Uzbekistan, where he was deported for criticizing President Karimov. He later worked as a sports journalist for the *Moscow Times* and played professional baseball in Uzbekistan and Russia as well as professional basketball in Mongolia. He returned to the United States almost twenty years ago and founded a newspaper in Buffalo, but by 2004 he was covering politics for *Rolling Stone* and won a National Magazine Award for his work there. Two years ago, he launched the podcast *Useful Idiots*. He has written several books, detailed at the footnote above.

A recent article from last week[108] is a trenchant look at the media problems in the country, hardly consistent with any known "progressive" thought. Some of his best work involves interviews that take thirty or sometimes sixty minutes to listen to. In his case, I think listening is worth the effort. Try these: "The Need for Change in the American Media" (thirty minutes);[109] "Media & the Death of Objectivity";[110] and "So Much for the "Transformational" Joe Biden."[111] The more you know about and read Matt Taibbi the more you are likely to be captivated by his high level of common sense and grounding in facts: two qualities not normally associated with progressives or the Trump right.

Glenn Greenwald started out in 1995 as a Big Law lawyer[112] at the most profitable firm in America (Wachtel Lipton) but migrated to journalism via his blogging on national security issues. He wrote for the *Guardian* and the *Washington Post* (where he won a Pulitzer Prize). Along with two others, he founded *Intercept* in 2014 but resigned in 2020 and moved, as did many of those I mention, to Substack where his work is available to subscribers and in part to nonsubscribers. While he started out as a center-left liberal, he has evolved into a critic of the groupthink of the left in general. A listing of his older articles is here.[113] Recent articles from Substack are here.[114] He is not so much a contrarian or an ideologue as one who tends to follow the facts. One can, and I often do, disagree with his conclusions, but his facts are sound.

I only "discovered" *Sam Harris*[115] just recently via a nephew in Europe. He has a regular podcast (they are numbered 1 through 251) under the worthy title of *Making Sense*. His current podcast #251 focuses on "Corporate Cowardice." The first one I heard was # 217, "The New Religion of Anti-Racism," and that is what motivated me to become a subscriber. Most are conversations of up to an hour, low key, and calm. The opposite of cable TV. Number 223, "A Conversation with Andrew Sullivan" is worth a listen. The introductory part of each episode can be heard for free, but beyond that, the paywall kicks in.

C. J. Hopkins [116] is an American playwright, novelist, and political satirist who lives in and writes from Berlin. He began as a leftish thinker and writer but has evolved into something complex and unpredictable. He publishes via Substack now. It is not possible to categorize his journalistic work, but it is somewhat edgy and often hugely entertaining. He punctures bubbles and bloviation mercilessly. A link to several articles and essays is here.[117] Topics he has been dwelling on recently include: "The New Normal Reality Police," "The Criminalization of Dissent," "The Covidian Cult," "The Unvaccinated Question," "Are You Ready for Total Ideological War." [118] Topics include: "The Push toward a Totalitarian New Normal," "The Liberals' New Pasion for Snobbery and Censorship," "The War on Populism." My favorite interview at the moment is one he did last month with Matt Taibbi (called "Meet the Censored"), found at the footnote above.

Hopkins is an acquired taste, so a small amount of patience might be required to become acclimated to his sense of humor. Nothing gets him going though like the endless phenomenon of progressives analogizing everything they hate to the Nazis. He has done scores of satirical tropes on this.

Bari Weiss is an American opinion writer and editor.[119] From 2013 until 2017, she was an op-ed and book review editor at the *Wall Street Journal*. From 2017 to 2020, she was an op-ed staff editor and writer about culture and politics at the *New York Times.* Since her heavily publicized, politically motivated, and high-profile resignation from the *Times*,[120] she has worked as a regular columnist for *Die Welt.* Her focus has been on Israel and the anti-Semitism of the left in the US and Europe, although it was her being on the wrong side of "wrong think" that led to her controversial resignation from the *Times* a couple of months ago. It also led her colleagues to refer to her as a bigot and a Nazi (cue articles by C. J. Hopkins on this).

John Podhoretz,[121] *Noah Rothman,*[122] *Christine Rosen,*[123] *and Abe Greenwald*[124] are the brains behind the *Commentary Magazine* Daily Podcast, which I have found addictive. A selection of them may be found simply by Googling "Commentary Podcasts." They became daily last year but may one day return to twice weekly. You are unlikely to be disappointed by becoming a habitual listener to this podcast. They last in each case about fifty-five minutes or so, and they are generally thoughtful, and well-focused on a particular topic of the day. And while *Commentary Magazine* is avowedly neo-conservative, it is not annoyingly political. That is to say, neither the articles nor the podcasts present a consistent narrative into which facts have to be squeezed, twisted, or otherwise finagled to fit.

Much excellent material is behind a paywall, but that seems to be the way things are today. It seems now that we have to pay to find journalism that is not part of herd think. It is worth the price.

Bill Maher is a comedian. One thinks of comedians these days as the most politically correct of people, rarely venturing into making fun of the sacred cows of the left. Bill Maher is not such a comedian, and he seems now almost the only one. It is no accident, one supposes, that his program is not on any mainstream network, but rather behind the paywall of HBO. Yet his comedy and his targets are serious and seriously important. A recent show closed by sounding the alarm on China's growing dominance over the United States.

> You're not going to win the battle for the 21st century if you are a silly people. And Americans are a silly people, … Do you know who doesn't care that there's a stereotype of a Chinese man in a Dr. Seuss book? China. All 1.4 billion of them couldn't give a crouching tiger flying f— because they're not a silly people. If anything, they are as serious as a prison fight.

Maher acknowledged that China does "bad stuff," from the concentration camps of Uyghur Muslims to its treatment of Hong Kong. But, he stressed,

> There's got to be something between an authoritarian government that tells everyone what to do and a representative government that can't do anything at all. In two generations, China has built 500 entire cities from scratch, moved the majority of their huge population from poverty to the middle class, and mostly cornered the market in 5G and pharmaceuticals. Oh, and they bought Africa.

He also pointed to China's global Silk Road infrastructure initiative. He continued:

> In China alone, they have 40,000 kilometers of high-speed rail. America has none. … We've been having Infrastructure

> Week every week since 2009 but we never do anything. Half the country is having a never-ending woke competition deciding whether Mr. Potato Head has a d— and the other half believes we have to stop the lizard people because they're eating babies. We are a silly people. "Nothing ever moves in this impacted colon of a country. We see a problem and we ignore it, lie about it, fight about it, endlessly litigate it, sunset clause it, kick it down the road, and then write a bill where a half-assed solution doesn't kick in for 10 years, China sees a problem and they fix it. They build a dam. We debate what to rename it.

The HBO star cited how it took "ten years" for a bus line in San Francisco to pass its environmental review and how it took "16 years" to build the Big Dig tunnel in Boston, comparing that to a fifty-seven-story skyscraper that China built in "19 days" and Beijing's Sanyuan Bridge, which was demolished and rebuilt in "43 hours."

> We binge-watch, they binge-build. When COVID hit Wuhan, the city built a quarantine centre with 4,000 rooms in 10 days and they barely had to use it because they quickly arrested the rest of the disease. They were back to throwing raves in swimming pools while we were stuck at home surfing the dark web for black market Charmin. We're not losing to China, we lost. The returns just haven't all come in yet. They've made robots that check a kid's temperature and got their asses back in school. Most of our kids are still pretending to take Zoom classes while they watch TikTok and their brain cells fully commit ritual suicide.

Maher then blasted Democratic New York City Mayor Bill de Blasio, accusing him of degrading school standards by eliminating merit and substituting a lottery system for admittance to schools for advanced learners. "Do you think China's doing that, letting political correctness get in the way of nurturing their best and brightest?" Maher continued. "Do you think Chinese colleges are offering courses in 'The Philosophy of Star Trek', 'The Sociology of Seinfeld,' and 'Surviving the Coming Zombie Apocalypse'? Those are real and so is China. And they are eating our lunch. And believe me, in an hour, they'll be hungry again." The film clip is here.[125]

I recommend that you take a bit of time and try out these writers, perhaps following them on Twitter to see if they capture and keep your attention. You will probably feel much better (and likely be better informed) than watching anything on cable news or other news sources.

19

The Present Ambiguity of July 4, the Rise of China as the CCP Hits 100, the Decline of the United States as a Serious Power, and the Politics of Everything

July 7, 2021

At the confluence of the 245th anniversary of the Declaration of Independence and the one-hundredth anniversary of the establishment of the Chinese Communist Party we seem to be living under the ancient Chinese curse: *May you live in interesting times.* Who would have thought that much of the population of the United States would now be viewing the July 4 holiday as a holiday not to celebrate but to be embarrassed about? The Founding Fathers and everybody associated with them have been condemned by much of the country, not just in academia but in the halls of government, too, as white racists or worse.

Government buildings, especially the US Capitol's rotunda, are candidates for being emptied of their portraits, their statues, and their busts. The Founding Fathers -- soon to be "Founding Persons"-- are increasingly persona non grata in public spaces, to be replaced by new acceptable symbols of current progressive ideology that would turn all public spaces into "safe spaces" monitored by a supposedly benign government much in the way that preschool classes are monitored by supposedly benign teachers. Our students are increasingly taught to be ashamed of their country and its founders and, similarly, ashamed of their own whiteness. Like homosexuality decades ago, whiteness is now like a disease to be treated. Many of our urban and suburban schools, and indeed corporate employers have become the reeducation camps of our time.

And so in the frenzy of shame, apology, and embarrassment for our past, we have become a country that no longer has any discernable, coherent, articulated, or pursued present national interest; no immigration policy; no policies to manage the nation's violent urban slaughter beyond "defunding the police" and blaming centuries of white supremacy; and indeed no national policies other than to be *for* racial equity and social justice and too be *against* white racism and climate change—even nature itself—as if our population of 350 million souls could address the human contribution to climate change by the other 7.5 billion souls who occupy planet Earth.

Sadly, we are a country in swift and steep decline: unserious, intellectually and physically flabby, self-indulgent. Politically, we are pandering to progressivism in its current incarnation. In order to invest in "infrastructure" (defined in many ways but always to include social justice, racial equity, and reparations for slavery) our federal government makes no secret of its intent to transfer trillions of dollars of wealth from the largely old and white segments of the population to the relatively young and POC segments of the population.

Meanwhile, on the other side of the planet, there is the People's Republic of China. China is ascendant, focused, and purposeful. It has the largest population on Earth; the largest navy; the largest military; an economy that is only $6.2 trillion less than the American GDP and poised soon to become the largest economy in the world (and the largest polluter, too). Somewhat more surprisingly to American sensibilities, while China is an autocracy, indeed a dictatorship, it is in many day-to-day ways "freer" than the United States. Putting aside political expression, especially political expression hostile to government views, the Chinese people can do pretty much as they please. They can travel overseas, be educated overseas, purchase the same goods available in the West; and so on.

And notwithstanding China's total subjugation of Hong Kong (which was wholly free just a year ago) and other regional bullying and atrocities, their populace does not seem to suffer the societal divisions that plague, indeed define, the United States today. In China one does not see homelessness or opioid/drug addiction on a massive scale; the Chinese border is secure such that those crossing it unlawfully are in jail or deported within hours. Yet remarkably, many or most Chinese expatriates, whether temporary or permanent, seem to maintain a strong respect and affection for their country and their Chineseness. They tend in general not to be critical of the country even when doing so would be completely unthreatening to them. They are proud of the military, political, and economic strength of their homeland on the world stage. They are unapologetic about their country and its leaders, notwithstanding the murderous bloodshed of Mao Tse Tung in the 1930s and 1940s so thoroughly documented by Jung Cheng in her published masterpieces *Mao* and *Five Swans*.

Whether for want of a decent education or otherwise, today's mainstream journalists and other members of the *commentariat* in this country seem to have lost sight of the visionary radicalism of the Declaration of Independence. To be sure, it contains a certain amount of hypocrisy. Its shining statement that "We hold these truths to be self-evident, that all Men are created equal, that they are endowed by their Creator with certain unalienable rights, and that among those are Life, Liberty, and the Pursuit of Happiness" did not include slaves (although it probably did include women, as the term "men" in the document was generally understood to include all genders). Today, of course even the use of the word "men" or "women" is controversial. The Declaration of Independence is even more astonishing in its radicalism considering what the world was like elsewhere in the late eighteenth century. There were no republics or democracies. Moreover, the document was created and adopted through negotiation, collaboration, and compromise and embraced by the Continental Congress unanimously. These men incepted the greatest explosion of freedom in human history, birthing almost immediately the French Revolution for example. And the ringing last sentence of the Declaration stated: "And for the support of this Declaration, with a firm Reliance on the Protection of divine Providence, we mutually pledged to each other our Lives, our Fortunes, and our sacred Honor." It is, quite frankly, impossible to imagine any elected officials expressing such a sentiment today, much less partisans of all factions doing so.

We have often been told how fragile our unique republic might be. Now we see it in disrepair. Who would have thought that the murder of George Floyd by Officer Chauvin in Minneapolis during the summer of 2020 would be the pivot point that would cause the legacy of the founders of this country to become so disrespected, indeed mauled. Massive segments of the country are now acting as if the legacy of the founders is a poison chalice, an idea that follows a fairly short but straight line from critical race theory to the 1619 Project, to the BLM movement and all of its negative nuances. Last week, during the run-up to the July 4 weekend, newspapers nationwide carried stories about the divisiveness of the American flag. It has become associated with the current Republicans, who in turn have become associated with racists and Nazis. A farmer in deep-blue New York with a large produce truck painted on one side as an American flag found that his business collapsed—until he advertised that he was a Democrat and a liberal.

Consider a recent poll: 99% of self-described Democrats believe that the COVID-19 pandemic is not over, while 52% of self-described Republicans believe that it is over. A different poll finds that some 75% of Republicans believe that the 2020 election was marred by massive fraud, whereas roughly 99% of Democrats believe that there was no fraud associated with the 2020 election. We have become a tribal country and each tribe has beliefs that are more faith-based than fact-based. One evidently cannot be a Democrat and express a belief that the pandemic is over. As a result, wearing a mask is a political signal and symbol. Not wearing a mask likewise. One cannot be a Republican and express the view that the 2020 election was not tainted by fraud. The facts of the matter don't really come into play anymore. Our tribes "celebrate" July 4 now in entirely different ways. For progressives and the left, the July 4 holiday is becoming more like an anti-American teach-in of the sort that was so prevalent during the Vietnam War. For many conservatives, the July 4 celebration is a celebration of like-minded partisans.

Not only have we become an unserious tribal or factionalized country, but our political parties through their favored media conduits (MSNBC on the left and Fox on the right) announce every hour of every day that we are in a state of permanent emergency or permanent crisis in this country. This ongoing and never-ending state of emergency justifies any and all curative political measures, and it justifies a determination not to compromise in any quarter. Yet as a podcast I listened to last week noted, if one turns off the news and generally ignores the media, and if one opens the window or walks around outside, one hears birds chirping and dogs playing; one smells freshly cut grass; and one feels gentle sea breezes coming off the Chesapeake Bay, or one of its many tributaries. If we did not live in a politically dysfunctional country, this would be a pretty nice place.

20

While You Were Out

August 16, 2021

Like many, I have been away for a few weeks, away on summer holiday just when society began to appear to be opening up. It was a glorious few weeks, unplugged as I chose to be from television, newspapers, and most of social media. Well, children and grandchildren have departed, and I have been scrolling around the internet to take a peek at the recent past to find out what has been going on and what sort of interesting things may have happened while I was happily unaware of them. As it turns out, things have gotten much worse while I was out.

Recent Catastrophes owned by the Biden Administration.

Any one of the circumstances mentioned below might not be enough to bring down some administrations. But it is hard for me to imagine that these four disasters, taken together, will not bring about a major midterm defeat for the Democratic Party and very possibly a presidential defeat in 2024, subject to the at present unknowable Trump factor.

1. The Afghanistan Fiasco. One hardly knows where to begin on this depressing topic, and the facts are changing by the minute. Overnight, Kabul, a city of more than 4.5 million, fell to the Taliban, and the entire country is now under Taliban control. The president has fled the country, while US citizens and their facilitators are stuck there. Troops and helicopters are frantically trying to evacuate diplomats, journalists, and others. We seem to be on the verge of abandoning Afghan citizens who have had some connection with in-country Americans (cooks, drivers, translators, military personnel, and others) as we have made a habit of doing to our allies for a long time. Meanwhile, our president is hiding at Camp David and apparently has no plans to return to the White House for several days. Not a Profile in Courage at all. It is a far greater catastrophe than April 1975 and the chaotic evacuations from Saigon. Yet as Matt Taibbi put it yesterday: "As the Taliban waltzes into Kabul, the look of surprise on the faces of top officials should frighten us most of all." And further:

> Down to their own stunningly (perfectly?) inaccurate mis-predictions of what would take place once our military forces left the country, Biden administration officials could not have scripted a worse ending to the twenty-year disaster that has been our occupation of Afghanistan.

Every image coming out of Afghanistan this past weekend was an advertisement for the incompetence, arrogance, and double-dealing nature of American foreign policy leaders. Scenes of military dogs being evacuated while our troops fire weapons in the air to disperse humans desperate for a seat out of the country will force every theoretical future ally to think twice about partnering with us.[126]

It is too early to make snap judgments, but it appears that the media, just a few days ago fawning over Biden's decision to leave Afghanistan, may now be finally turning on him not for the departure but for the incompetence associated with its execution. The implications of this are wholly unclear for now, and the Republicans must take care since their fingerprints are all over the decision to leave Afghanistan. While Biden ended up looking like a fool, and perhaps he is, the situation might not be much different if Trump had won the election and carried on with his stated policy, which was applauded by most US citizens.

Nonetheless, the events of the last few days do bring home the observation from former defense secretary (under President Obama, among others) Robert Gates, as set forth in his 2019 memoir: "Biden had been wrong on virtually every major foreign policy and national security issue over the past four decades." This dismal record of incompetence in foreign policy affairs continues apace with catastrophic consequences for America's standing in the world and even more catastrophic consequences for the citizens of Afghanistan who are not affiliated with the Taliban.

A forty-four-minute *Commentary* podcast from Last Friday (entitled "Decline is a Choice, and We've Chosen It") [127] lays out the many layers of disaster brilliantly. It is too much to try to repeat here except to say that it was only a couple of months ago when Biden so precipitously and unexpectedly announced the near-immediate departure of American troops (the roughly three thousand of them) by a certain date. The government of Afghanistan was not informed, and the military leaders of Afghanistan were also not informed. This was a pure political act. In making this announcement, the administration assured the American population that *it would take at least a year for the Taliban to take over the entire country*. This is independently quite astonishing. So, after fighting the Taliban for twenty years, the administration intended to hand the keys of the country to the Taliban, but after a twelve-month decent interval.

Biden also gave great assurances that this would be nothing like the fall of Saigon, and there would be no helicopters taking out Embassy personnel from the roof. The photos at the following footnote demonstrate how wrong he was. Saigon 1975 (top) and Kabul 2021 (bottom).[128]

So, the troops were pulled out, chaos has ensued, and just yesterday the administration said it was sending three thousand troops back to Afghanistan, later adding another three thousand for a total of six thousand. But these troops are not being sent back because of any change of policy. They are being sent back to permit embassy personnel and staff to bug out quickly—and out of the sight of any cameras—so that there will be no images similar to those of April 1975, when the final days of departure from Vietnam were so painfully and powerfully recorded, causing a decade of psychic pain for the entire nation. Like so much that happens with this administration, it is performance art—political theater—behind which might be hiding a smidgen of incoherent policy. Even in the face of the ongoing catastrophe, Biden seems to believe that his precipitous and unexpectedly immediate departure from Afghanistan will "bring America back to the leadership of the free world." Fat chance. It would be hard to imagine a more delusional thought in the current circumstances. See this footnote for the early propaganda fallout and the Chinese crowing.[129]

Beneath it all, it is not clear that the Afghanistan adventure was a complete failure. Many people even think it successful in a limited way, especially in the past few years, including the Obama years. With a minuscule footprint of three thousand troops, sophisticated drone defensive actions, and on a shoestring budget, the Taliban were kept at bay for years protecting a nascent form of democracy and the liberation of women and girls, especially with regard to education and the professions. Outside the cities, though, there was never success. But the timing and the rationale behind the timing were horribly misguided. The Taliban fighting season is dictated by the weather. The fighting season is the spring, summer, and early fall, not late fall, or winter, when the Taliban retreat to the mountains. So, for the American bugout to occur at the height of the fighting season amounted to either strategic and tactical malpractice or insanity. And it was dictated by the delusional notion that our country would heartily celebrate the twentieth anniversary of 9/11/2001 by being out of Afghanistan before 9/11/2021. Instead, we will see the domination of Afghanistan by the Taliban and the resurrection of terrorist cells capable of operating outside of Afghanistan, all in place by 9/21. Not the celebration Biden had in mind.

The words "catastrophe" and "fiasco" are not strong enough to articulate the magnitude of the negative impact of Biden's decision, made on purely political optics grounds. In just months, this will be revealed as a tragedy of Shakespearean proportions (see the comment about wokeness below). It will be defended no doubt on the grounds that it was the implementation of a policy first articulated by President Trump. But for a Democratic president and the Democratic Party to invoke the despised Donald Trump is a most pathetic defense of incompetence (although it does protect against the most devastating Republican criticism, so there is that). Equally pathetic were the US efforts to beg the Taliban to spare the American Embassy, offering a bribe to the new Taliban government. President Biden and his administration will own this fiasco, and the hundreds of thousands of deaths of innocent people, and the virtual re-enslavement of Afghan women that was not inevitable under any administration.

2. The CDC's Extension of the Eviction Moratorium. Background: a few weeks ago, the Supreme Court found that the eviction moratorium was illegal, but because it was about to expire on July 31 shortly after their decision, it was allowed to stand and expire by its own terms but also to give the legislature a chance to take such action to extend the eviction as might be necessary, appropriate, or politically palatable. The legislature did not act, doubtless because of the inevitable failure of any effort to legislate a further extension of the prohibition on evictions. President Biden candidly confessed that he had sought advice from constitutional scholars all over the place and that it was pretty much unanimous that the eviction moratorium could not be extended by executive fiat but rather required congressional legislation to be constitutional.

The reaction from the progressives was instantaneous. There was howling. There were demonstrations. There were all manner of speeches given in condemnation of President Biden's claim that he was constitutionally limited. A senior official advised President Biden that he should seek another opinion from a once respected constitutional scholar: Harvard's Laurence Tribe. Tribe provided a convoluted explanation for the possible constitutionality of executive action, and so the president instructed or allowed the CDC to extend indefinitely the eviction ban. A particularly trenchant comment on all this by Jonathan Turley is here.[130] Our elected officials, while declining to address the matter legislatively as the Supreme Court had invited them to do, urged the president to take executive action and thereby supplant the legislature itself. This abandonment of legislative responsibility is independently problematic and is the subject of a separate comment below on legislators abandoning legislation in favor of activism. There are approximately eight million landlord victims of the ban (many homeowners who rent a basement) and perhaps a million tenant beneficiaries, although data on these things are hard to come by.

When the eviction ban was first announced more than a year ago, the country was in lockdown, and people were urged or even required to stay at home indoors. Under such circumstances, the ban at least made sense. It was not a political stunt. Now, there is no mandate or suggestion that we should all be locked up inside our homes under house arrest, as we were for so much of 2020. And the pressure to extend the eviction ban from the progressives had nothing whatsoever to do with public health or safety. The progressive point of view is quite literally a Bolshevik point of view to the effect that private property rights are illegitimate and contract rights no less so. And so, we now have a ban in place (soon to be reversed by the courts no doubt) that is based on a denial of property rights and a denial of contract rights. Properly understood, this is a huge issue and, standing alone, should cause political upheaval even within the Democratic Party and material segments of its constituency. Even the uber-liberal *Washington Post* seems to have awakened to the dangers of what the Biden administration is doing, publishing an excellent piece by David Von Drehle entitled: "The Eviction Moratorium Mess Exposes the Decay in American Politics."[131]

3. A Multitrillion-dollar Game of Three-Card Monte. The capture of the president and the administration by three or four progressive/Bolshevik members of Congress ("the Squad") has created a weird legislative situation. With considerable Republican support, the Senate has passed a $1 trillion infrastructure bill, which involves only $250 billion of "new spending." But now, in the House, the Squad has vowed not to vote for this bill unless it also includes $3.5 trillion worth of new spending on the progressive wish list. So, the Squad seems to be on a path to blow up the Biden presidency. All of this is because Biden has deferred a few too many times to the progressives in his party. Recall that the last time anything of vaguely comparable magnitude was passed, it was 1964–1965 when, under Lyndon Johnson, the Great Society legislation was passed, which included among many other things the Civil Rights Act of 1964. At that time the Democrats held a 120-seat advantage in the House and a filibuster-proof 18-vote majority in the Senate. The Great Society programs, therefore, enjoyed a political mandate unprecedented in the United States, even greater than the mandate that brought about Social Security and other reforms during the Roosevelt era. Now we have a 50/50 Senate and a [likely fleeting] three-vote Democratic majority in the House.

As of this writing, it is unclear how this will play out, but Biden's hoped-for signature "unity legislation" could well go down the drain. This is due to a complete lack of leadership on the part of the president, amplified by his lack of influence on the progressive left. Also to the point, nobody really knows as yet what is in the $3.5 trillion spending bill because it is too long to read in a week. But we do know that it throws money around as if we had it, and it would raise taxes on "the wealthy," defined as anybody making more than $250,000 per annum, it will get rid of most estate tax exclusions and thereby vastly increase the so-called death tax, and by some accounts it will increase the capital gains tax to an even higher rate than the ordinary income tax, which would be astonishing. It would bring about a century-long desire on the part of Bolsheviks to value labor more than capital.

The outcome of this multitrillion-dollar adventure will either be a catastrophe for the Biden administration or a catastrophe for the country. One suspects that the country could survive the former but perhaps not the latter. We will just have to wait and see. In either case, my always cloudy crystal ball says that the Republicans, whatever they may stand for, will control the House and maybe even the Senate after the 2022 election.

4. Covid, Masks, and Vaccination. The governors and administrators of many large blue states have ordered a return to 2020 insofar as mask mandates are concerned, much to the displeasure of their vaccinated constituents. Many are also demanding proof of vaccination (vaccination passports) as a ticket to enter indoor public spaces, such as restaurants, buses, subways, concerts, sporting events, and so forth. These governmental apparatchiks give no credit to those who have become infected with COVID-19 and therefore seem to have generally the same immune capabilities as vaccinated individuals. But they are nonetheless treated in all respects as "unvaccinated."

All of this is due to the emergence of "the highly contagious Delta variant" (it is now compulsory to say it that way, without mentioning that it is in nearly all cases harmless). The current circumstances have provided the CDC with the opportunity to take its umpteenth position on the importance of masking indoors, outdoors, at home, in front of unvaccinated children, etc. And then there is the fact that roughly half of US citizens are unvaccinated. It is becoming increasingly clear that the choice to remain unvaccinated is not based on ignorance, stupidity, the desire to infect others, libertarianism, or any other single explanation. There is a wide range of explanations. And so we have a new and significant divide in this country between the vaccinated and the unvaccinated. Few generalizations are possible or accurate except that the masking policies of the largely blue states seem bent on punishing the vaccinated for the existence of the unvaccinated. And there is no medical consensus on the benefits of immunity received as a result of having been infected. There are many such people, but they do not get the "passports" of the vaccinated.

There also has been exposed a complete lack of medical consensus on the risk or danger of so-called breakthrough infection. The data do seem to point to the proposition that the Delta variant, while very transmissive, causes mild symptoms and very few fatalities. I predict that the era of Dr. Fauci is close to over as he seems to be more responsive to political policy than to "science" and his secret role in funding the Wuhan lab is coming to light.

Among the many curiosities of all this is the lack of attention given by the media to huge demonstrations in France, Germany, and elsewhere in

Europe instigated by the unvaccinated protesting the spread of vaccination passports as essential tickets to indoor public spaces. We seem inevitably headed toward compulsory vaccination as a condition of employment. One might have thought that people could unite against a potentially deadly virus, but the fact that such unity requires faith in government proclamations and adherence to government policy creates its own serious issues, given the inconsistent and contradictory "facts" presented by government in general over the last eighteen months. And then there is the obvious collaboration between governments and big pharma, whose profits have soared and will continue to do so as long as vaccines are more or less mandatory. Moderna has seen its market capitalization grow from about $6 billion in January 2020 to about $180 billion today. Following the money may not always be the complete answer, but it sure is informative.[132] Biden's kowtowing to the forces demanding constant masking is making him very unpopular.

Then there is Andrew Cuomo, whose resignation was most unexpected given his Clintonesque defiance. Not long ago he was the toast of the left for his "heroic" handling of COVID-19 while governor of New York. The fact that his policies and their accompanying prevarications killed thousands of elderly people in nursing homes was conveniently overlooked by a hospitable and compliant media. But just as Al Capone was brought down by income tax evasion instead of a lifetime of bootlegging and murder, so was Andrew Cuomo brought down by his narcissistic view of his own power and his fully developed belief that he could lie at will to anybody about anything or everything. His bullying and intimidation of associates were apparently legendary. The media, nonetheless, professed itself, like the French Inspector in *Casablanca*, to be "shocked, shocked" that Cuomo was a devoted sexual predator and power-hungry, bullying, autocrat.

Mind you, his downfall was engineered by the New York Attorney General Letitia James, a woman who undoubtedly lusts after his job, and so there is much in the lengthy report that one might consider trivial and not really of a sexual nature at all. Indeed, his conduct seems more about power than sex, although they are quite commingled. Yet mixed in with all this was enough that *was* of a sexual nature to taint everything else. And so his personal assistant of many years has now become another female enabler like Ghislaine Maxwell, Hillary Clinton, and the women who facilitated Harvey Weinstein's escapades, among others. Maureen Dowd's column last weekend, "The Quislings of Albany," focused on the enablers. The *Times* also ran an op-ed piece on "How Cuomo Got Away with It for So Long." Old story, new players. Cuomo turns out to be a sort of doppelgänger of Bill Clinton, Harvey Weinstein, Jeffrey Epstein, and even Prince Andrew. It will not end well for the governor.

Wokeness has not died, but it seems to have moved below the fold if not into the back pages for the moment. This is, no doubt, because so much of it is somewhere in the neighborhood of silly or ridiculous. The University of Wisconsin–Madison determined, in its woke wisdom, to remove (and I'm not making this up) a fifty-thousand-pound "racist rock." The removal and relocation of this particular rock cost $50,000. News reports say that privately donated funds were used for this purpose. How very peculiar that someone would direct a contribution of that amount to a public university for that purpose. The "racist rock removal" story is here.[133]

Then there is the rebranding of vocabulary. The words "men" and "women" are verboten. Women do not get pregnant, people do. There are no "mothers" anymore in this country, just "birthing people." Christine Rosen wrote lucidly about this a few days ago for *Commentary*[134] and it is another step down the slippery slope of vocabulary control, an early form of mind control. It is time for us all to reread George Orwell, and not just *1984*. In the current milieu, his books will resonate much more than your vague memory of them.

In the end, perhaps the most disheartening aspect of national wokeness is the existence of persistent sustained outrage over the trivial. This inability to distinguish between the important and the unimportant, the serious and the silly, and indeed good and evil, has produced a populace that is unwilling or unable to recognize *real evil* in the world. For those who pay attention, and that will be only a few, we may well see and hear real evil in Afghanistan on par with Hitler, Stalin, and Mao. Young girls and women who have embraced Western ways will be stoned to death, hanged, beheaded, shot, and otherwise executed in public stadia; attendance may again be compulsory for the subjects of the Taliban. One wonders whether our woke media will have the stomach or the courage even to report on this activity much less pass judgment on the current administration for bringing it about. More likely, this true evil will be treated as less important than microaggressions in the classroom; persistent whining about centuries of white privilege; improper use of chosen genders; and other trivialities that have come now to so dominate our country thanks to our social justice warriors, led by social media, elected officials, and even our most successful corporations and law firms.

A curious sidelight of all this is the accelerating departure of wealthy people from the United States. The geese are leaving.[135] No more golden eggs to feed people and no geese to tax.

5. Legislators Have Abandoned Legislating in Favor of Activism and Political Performance Art. A *Commentary Magazine* podcast last week on the subject of the evictions was interesting for its short discussion of how federal legislators have in many ways given up on legislation and devoted themselves to becoming activists. And as activists and performance politicians engaged in a sort of Kabuki theater, they ask the executive branch to approve rules and regulations by executive order or fiat. The fascinating discussion begins five minutes into the August 5 podcast. The activists' performance politics aspect of this is even more striking when one considers that the entire brouhaha over evictions was too much of a political hot potato for the legislative branch, and so it was left to the executive branch to act, despite knowing with near certainty that the action to be taken would be ruled unconstitutional by the judicial branch (because the Supreme Court had already so held). So, two branches of government can blame the judicial branch for the failure of the progressives' aspirational Bolshevism. This is a seemingly new phenomenon, and it is deeply unsettling to anyone who values or has a sense of constitutional order. One can also imagine this sort of thing being called into play as an excuse to defang the judiciary in a variety of ways.

6. Tucker Carlson, Viktor Orban, and Hungary. Tucker Carlson has long been the bête noire of the liberal elite as well as what is left of the country club republicans, but he has been getting a certain amount of interesting press recently[136] because the inspector general of the NSA has opened an investigation into whether the agency "improperly targeted the communications of a member of the U.S. news media" following Carlson's claims that the NSA tried to shut down his show. While it seems unlikely that the NSA was interested in "shutting down" his slot on Fox News, it will be interesting to find out how it came to be that the NSA first ended up monitoring Tucker Carlson's emails or telephone calls and, second, how the administration (unclear which administration) came to "unmask" those intercepts.

Probably more substantively, Tucker Carlson spent a week in Hungary praising Hungary and its leader Viktor Orban, while at each step comparing Hungarian orderliness, cleanliness, absence of illegal immigrants, and general lack of visible political dysfunction to the presence of those qualities in the United States. Hungary quite famously closed its borders to immigrants, mostly from North Africa, at about the same time that Germany was pressuring countries to take such immigrants. The press around Carlson's week in Hungary has been fascinating. A *Washington Post* op-ed view was that the interview and surrounding reporting provided

> a deeply unsettling glimpse into the true nature of the authoritarian nationalist future that Carlson and his fellow travelers envision for our country. Carlson fawns over the "free" nature of Hungarian society — contrasting it favorably with the supposed repression of widespread anti-liberal yearnings in American society — while saying little to nothing about the autocratic nature of Orbanism. In this lurks a sort of dream combination: ethno-nationalism secured via autocracy.[137]

This reaction was to be expected and was 100% predictable. But far less expected was the *New York Times*'s publication of a piece by Ross Douthat, which contains the following:

> I was struck by an observation from *The Atlantic*'s David Frum, a fierce critic of the right's Orban infatuation. As part of a Twitter thread documenting corruption in Orbán's inner circle, Frum wrote: "I visited Hungary in 2016. Again & again, I witnessed a gesture I thought had vanished from Europe forever: people turning their heads to check who was listening before they leaned forward to whisper what they had to say. They feared for their jobs, not their lives — but still …"
>
> On the one hand, there's the fear that Trumpian populism will someday gain enough power to make its critics fear for their livelihoods. On the other, there's the fear that progressivism already exerts this power in the United States, and that what Frum describes in dire terms, the cautious *sotto voce* conversation, is an important part of American life right now.

You can document this fear of sharing strong opinions, especially ones that conflict with progressive orthodoxy, by looking at opinion polls. For example, a 2020 survey conducted by the Cato Institute found that 62 percent of Americans felt uncomfortable sharing their views because of the political climate, and "strong liberals" were the only ideological group where the majority felt free to speak their minds. To the question, "Are you worried about losing your job or missing out on job opportunities if your political opinions became known?" highly educated Americans were the most anxious, with 44 percent of respondents with a postgraduate degree and 60 percent of Republicans with a post-grad degree saying yes.[138]

Douthat is not a big fan of Viktor Orban, but he does wonder aloud how one can fight the social or cultural totalitarian forces of today. Where can you go to vote for a different ruling ideology given the interlocking American establishment, all its schools and professional guilds, its consolidated media and tech powers? The old liberal idea that we could fight these social and technical forces through debate is implausible when debate is no longer actually allowed on campuses, in schools, by employers, and so forth. Douthat describes this as a naïve form of cultural surrender, like telling a purged screenwriter during the Hollywood Blacklist, "Hey, just go start your own movie studio."

Douthat explains his sense that it is this real feature of the United States today that makes the Carlsonian view of Orban appealing to American conservatives.

> It's not just his anti-immigration stance or his moral traditionalism. It's that his interventions in Hungarian cultural life, the attacks on liberal academic centers and the spending on conservative ideological projects are seen as examples of how political power might curb progressivism's influence.

At a somewhat higher level, the idea that our democracy has failed and needs to be replaced by a benevolent but nonprogressive authoritarian leader seems at least understandable if not a permanent solution.

Short Takes

1. The Death of Meritocracy and the Abandonment of Standards (Oregon). A new Oregon law suspends a requirement for a basic-skills test in math, reading, and writing to graduate high school.[139] This law is praised by advocates as a way to rethink education standards. This of course will create a permanent underclass of uneducated people, many of them people of color, and thereby perpetuate inequality and even the notion of white supremacy. It will create a whole generation of illiterate students without job skills who will be dependent on the state from cradle to grave. A perfect way to implement Bolshevism. This is a policy, one might note, not all that different from the policies that the Taliban will bring to the "education" of Afghanistan women in the months to come.

2. Mass Psychosis and Societal Insanity Might Now Be Real. This short video, put out by something called the Academy of Ideas,[140] presents the hypothesis that America is in the midst of a mass psychosis (societal insanity) not altogether unlike the mass psychosis that overwhelmed the nation and led to witch burnings in Salem and elsewhere. It is a twenty-two-minute artistic cartoon presentation that starts off sounding very simplistic but develops by the end into something more complex and quite troubling. But beginning at about minute eighteen there is a short discussion of how to escape or resist society's madness.

3. On the international front, the Olympics came and went. But since everything happened on the other side of the world, and since no spectators were allowed actually to witness the events in the physical presence of the athletes, it was hard for most people to become particularly engaged. Now that professionals have taken over the Olympics, they have an element of pointlessness to them (said the curmudgeon). But the fact that France beat the US team in basketball (although not for the gold) was amazing, and it was interesting to learn that so many French players came from the NBA.

4. Back to the Future with Masking Mandates. The governors of two of the four largest states, Texas and Florida, are in open revolt against federal mandates. This has resulted in the Biden administration declaring war on Florida and its governor based on statistics showing that Florida has more

Delta variant infections than other states, despite having hardly any deaths at all as a result. The only thing that is newsworthy about this is its revelation that Biden administration is terrified of Governor DeSantis in his capacity as a possible 2024 presidential candidate, assuming away for now the unknown Trump factor. There is a separate panic going on in the Biden administration: namely, the suddenly obvious incompetence and unpopularity of Vice President Kamala Harris.[141]

5. The Anti-Trumps Cannot Stop Seething and Writing about Their Hatred. A fascinating insight from the European publication *Le Monde Diplomatique* [142] by Thomas Frank gives more insight into the American psyche than is found in American publications. The article, entitled "US Liberals Hysteria Outlives Trump," seeks to address the question: Why did President Trump induce such fear and loathing among the nation's highly educated elite? Mr. Frank details some notable successes of the Trump administration, while being deeply critical of Mr. Trump himself. Yet the hysteria led leading publications, radio outlets, and TV channels to describe Trump as authoritarian, a tyrant, a nuke-crazy warmonger, a fascist, a Nazi, and the worst leader of any nation since Hitler. The hysteria was universal, hegemonic. To be on the left and hold some other interpretation of events was not only impermissible; it was a career-limiting gesture. To refuse hysteria was to silence yourself. This phenomenon parallels the mass psychosis diagnosis introduced in ¶2 above. Mr. Frank points out that there were so many conspiracies (Russian conspiracy, and other conspiracy speculations) that it led Matt Taibbi to suggest that the high-speed succession of "bombshell" Trump-outrage news stories—each of them accelerating the audience's Trump hysteria, each of them turning out to be misleading in some way, and each of them instantly forgotten when the next bombshell appeared—became the business model for the news industry.

The article does not lend itself to ready summation and should be read. It is replete with extraordinary insights into the recent past. Its concluding paragraph is this:

> Longing for the dictatorship of the expertariat is just a slightly more vivid expression of the authoritarian tendencies that now, post-Trump, make up more and more of the liberal faith. Look around at American politics today and

you will see prominent lawyers expressing their disgust with free speech.[143] You will find banks[144] and defense contractors [145] declaring their allyship with the oppressed, liberal legislators pushing for censorship on social media,[146] and everywhere a belief in the essential villainy of the white, working-class population. These are the views of an elite that now regards as intolerable many of the millions over whom it presides. The only norms that matter, it now seems, are the ones that keep the right people on top.

6. Obama's Fast Fall from Grace. The occasion of the sixtieth birthday of former President Obama, taking place at his $14 million-dollar mansion on Martha's Vineyard, led to criticism from Massachusetts authorities that it was too large for an unmasked event. So, the former president uninvited all of his close personal aids and hundreds of almost A-listers and limited the guests to the truly rich and famous, largely from the entertainment community. Uninvited were people who once had influence such as Stephen Colbert and Larry David. All of this led to a couple of extraordinary articles by people who had been strong supporters of President Obama in the early days.

The first of these articles, by Matt Taibbi, is biting and trenchant. It is entitled "The Vanishing Legacy of Barack Obama" and subtitled: "On the Road from Stirring Symbol of Hope and Change to the Fat Elvis of Neoliberalism, Birthday-Partying Barack Obama Sold Us All Out."[147] It gets way more biting from there.

The second of these was Maureen Dowd's "Behold Barack Antoinette" in yesterday's *New York Times*.[148] While covering some of the same ground from different angles, her take is different from Taibbi's but a clear sign that Obama can and will now be viewed even by the left through an altogether new and more critical lens, not all that different in fact from the lens through which he is seen by many conservatives.

21

Afghanistan, Mr. Biden, and Coming Full Circle

September 11, 2021

Next year we are to bring all the soldiers home
For lack of money, and it is all right.
Places they guarded, or kept orderly,
Must guard themselves, and keep themselves orderly
We want the money for ourselves at home
Instead of working. And this is all right.

It's hard to say who wanted it to happen,
But now it's been decided nobody minds.
The places are a long way off, not here,
Which is all right, and from what we hear
The soldiers there only made trouble happen.
Next year we shall be easier in our minds.

Next year we shall be living in a country
That brought its soldiers home for lack of money.
The statues will be standing in the same
Tree-muffled squares, and look nearly the same.
Our children will not know it's a different country.
All we can hope to leave them now is money.

—Philip Larkin, "Homage to a Government" (1964)

My wife and I flew over Afghanistan in 2019 on the way back to London from a three- week stay in Vietnam as a sort of pilgrimage to observe the fiftieth anniversary of my own departure from Vietnam after my second tour of duty with the Navy. We seemed to be flying over Afghanistan for hours, but it never looked much different. As we looked down at this extraordinary gray and mountainous landscape, we took note of the fact that no central authority could ever hope to govern this vast and inhospitable region, where thousands of towns and villages appeared to be cut off from any infrastructure connecting them to any other town, village or city. It was, frankly, an extraordinary and memorable sight, even from forty thousand feet. But before getting into Afghanistan proper, it is important to note a thing or two about President Biden.

1. Memories of Joe Biden from His Past Life

I am beyond old enough to remember well Mr. Biden's run for the presidency in 1987. I traveled by train regularly from Washington to New York, Philadelphia, and Wilmington. In the late 1970s and early 1980s I also used to bump into Mr. Biden from time to time on the train, the Metroliner as it was then called. Our interactions were limited to pleasantries. But based on these, and much more on his public persona, I always perceived him as an amiable but relatively harmless dunce. To be sure, he demonstrated in his 1987 run for the presidency a strange combination of fecklessness and bold (what we might today call Trumpian) dishonesty.

During that campaign, Mr. Biden made headlines for serial lying about his academic credentials. He claimed to have been a top graduate from Syracuse Law School when in fact he graduated seventy-sixth in a class of eighty-five; he claimed to have gone to law school on a full scholarship, but this was untrue.[149] He also was accused of and admitted to plagiarism in law school but defended it on the grounds it was not "malevolent" (see a September 1987 *New York Times* story written by E. J. Dionne Jr.[150]). The final straw for Mr. Biden's 1987 presidential campaign was his word-for-word and gesture-for-gesture plagiarism of chunks of a famous speech given in Parliament by Neil Kinnock, then a British Labour Party politician. He plagiarized others as well, to the annoyance of Robert Kennedy's speechwriter, who thought Biden "counterfeit." Story here;[151] film here.[152]

But much as Presidents Nixon and Clinton redeemed, or at least normalized, themselves in various ways, so it appeared that Joe Biden had matured and grown up and out of his old self. His rehabilitation was facilitated by the fact that everyone felt pity for him because of the death of his first wife and daughter (car accident in 1972 just after Mr. Biden had won election to the Senate). Decades later, by the fall of 2020, he appeared to be nearly the only semi normal person in a crowded Democratic field composed mostly of relatively hard-left progressives. He was amiable; he was "Uncle Joe" "Joe Six-Pack" he was full of hair- sniffing empathy, especially for womankind.

While perhaps a boob, he was hard to hate. And given that the country was suffering from a high level of "Trump fatigue," and Trump was easy to hate, it was hardly a shock (other than perhaps to Mr. Trump) that Mr. Biden won the presidency. The campaign was marked by several Trump blunders and by what at the time appeared to be the political genius of Mr. Biden's campaign managers: keeping him out of sight in the basement of his Wilmington residence, while leaving the stage completely to President Trump, who used his months alone in the public eye to demonstrate to independent and suburban voters why they so disliked him. Suddenly, however, and for the last many weeks, Mr. Biden has been in full view, and we have seen the raw Biden unsheathed. To my eyes, it has not been a pretty sight. But I am getting ahead of myself.

2. Afghanistan: Why Were We There, What Did We Do?

We all need to step back from the last few weeks for a few paragraphs. First of all, it has emerged as a conventional view in this country that we needed to get out of Afghanistan with all deliberate speed because it was an "endless" or "forever" war and therefore "bad." The slogan was all one needed to know to reach a conclusion: very Madison Avenue and very American. Yet, mercifully, one of the things I learned from my parents, and my formal and informal education, was never to accept the premise of a statement or a policy unblinkingly. Indeed, as I have grown older, the more widespread or conventional a view is, the more I tend to wonder whether it is likely to be the product of "the lemming effect" of peer pressure or something like that. So, I want to make a point that has been made by no one in recent weeks or months (so far as I know), the point being that the military action in Afghanistan began, indeed continued for a long time (perhaps even right up until the end) as the most legitimate foreign military action in American history since at least World War II. After you finish scoffing, consider the facts below.

In response to the attacks of twenty years ago today: (1) the United States Senate and the United States House of Representatives voted 534–1 in favor of military action in Afghanistan to remove Al Qaeda as a terrorist threat to the United States, which meant removing their protectors the Taliban who had taken over Afghanistan militarily in 1996; (2) NATO invoked Article 5—the common defense clause—for the first and only time in NATO's seventy-five-year history; (3) the United Nations passed a Resolution authorizing the United States to respond "by any means necessary," UN-speak meaning the United States was authorized to utilize such military force as it might find appropriate to deal with the Taliban; (4) and fifty-one (51) countries (!) sent troops to Afghanistan, with a combined 130,000 troops at the deployment's peak.

NATO's combat mission ended in 2014, but thousands of coalition troops remained to help train and advise Afghan security forces. Many (about seven thousand as best as I can learn) of those allied troops were there until last month. They shed much blood and spent much treasure. And Mr. Biden never consulted with them (or the Afghan government or Afghan Army) before deciding to bug out of Afghanistan in the manner he chose. The prime minister of one such country, Australia, happened to be in Washington on 9/11 and observed the smoke rising from the Pentagon. He immediately flew back to Canberra, telling his cabinet to meet him planeside so that they could promptly declare war. Other countries acted similarly. President Bush enjoyed a favorable rating of an astonishing 89% in the polls.

While the NATO combat mission ended in 2014 and while the US troop decline began then and continued such that by the end of the Obama administration troop levels were reduced to eighty-four hundred. But due to security concerns on the ground, Mr. Obama decided not to remove all the troops by the end of his second term.[153] In August 2017, President Trump warned against a "hasty withdrawal," stating that conditions on the ground, not arbitrary timetables, would guide American strategy. Mr. Trump, in fact, raised the number of troops to some fourteen thousand later that year and into 2018. Then, in the fall of 2019, Mr. Trump's representative negotiating with the Taliban announced that under a deal reached "in principle" with the Taliban, the first five thousand US troops would withdraw within 135 days of the agreement becoming final.[154] According to CENTCOM, the United States had reduced its Afghan troop numbers to eighty-six hundred by June 2020 "in accordance with the February 2020 Taliban peace deal." On November 17, 2020, acting US Secretary of Defense Christopher C. Miller announced further troop withdrawals, leaving 2,500 troops across both Afghanistan and Iraq, down from the previous amount of 4,500 and 3,000, respectively.[155]

So, when Mr. Biden took office, we had about twenty-five hundred troops in Afghanistan. American allies still had seven thousand troops there according to Sam Harris's *Making Sense* podcasts 258–59. There had been few if any US casualties from and after January 1, 2020, and only a modest number of casualties after 2015 according to Pentagon data cited below. Some 66,000 Afghan soldiers died, as did more than 47,000 Afghan civilians. Taliban and other opposition fighters killed numbered about 52,000. According to the Defense Department, total American military combat deaths in Afghanistan for the twenty years from inception to the end of 2014 were 1,847. From January 1, 2015, to date only twenty were killed in action according to a DoD Release dated August 31, 2021. Nonhostile deaths (illness, accidents, and the like) were 505 and 88 during these two time frames according to the same release. In addition, 1,145 allied troops died in Afghanistan.[156] To put this in some pertinent perspective, there were 10,120 deaths by murder in Chicago during the same twenty-year period. One might readily conclude that a year of combat duty in Afghanistan would be safer than spending a year in Chicago. Sadly, the street war in Chicago really *is* a "forever war."

A different pertinent point of comparison is that we have had more than 28,500 military troops stationed in South Korea for roughly 65 years and we have had some 55,000 troops stationed in Japan and more than 65,000 troops stationed in Europe, in each case for 75 years. It is not unreasonable to believe that the maintenance of a small force in Afghanistan did more to protect the security of Americans in this country than did the maintenance of nearly 150,000 American troops in Europe and Asia. Our allies, especially in Europe, tend to believe that their own security was enhanced by the presence of the small military presence in Afghanistan. See "Biden Refusal to Acknowledge Error Dismays Supporters and Allies."[157] That presence had little or nothing to do with combat, but it had almost everything to do with training and intelligence gathering through both human sources and drones. In moderately well-managed circumstances, it would have been possible to leave Afghanistan without our own conduct and words triggering the immediate collapse of the military and the government: facts that Mr. Biden and his administration now turn upside down in arguing that the very chaos they caused proves the wisdom of their actions. But I get ahead of myself again.

One reason offered by Mr. Biden and his administration for their ill-conceived departure was that having spent twenty years, considerable American treasure (approximately $1 trillion over two decades), and having lost American blood on foreign soil, it was time to end this "forever war," given the supposed choice of either leaving or committing "tens of thousands of American men and women" to combat in an unfamiliar foreign land. But as became so common this past summer, Mr. Biden spoke with forked tongue: he used false hyperbole and offered phony choices. The $1 trillion number is a mere fraction of what Mr. Biden and his progressive colleagues in Congress and in his administration are trying to commit to spend in a single bit of pending legislation. To digress for a moment, it should be sobering (but apparently it is not) that in 2000 US federal debt amounted to 56.5% of Gross Domestic Product (GDP). Today, US federal debt represents 125.73% of GDP. At today's rock-bottom interest rates, the interest on our roughly $29 trillion of federal debt is $405 billion per year. See "US Debt Clock."[158]

Mr. Biden is throwing around his $1 trillion number, spent over twenty years, as if it is shockingly large when actually it is pretty modest considering the absence of significant terrorist activity on US soil since 9/11. If and when Al Qaeda or other terrorist jihadist groups are able to operate freely in Afghanistan (and there is no reason to believe they will not) and if they again do great damage on American soil (one hopes not, but given the absence of border security in this country it seems a distinct possibility), then Mr. Biden will be remembered as the man who surrendered Afghanistan to the Taliban and increased American vulnerability to terrorist jihadist attack. In such an event, he will be remembered as far worse than even Neville Chamberlain. And why did he do this? He did this to score a political photo-op on 9/11 so that he could heroically celebrate the twentieth anniversary of 9/11 and the "extraordinarily successful" departure of American troops from Afghanistan. Even today, on the twentieth anniversary of 9/11, he has the effrontery to continue congratulating himself on the "extraordinary success" of his grotesquely bungled disengagement from Afghanistan.

I cannot go further on this topic without generally aligning myself with the comment by former UK Prime Minister Tony Blair to the effect that Mr. Biden's withdrawal was driven "in obedience to an imbecilic slogan about ending 'the forever wars.'" BBC story and footage here.[159] I also cannot go further without making clear my view that Mr. Trump, no less than Mr. Biden, was making ill-considered decisions about withdrawal from Afghanistan based on short-term domestic political considerations and not based on the long-term interests of the United States. The same was true of Mr. Obama to some extent, except that he did not go forward with his preferred course of action (withdrawal of troops) given the situation on the ground in Afghanistan in 2014 and even in 2016.

I believe the concept of "forever wars" has its roots in the Iraq fiasco far more so than in Afghanistan and also in the slogan-driven system we call politics in this country. The idea of "forever war" is the antithesis of "forever peace" and hence not possible to support. And on the flip side of that, of course, only a hard-bitten soul, probably a fascist, would be against "forever peace." But as one of the editors of *The Chesapeake Observer* wrote last week: "Endless war can end when the endless jihad does." A country does not stop defending itself unless it is simply too tired, too lacking in will, too defeated to soldier on. The United States seems to have reached that place, well captured in the Philip Larkin poem at the top of this piece.

Where was I? Yes, from start to finish Iraq was built on a founding lie about WMD, compounded by monumental ineptitude. Afghanistan was completely different. Afghanistan was successful in its initial mission to remove the Taliban and hence deny Al Qaeda and other jihadists free rein in Afghanistan. The mission crept to something different thereafter and had a "nation building" feature to it, but it was hardly a total failure on that account. That mission, which I shall refer to as the "middle mission," resulted in a workable and relatively stable Afghan government, democratically elected. There was to be sure much corruption, but it was as much American as Afghan.[160] This middle mission resulted in the creation (mostly by the Afghans themselves) of a viable economy and educational system that in the past generation have pulled the country out of illiteracy to a very large extent and brought women (and men, too, one must remember) from the seventh century into the twenty-first century (at least temporarily). It was hardly a failure compared to, say, Iraq, Vietnam, or Cuba.

It was because of this "success" of the middle mission, imperfect but not trivial, that the mission changed during Mr. Obama's second term to move altogether away from nation building and to also move away from being in any true sense "a war." As in Korea, and also Germany for some decades, we were in a somewhat stable standoff: a stalemate with the Taliban. Beginning in 2015 or thereabouts, our mission was fairly understood to keep the Taliban and other terrorists at bay. The American presence was to support the Afghan army with air support, intelligence, war material, and "over the horizon" drone and satellite capability. Neither the media nor many consumers of media output took the trouble to pay very much attention to Afghanistan though.

And, for reasons that were never altogether understandable, the polling on Afghanistan suggested that most Americans thought we should simply leave. I do not know what precise question was asked in such polls, but I doubt that it had much context (or, more likely, none). If people were asked the question in a certain way, they would no doubt state their opposition to maintaining troops in Europe, Korea, or Japan. Doubtless people were not asked whether we should surrender to the Taliban and give Afghanistan back to jihadists as a safe haven for them to terrorize America and the West.

Notably, until Mr. Trump was elected there was no constituency in this country for bugging out of Afghanistan immediately or precipitously. It was the far-right isolationism (Trump's America First view) that gave voice to the notion that indiscriminate retreat from foreign affairs was desirable. Unexpectedly, perhaps, this piece of Trumpism was embraced by the far left, with its evolving view that the United States is and has been from its inception an Evil Empire and has no business imposing its views about anything on any other countries. This Trumpian urge to retreat from foreign affairs was not just Afghanistan, it was Europe and NATO as well. It was politically convenient, but otherwise beyond astonishing, that Mr. Biden should claim that he had "no choice" but to follow through on Mr. Trump's arrangements with the Taliban. This was dishonest first because Mr. Biden felt no obligation to do anything but undermine and undercut every other agreement or executive act of Mr. Trump to the extent he could. It is even more dishonest because in essentially the same breath he claimed to his European allies that "America was back," whereas those allies all said and felt that his chaotic bugout from Afghanistan was a monumental betrayal and possibly the death knell of NATO.[161] One suspects that many in Europe may soon yearn for the "good old days" of Mr. Trump.

It also strikes me as remarkable that both the isolationists of the right (Trump supporters) and the isolationists of the left (progressives, now including Biden) seem to be paying no attention to the fact that the Pakistani government has proved itself at once fearful of, yet hospitable to, the Taliban. Pakistan, of course, is not Afghanistan. And one thing that makes it different is that the Pakistani government controls 165 nuclear warheads. The American presence in Afghanistan, tiny as the footprint was, and as modest as was the annual cost in recent years, included Bagram Air Base, one of the most strategically well-located airfields in central Asia and one now denied to American airplanes. As a practical matter, this means the United States will have virtually no intelligence capability on the ground or in the air over Afghanistan or near Pakistan. It is difficult to imagine anything good coming from all that.

Indeed, under more astute leadership both on the military side and in the White House, it would be hard to imagine an orderly withdrawal from Afghanistan that did not include continued rights to utilize Bagram Air Base for some nontrivial period. Instead, Mr. Biden made the decision to sneak away from Bagram, against the advice of his military commanders, and to abandon Bagram at three o'clock in the morning over the July 4 holiday weekend. This was done without advising the Afghan military or our NATO allies that it was happening. Talk about pulling the rug out from under our friends. And the United States simply left five thousand terrorist prisoners at the facility as it abandoned the place. As the Associated Press reported on July 2, weeks before Mr. Biden and his administration were completely overwhelmed by their own acts:

> Afghanistan's district administrator for Bagram told The Associated Press that the U.S. departure happened overnight and without coordination with local officials.[162] As a result, dozens of looters stormed through the unprotected gates. Taliban spokesman Zabihullah Mujahid called Friday's departure from Bagram "a positive step" and told NBC News that "for now" the Taliban does not plan on seizing the sprawling airbase, which is located some 40 miles north of Kabul.

The people of Afghanistan have been engaged in a civil war since 1978. This civil war began even before the Soviet invasion of the 1980s. When the Soviets finally departed in 1992, Kabul and the Afghanistan provinces fell into the hands of various tribal Warlords: Pashtun, Tajik, Uzbek, Hazura, Turkmen, and many others. Four years later, in 1996, Kabul and Afghanistan fell to the Taliban, most of whom are Pashtun. In 2001, Kabul and most of the country fell to the Americans. Now, in 2021, Mr. Biden and his administration chose to surrender the country to the very group of people we ousted in 2001, preferring the uncertainty of the future to the stalemate with terrorist jihadists of the present. Mr. Biden and his administration have traded a faux forever war for a very real forever jihad. Mr. Biden has made the perfect the enemy of the good. Having run on the antiwar slogan "Build Back Better," one of Mr. Biden's very first acts was to build *the Taliban* back better. What could possibly go wrong?

All of this said, I am to a degree persuadable that it might have been necessary or desirable to leave Afghanistan at some point in the near or medium term. Maybe we even should have left after the December 2001 failure to capture Bin Laden at Tora Bora, where he had been cornered but slipped away largely due to military blundering. But that is a whole other story, well summarized by Maureen Dowd more than a decade ago in her *New York Times* column "Blunder on the Mountain."[163]

The polling notwithstanding, the stated reasons for our immediate and recklessly chaotic departure (whether by Mr. Trump's administration or Mr. Biden's administration) do not at this moment strike me as strategically sound or even rational, except as an act of political pandering. Rather, in each case, the precipitous decision to abandon Afghanistan seems to have been made *solely* for domestic political reasons. Both Mr. Trump and Mr. Biden seemed perfectly willing to sacrifice national interests for potential personal political gain. History will judge this point, and it may take time before that historical judgment can be rendered. Or it might be swift. If terrorist jihadists find Afghanistan to be a suitable platform for attacks on the United States and Europe and we will know that timing of the decision to leave was as catastrophically incompetent as the method of departure. And it is now to that event, and the multiple layers of bad judgment surrounding it, that I now turn.

3. The Timing and Manner of the American Departure

One seemingly positive outcome from the 2020 presidential election was that we would return to executive competence in the presidency. There would be adults in the White House who could engage in foreign policy matters with a steady hand. While Mr. Biden had no legislative achievements to point to over his four decades of legislative experience, he has not left behind evidence of management incompetence. It is true that former defense secretary Robert Gates opined publicly, and in his memoirs, that "I think Mr. Biden has been wrong on nearly every major foreign policy and national security issue over the past four decades," but nobody had ever seriously questioned his management competence in the same way that, for example, Mr. Trump's management competence was questioned nearly every day. In hindsight, it seems that Mr. Biden never actually had any management experience, which would explain the absence of demonstrated incompetence in that area.

And from his inauguration in late January through roughly the end of June of this year 2021, Mr. Biden did not demonstrate utter management incompetence. While he transmogrified from a centrist Democrat to a progressive Democrat during this five-month period, most people I know felt that at his core he was just being influenced by the political situation on Capitol Hill. But the notion of being transformative seemed to grow in his mind as time went on and seems to have given him the delusion that if he played his progressive cards right, he could be recognized by the media, indeed history, as the second coming of FDR. This delusion seemed to give him a wholly unwarranted level of confidence in his own judgment about many things, including Afghanistan.

Anyway, as I come at last to the events of July and August of this year (2021), I can hardly bear to think about them, much less write about them. Vocabulary sometimes seems inadequate to communicate the shame, the disgust, the horror, the embarrassment I feel about President Biden and his military and civilian advisors for their total mismanagement of the withdrawal. In most parliamentary systems, our secretary of state and our chairman of the joint chiefs of staff would have resigned by now, along with the president's national security advisor. But without doubt we can look forward to some interesting finger-pointing books. Few presidents can get away with blaming the military, the state department, and the intelligence services for their own essentially political choices. There will probably be retribution in due course via leaks, books, and otherwise. A book is a ready-made bestseller for Bob Woodward, too, if he still has good sources. In the long run, few reputations will emerge unscathed.

One must, I suppose, begin with Mr. Biden's July 8 press conference.[164] The speech, and the responses at the press conference, were laced with false premises, false choices, and a level of blind faith in his own judgment that has not since wavered, and I do not mean that as a compliment. The italicized commentary in the bloc quotes are mine.

> Our military commanders advised me that once I made the decision to end the war, we needed to move swiftly to conduct the main elements of the drawdown. And in this context, speed is safety. *Speed was chaos and death to many.*
>
> In our meeting, I also assured [Afghan President] Ghani that U.S. support for the people of Afghanistan will endure. We will continue to provide civilian and humanitarian assistance, including speaking out for the rights of women and girls. *Virtue-signaling falsehood.*
>
> I intend to maintain our diplomatic presence in Afghanistan. *Fat chance.*
>
> We're also going to continue to make sure that we take on the Afghan nationals who work side-by-side with U.S. forces, including interpreters and translators — since we're no longer going to have military there after this; we're not going to need them and they have no jobs — who are also going to be vital to our efforts so they — and they've been very vital — and so their families are not exposed to danger as well. Our message to those women and men is clear: There is a home for you in the United States if you so choose, and we will stand with you just as you stood with us. *If only that had turned out to be true.*
>
> But for those who have argued that we should stay just six more months or just one more year, I ask them to consider the lessons of recent history. In 2011, the NATO Allies and

partners agreed that we would end our combat mission in 2014. In 2014, some argued, "One more year." So we kept fighting, and we kept taking casualties. In 2015, the same. And on and on. *He has airbrushed out of the storyline everything after January 2015. Post 2015, there were almost no deaths of US troops.*

Q. Mr. President, thank you. But we have talked to your own top general in Afghanistan, General Scott Miller. He told ABC News the conditions are so concerning at this point that it could result in a civil war. *So, if Kabul falls to the Taliban, what will the United States do about it?*

THE PRESIDENT: Look, you've said two things—one, that if it could result in a civil war—that's different than the Taliban succeeding, number one. Number two, the question of what will be done is going to be implicated—is going to implicate the entire region as well. There's a number of countries who have a grave concern about what's going to happen in Afghanistan relative to their security. The question is: How much of a threat to the United States of America and to our allies is whatever results in terms of a government or an agreement? That's when that judgment will be made. *The answer to the question stated was "nothing."*

Q. Mr. President, some Vietnamese veterans see echoes of their experience in this withdrawal in Afghanistan. Do you see any parallels between this withdrawal and what happened in Vietnam, with some people feeling—

THE PRESIDENT: None whatsoever. Zero. What you had is — you had entire brigades breaking through the gates of our embassy — six if I'm not mistaken.

The Taliban is not the south—the North Vietnamese army. They're not— they're not remotely comparable in terms of capability. There's going to be no circumstance where you see people being lifted off the roof of a embassy in the —of the United States from Afghanistan. It is not at all comparable. *No doubt Mr. Biden would like a mulligan on that answer.*

From and after that press conference, we saw a President Biden cornered, querulous, combative, pig-headed, defensive, mean, and in many ways just plain unlikeable. He morphed away from amiable Uncle Joe to Mean Joe. He had run in some large part on his "likability," an asset that he squandered almost completely during the summer of 2021. He also squandered his credibility. He seems still in denial about the possible undermining or destruction of NATO and the concomitant (and quite sudden) distrust of the United States by virtually all other nations. The reaction from Europe and Germany was disbelief and betrayal. This sort of reaction was ubiquitous among European leaders either privately or publicly. See "How Biden Broke NATO"[165] and "The Allies Retreat from Afghanistan is a Monstrous Act of Self-Harm," Daily *Mail (UK)*. "[166]

As for Mr. Biden's well-known and politically marketable empathy, he has demonstrated an uncharacteristic heartlessness in his public utterances about stranded Afghans (and even Americans), who have been left in Afghanistan to, as Mr. Biden put it, "shelter in place," an odd and vapid choice of words for citizens stranded in a deadly totalitarian environment.

He also demonstrated a similarly puzzling tone-deafness in his trip to Dover Air Force Base in Delaware to greet the bodies of the thirteen young American men killed by a suicide bomber just days before the final pullout. He seemed bored by the whole event and looked at his watch almost constantly. And when confronted by parents of dead young Marines, Mr. Biden tried to show his empathy by talking about the fact that his son Beau had been in the military in Iraq (Beau was a lawyer in the military not a combatant) and then wrongly implying that it was his son's military service as a lawyer that caused the brain tumor that killed him much later at age forty-seven or so.

The families did not take well to Mr. Biden's callousness and pretend empathy. The parents of the young Marines were offended by his demonstrated lack of respect. Some lashed out at him publicly after their meetings with him.[167] He did not rise to the occasion; he simply sank. The mother of one of the young Marines killed that the Kabul airport told a radio station: "I never thought in a million years my son would die from nothing, for nothing, because that feckless, dementia-written piece of crap decided he wanted a photo up on September 11th." This is of a piece with his failure to rise to the occasion to take account of the immiseration of Afghan women, girls, and Afghan citizens in general. So much for a foreign policy centered on human rights and supporting allies as full partners. We can thus add hypocrisy on a Trumpian scale to Mr. Biden's character.

Rarely have words such as *bungling, fiasco, catastrophe, reckless,* and *betrayal* been tossed around with such regularity by the media to characterize an American president and his administration. And not just the right-of-center media, but the left-of-center media as well. The cover story for *The Economist* was "Biden's Debacle." *The Week* magazine ran with "A Shameful Ending"; the *Washington Examiner* went with "Biden Runs Away: Self-delusion and Humiliation in Afghanistan." The mockery to which the nation was subjected by the Taliban, China, Russia, Iran, and others was unprecedented. The faux Iwo Jima flag raising, reenacted by Taliban soldiers wearing American uniforms left behind was one of the tamer symbols of humiliation.[168]

Mr. Biden and his administration are widely accused of a frightening, even grotesque, lack of preparation and foresight, not to mention their total failure to consult with our allies who had several thousands of their own military personnel on the ground, plus many more civilians. To me, it beggars' belief that our president should lie behind such a shocking betrayal of our obligations and, just as importantly, our own American interests. It is almost impossible to imagine a greater indication of American decline or a greater gift to our enemies, who must now know to a moral certainty that they can always call our bluff because we are simply no longer a competent superpower. If Russia soon challenges the NATO alliance through further advances in Ukraine or China invades Taiwan in the next few years, our frantic and chaotic withdrawal from Afghanistan (and the empty rationale for it) will surely be one of the reasons they felt they could. As Sam Harris put it in a recent *Making Sense* podcast:

> The way we left is astonishing; it will hurt us. Who will trust us? If you don't think we want our friends of trust us and our enemies to fear us, what planet have you been living on?

It was surreal to hear our president say that the deadly and chaotic withdrawal was an "extraordinary achievement." It certainly was "extraordinary" but not any form of "achievement." To the extent there were problems (such as being forced to turn over to the hated Taliban 100% of all responsibility for the security of Americans and their Afghan allies during the last days of the bugout—not to mention bequeathing to them either $20 billion in military hardware or $60 billion depending on the source), they were blamed on President Trump for having initiated the negotiations with the Taliban that led to the initial agreement to withdraw by May 31; they were blamed on the intelligence community; they were blamed on the Afghan government; and they were blamed on the failure of the Afghan Army to live up to its potential even after they had been unexpectedly and precipitously abandoned by the United States and left without incoming intelligence, drone support, or any other kind of support.

I fear, no I see, that the wheels have finally come off this country. They have been wobbling for a few years now, beginning at least during the Trump administration, and likely before that. The social order has no cohesion. Government has no cohesion. Institutions have no cohesion. We are living in the space where there is a complete distrust of nearly all institutions: the government, the media, corporations, schools, universities, courts, everything. It has become depressingly evident that we have become a divided country and we cannot address common threats to our society or even our civilization. Just as bad, in a way, is that nobody in this country knows what it means to be "American" anymore. Foreigners all want to come here, but we as a people seem to have lost any idea of who we are, why we are here, and what if anything we stand for. So, whether it is terrorist jihadists, COVID-19, social upheaval, cancel culture, climate change, or any other number of internal or external existential threats, we as a people have chosen disunity over unity, chaos over order, individual rights over broad social rights and obligations, and so on and so on.

Journalists have been writing about the reckoning to come for the US foreign policy elites,[169] and surely this is deserved no less for the state department personnel and the military then for the president. News outlets from the *New York Post* to the BBC have recently published stories about the president's bending of reality and the truth (*NY Post*: "Biden Lies Piling Up";[170] BBC: "Fact Checking Biden on Afghanistan."[171] An especially thoughtful podcast is Sam Harris's *Making Sense* no. 260 from two days ago entitled "The Second Plane"[172] a thirty-minute remembrance of 9/11 and also a rumination on the impact of 9/11 and the bungled withdrawal on US foreign policy in the coming years.

The polls, which seem quite consistently to be off a few percentage points in a center-left direction, have shown a drop of more than ten points in the president's approval in the last few weeks: from 55% to 45% as of this writing. What both surprises and in a way depresses me is that his ratings are still so high. I expected them to be deservedly far lower. I must be out of touch with the mainstream. But I sense a general social comfort on all ends of the political spectrum, and maybe even in the middle, too, that we should be quite all right retreating from foreign and world affairs so that we can repair our roads and bridges, get the lead out of our water pipes, attend to tearing down historical statues and symbols, provide a better life (or at least money) to the poor and uneducated, police each other's societal behavior on social media, and make sure that people use the correct pronouns for each other. In such an isolationist and self-centered world, we can all lie in our own warm bathtub, pour a glass of nice wine, put on our headphones, and tune into our social silo of choice, hoping at least for a time the world will not require us to pay attention to large or microaggressions outside our borders that might annoy us. And if we have no life lessons to bequeath to our children, well, as Philip Larkin wrote, "We can leave them money."

22

Mr. Magoo as President and the Collapse of the President's Poll Numbers

October 12, 2021

I have been thinking about the performance of our president in the wake of my last article about the debacle involving Afghanistan. Since then, the Biden administration has been through one embarrassment after another, demonstrating a startling incompetence at managing the basics of government. Virtually everything that the president has touched has turned to chaos; his policies have had obvious unintended adverse consequences, both economic and political.

As I sat down to begin writing about this, the image of Mr. Magoo as president popped into my head and made itself home there, immovable. Not only does Mr. Biden bear an uncanny likeness to the nearsighted Mr. Magoo, but both leave mayhem in their wake, and both are completely oblivious to the consequences of their actions. The main difference is that Mr. Magoo seems always to come across as a likable nearsighted old soul who means well. Compare the images here[173] and here.[174]

But contrary to his appearance during the campaign of 2020, Mr. Biden now comes across as an unlovable, mean, and mean-spirited person. He has transmogrified completely away from his "Lunch Pail Joe" and "Uncle Joe" good-ole plain folks' persona. He has revealed himself as part of "the elite" who will tell us all not just how to live and what to do but how to think. He also is no longer believed. Worse, he is thought to be dishonest. And as we shall see shortly, all of this comes through with a crystalline clarity in polls released late last week, especially the Quinnipiac poll. Here are the main specific events of recent weeks.

Inflation is increasing at a rate unseen in many years, having been below 1.5% for years, it has shot up since March of this year to its current monthly level of 5.4% with no end in sight, while wage growth lags behind. [175] It took the minority leader of the Senate and ten Republican senators to increase the *debt ceiling* because the majority leader and the president simply did not have fifty Democratic votes in the Senate and could not therefore lift the debt ceiling. Astoundingly, the majority leader of the Senate—immediately after the Democrats' problem was solved by the Republican minority leader—took the floor to condemn Sen. McConnell. Mr. McConnell was also by the most conservative elements of his party for what will doubtless be seen in hindsight as an act of political courage and indeed statesmanship.

I must digress for a moment. Columnists like Paul Krugman ("Wonking Out: Coins and Money"[176]) and politicians like Mr. Schumer all engage in *faux* hysteria when the debt ceiling becomes political, although in each case the outrage is reserved for Republicans. High-position Democrats have been very public in their opposition to lifting the debt ceiling when it has suited their politics. One such Democrat who cast a vote against raising the debt ceiling was current Senate Majority Leader Chuck Schumer during the Bush administration[177]. Now, with the shoe on the other foot, he says, "As default gets closer and closer to becoming a reality, our Republican colleagues will be forced to ask themselves how long they are going to keep playing political games while the economic stability of our country is at risk." As the *New York Post* put it in its own inimitable style: "Square that Circle, Boychick." One might have thought that Mr. Schumer should have kissed Mr. McConnell for bailing Schumer out of his dilemma rather than condemning him given that Schumer was simply unable to muster even fifty Democrats in favor of raising the debt ceiling.

And what of the president? Here's what Senator Joe Biden said in 2006: "Because this massive accumulation of debt was predicted, because it was foreseeable, because it was unnecessary, because it was the result of willful and reckless disregard for the warnings that were given . . . I am voting against the debt-limit increase."

Then there was Senator Obama in 2006: "The fact that we are here today to debate raising America's debt limit is a sign of leadership failure. ... I therefore intend to oppose the effort to increase America's debt limit." But at least Mr. Obama admitted his prior lack of leadership and rued what he had done. "That was just an example of a new senator making what is a political vote as opposed to doing what was important for the country," Obama said. "And I'm the first one to acknowledge it." End of digression.

The number of illegal immigrants pouring across the southern border monthly is now exceeding 200,000, a twenty-one-year high. On an annualized basis, *illegal border* crossings now exceed the populations of Boston and Washington put together. See Pew Immigration stats.[178] *Unemployment* has snuck below 5%, but the numbers are not as strong as they appear in part because so many employers cannot find people willing to work, mainly because the available federal benefits provide an incentive not to work, especially in food service. The containers are backed up at US ports for want of enough truck drivers to take them away, hence looming shortages (again) of toilet paper and other manufactured goods are on the horizon.

Food is also in short supply. The largest increase in the Consumer Price Index this year was for meats, poultry, fish, and eggs.[179] They increased 8.0% year over year, and the index for beef rose 12.2% over last year. My observation is that at local markets shelves for all goods are sporadically empty, and for the same cut of beef prices have doubled in a few months. That is consistent with the BLS data, because all indexes have problems when consumers substitute lower quality to save money.

Energy barely exists except to pander to greens. We are witnessing a rapid unraveling of the energy revolution that made the United States the world's strongest producer of energy, and it is very clear that is exactly what this administration wants.[180] Its green supporters have always wanted to restrict the production of oil, gas, and coal in order to drive prices up enough to make their favored "green" technologies profitable. Their program of halting pipeline construction that would have delivered cheap natural gas; threats of regulation that are chilling investment in oil and gas production; cutting back or eliminating leasing of federal lands for oil and gas development; and promising to eliminate these fuels within twenty-five years has its predictable effects.

Putting aside the unreality of the world abandoning carbon fuels within decades, and then only in part, it is no wonder the Bureau of Labor Statistics reports that energy prices are up 25% this year over last. Probably less obvious but more importantly, we are turning over marketplace power in petroleum to Saudi Arabia, Iran, Iraq, Venezuela, and other countries on whom our dependence would be geopolitically unhelpful and unhealthy, to be understated about it. What could possibly go wrong?

In the areas I have been frequenting, nearly every restaurant or retail outlet has a sign in the window apologizing for the lack of available help. This is a complex situation amplified by huge stimulus payments but also heavily influenced by a combination of baby boomer retirements and the unusually low birth rate in this country. See this fascinating video on the "Help Wanted Crisis."[181] Whatever the causes, the administration has demonstrated its obvious inability to manage the situation or even comprehend the consequences of its actions.

Then there was the decision to continue by executive directive from the CDC the program relieving tenants from honoring their *rental contracts*. The Supreme Court had already ruled that this was unconstitutional but kept the moratorium in place for two extra months to allow the administration time to come up with a lawful legislative solution. But the Democrats on Capitol Hill could not come up with any legislative solution, and so the president, with knowledge of the illegality of the action he authorized, claimed to have "discovered" a constitutional loophole that would permit the CDC to declare rental contracts unenforceable by landlords. At the first challenge, however, the action was found to be illegal and unconstitutional, as those who kept watch on the situation, including inside the administration, knew would happen.

The administration did little better in its handling of the COVID situation, sending all manner of mixed messages. On the one hand, the administration wanted to get everybody vaccinated, by and large a commendable goal. On the other hand, in order to protect the vaccinated from the unvaccinated, we have seen a return to universal masking requirements, including in schools for children. All of these directives and policies seem at odds with each other. If the vaccinated are protected, why should they wear masks since they are neither at risk nor a risk to others? If the unvaccinated are unprotected, then it would be rational that they should be required in some sensible way to avoid infecting other nonvaccinated people? For a seriously fascinating critique of the situation, see Matt Taibbi's "Cult of the Vaccine Neurotic."[182]

In the middle of this unprecedented display of presidential management incompetence, the administration prompted the attorney general to issue a directive to the FBI that federal law enforcement should be deployed to investigate and prosecute the parents of school children who are supposedly "threatening" school boards over the curricula, characterizing these parents as *domestic terrorists*. So, on the right, we had Trumpists decrying the press as "enemies of the people" and Bidenistas calling out our neighbors with children as domestic terrorists, doubtless to keep them from PTA meetings and school board meetings lest they disrupt the agenda of the teachers' unions.

Now, with a surprising suddenness, all of these chickens seem to have come home to roost as evidenced by a series of polls released late last week. Virtually all of them show an astonishing collapse of confidence in the president across a broad front. The president's job approval rating bottoms out at 38% approval and 53% disapproval in the Trafalgar and Quinnipiac polls. The "Direction of Country" poll is at wrong track 59%/right track 29% in the *Economist* and wrong track 63%/right track 37% in the *Politico* poll.

The quite granular Quinnipiac poll provides a serviceable insight into the administration's crisis of the moment. While 55% of the respondents disapprove of the president's performance, 45% "strongly disapprove" and only 21% strongly approve. Fifty-eight percent of those polled disapprove of the president's handling of foreign policy. He gets similar disapproval numbers in his handling of his job as commander-in-chief of the US military. This seems to be a direct rebuke of both Biden's decision to leave Afghanistan, and the incompetence of the execution of that decision.

Commentary magazine ran a podcast late last week entitled "Is he a Fool or an Idiot?" The point was made by two of the discussants that even in real time, not to mention hindsight, there never was a meaningful constituency to depart Afghanistan under any circumstances. The Quinnipiac poll gives some heft to this proposition, reflecting that only 30% of registered voters thought the United States should have withdrawn all troops from Afghanistan. Stated the other way, 70% of all registered voters disapproved of the withdrawal of all troops. It is possible, of course, that the bungled method of withdrawal led to these poll numbers, and that if all troops had been successfully withdrawn without incident, and if the Taliban had not taken over the country even before the US departure, and if the president had not come to depend on the Taliban as his new best friends, the polling might have been different. But that is another way of saying that if pigs had wings, they could fly.

On the question of whether the Biden administration has been competent in running the government, 54% of registered voters say no; 44% say yes. Strangely, on the question of whether Biden is honest, 48% of registered voters say no, and only 46% say yes. On whether Biden has good leadership skills, 55% say no, 43% say yes. On the administration's handling of immigration, 67% disapprove while only 26% approve. Only 24% approve of the way Joe Biden's handling the situation at the Mexican border. Even on taxes, where it is almost universally believed that everybody thinks that *they* should pay no more taxes, but that everybody wealthier should, 39% of registered voters disapprove of the administration's policies on taxation and 54% disapprove. Mr. Biden's handling of the COVID response is the only area where his approval rating (49%) is better than his disapproval rating (48%). On the other hand, this is down from a 66% approval last spring, so his approval in this area is falling badly, but not quite as quickly as elsewhere.

Charles Blow of the *New York Times* had this to say:

> Battered on trust, doubted on leadership, and challenged on overall competency, President Biden is being hammered on all sides as his approval rating continues its downward slide to a number not seen since the tough scrutiny of the Trump administration.

But the Democrats' solution to the multifaceted problems—competence, policy misdirection, and general inability to perceive even dimly the consequences of their actions—boils down to spending trillions of dollars, on what it seems not to matter. Again, Charles Blow presents a representative center-left view:

> Maybe the Democrats will pass a massive spending bill and tout it well, and people will forget their disappointment on other issues and revel in the mound of cash the Democrats plan to spend. Maybe. There is no doubt that this country desperately needs the investments Democrats want to make. In fact, it needs even more investment than the amount Democrats have proposed.

We are seeing in real time a potentially perfect storm of higher food and energy prices; job losses imposed by ill-conceived COVID lockdowns; an out-of-control immigration crisis; an emerging tax regime that will stifle economic growth; a petroleum policy that takes us back to the 1970s; a resultant power shortage; and the promised giveaways (whatever they are—they are unknown) in the $4.5 trillion-plus package that the administration seeks by hook or by crook. All of this suggests more than just political distraction but rather fundamental institutional change, which is what is in fact intended.

It was not too long into the Trump administration that the *New York Times* ran an op-ed piece by an anonymous self-described "senior Administration official" entitled "I Am Part of the Resistance within the Trump Administration."[183] One wonders whether there is anybody at any level in the current administration who thinks of themselves as being part of a well-intended force of resistance against the incoherent and incompetent madness of the Biden administration. One hopes such a person will emerge, even while one doubts that the *New York Times* would publish any such article even if it were written. While Substack certainly would publish it, I am not holding my breath.

All of the circumstances suggest, and quite strongly, that the Democrats are poised to lose massively in the midterm elections next year. With one of the slimmest majorities in history, they are unusually aggressive in their determination to defend and advance a political agenda that is disapproved of by a significant majority of the electorate and across gender, color, race, religion, and even to a degree age. On the other hand, the Republicans have demonstrated an uncanny ability to grab defeat from the jaws of victory, and they already seem angling to do just that again. Mr. Trump attacked Mr. McConnell and the ten Senate leaders who acted responsibly to lift the debt ceiling in circumstances where absent such action the consequences could have been catastrophic. Trump loyalists in the Senate, such as Senators Cruz and Graham, piled on Mr. McConnell in the wake of Mr. Trump's criticism.

The idea of Trump back on Twitter, Facebook, and on the ticket in 2024 could well scare Independents and Democrats who have little or no confidence in Mr. Biden or anyone connected with his administration but who do not want to relive the daily drama of yet another Trump administration. So, just as the consequences of Mr. Biden's incompetence have come home to roost (at least for the moment), so it should not be presumed that the national memory of the chaos of the Trump administration will not also come home to roost in 2024.

23

Would Anyone Today Actually Fight to Preserve the Union?: A Thought Experiment

November 2, 2021

Since the turn of the new century, the American people have devolved into warring camps. People no longer have mere political disagreements. People have come to hate their opponents' political views. And while religion is rapidly disappearing from American life, it is being replaced by faith in one's tribe. This tribal faith is replacing reason, logic, critical thinking, and many other advances of the Enlightenment. In the circumstances, one can be forgiven for thinking we have devolved into a high-tech version of the twelfth century in our politics and governance. It is not fruitful right now to delve into the reasons for all of this. Suffice it to say that for present purposes, I take it as a given that the unification of the country through a political process is simply not possible in the foreseeable future. Neither of the warring parties (I shall call them the Reds and the Blues) are interested in solving the nation's problems. Both parties are instead interested in stirring up hatred for their opponents and perpetuating their own power by any means possible. Nearly all of our major institutions have been corrupted in this process, each in somewhat different ways. Neither individuals nor institutions seem to have a stake in agreeable unification.

Mind you, various straightforward modifications to our political system could probably bring about unification. Eliminating gerrymandering in simple ways (for example, each congressional district would have to be defined by no more than five straight lines and one nonstraight line but only to accommodate a border with another state) would be a decent start. Eliminating party-dominated primaries might also be a decent start. For example, having just one open primary with weighted voting would require candidates to seek votes in the middle and not at the fringes. Requiring voter ID but expanding the period for in-person voting would tend to assure ballot integrity while the same time go a long way toward opening the franchise to all truly eligible voters. Eliminating ballot harvesting and its inevitable corrupting impact also seems desirable.

But such solutions have been within reach for decades, and neither political party has taken any serious steps toward implementing them. The wars over immigration are more important to the parties as wars than as actual problems to be addressed and solved. Nobody has proffered a bipartisan solution in decades, even though to devise a solution would be rather simple. In other words, division has become a political necessity for both parties, and the rest of us have become largely observers.

All of this has led me to contemplate whether the Reds or the Blues would be more comfortable seceding or remaining unified. And what about the Purples or the Independents in the middle, a growing percentage of the entire electorate? This has been developing as a nontrivial question over the last year. See "America Could Split Apart."[184]

But before getting to my questionnaires to the combatants and the neutrals, a word about secession itself. I am no expert on secession, to be understated about it. But it is an interesting topic. In less than an hour I was able to stumble across several fascinating factoids. For example, it is likely news to most people that the Federalist Party briefly explored New England secession during the War of 1812. But since then, secession has become associated with the Southern states in the Civil War. On the other hand, it is also not well known these days that the Republic of Texas successfully seceded from Mexico in 1836. However, this took the form of outright rebellion against Mexico and was not done with Mexican consent. Nine years later, Congress admitted Texas as a state.

The Supreme Court in 1869 ruled that unilateral secession by a single state was unconstitutional, while commenting that revolution or consent of the states could lead to a successful secession. Most interesting of all perhaps is that secession apparently played a huge role in the decision of the government after the Civil War *not* to prosecute Jefferson Davis for treason. Cynthia Nicoletti, a legal history professor at the University of Virginia School of Law, examined the issue in a book published four years ago *Secession on Trial: The Treason Prosecution of Jefferson Davis.* Davis's trial would have served as a test case for the legality of secession. But it was delayed for four years before being dropped. Among government officials, there was concern that the prosecution could backfire. Superficially, it would have been simple to prove that Davis committed treason since treason is levying war against the United States by a US citizen. Certainly, Davis levied war against the United States: that was his job. But was he a US citizen? In 1860, many people in the North and the South believed that states had the right to leave a union they voluntarily joined. Davis was a citizen of Mississippi. Mississippi seceded from the Union in 1861. By many accounts, that removed his US citizenship. Four years after the end of the war, the government dropped his prosecution altogether for fear of a defeat in front of a Virginia jury that would effectively validate the right of any state to secede from the union.

Somewhat more recently, Alaska, California, Florida, Georgia, Hawaii, Minnesota, Montana, New Hampshire, Oregon, Texas, and Vermont have each toyed with secession, perhaps Georgia more seriously than others. On April 1, 2009 (the date might be important, given April Fools' Day) the Georgia State Senate passed a resolution almost unanimously that asserted the right of states to nullify federal laws under some circumstances. The resolution also asserted that if Congress, the president, or the federal judiciary took certain steps, such as establishing martial law without state consent, requiring some types of involuntary servitude, taking any action regarding religion or restricting freedom of political speech, or establishing further prohibitions on types or quantities of firearms or ammunition, the constitution establishing the United States government would be considered nullified, and the union would be dissolved. Details on the above at this Wikipedia entry.[185]

But the illegality, technical or otherwise, about secession is not the main focus of this article. I'm going to presume that secession by a single state, or a group of states, is possible if not as a matter of technical law, then as a practical matter. This does bring me to the point. I would very much like to see major polling organizations do some polling along the lines suggested below to explore whether there is some group of Reds, Blues, Purples, or others who would actually put their lives on the line and fight today for the preservation of the union. Would a US president gather and command an army of unionists to go to battle with secessionist states? Would secessionists states be able to command military resources to defend or enforce their secession?

Let's begin this simple thought experiment with two maps, one of the 2016 election and the other of the 2020 election.[186] They are quite similar, and they are a good starting point for thinking about all this. First of all, if the Blues or the Reds were to secede from the union, the Blues would control discrete geographies not connected to any other Blue jurisdiction. This suggests that the Blues might not choose to secede at all, and that perhaps they would have a greater incentive to fight for a union. The Reds, on the other hand, would control contiguous geography whether their secession was based on the 2016 map or the 2020 map. Secession based on the 2016 map would provide the Reds with considerable oil and natural gas, which the Blues tend to want to get rid of anyway. The Blues would be without much oil and gas extraction, transportation, or refining capability. They would be very dependent on imports from overseas or from the Reds. But secession based on the 2016 map would also provide both the Blues and the Reds with adequate port facilities for imports and exports and manageable food supplies. Citizens of each tribe would have to choose their citizenship; it could result in a mass migration of Reds to Blue jurisdictions and vice versa.

So, dividing the country into two countries (I'm not going to assume there would be a third country created) would be interesting in an academic sort of way. Like-minded people could engage in self-government of their own choosing, maybe based on something resembling the existing Constitution but with differences. What would happen to Washington, DC, and its various government institutions is beyond the scope of this thought experiment. So, finally, on to the questionnaires for Reds, Blues, and others.

Questions for those who self-identify as Reds, Blues, and neither.

1. I self-identify as: /__/ Red /__/ Blue /__/ Neither

A. For Blues only:

1. I am /__/ am not /__/ in favor of the Blue states (as described by either the 2016 or 2020 election) seceding from the Union to become a separate nation, governed in general by the same governing documents now in place, as perhaps slightly amended.

America in Turmoil

2. I /__/ would /__/ would not take up arms in support of such secession if the Reds would not agree to it.
3. I /__/ would /__/ would not oppose the secession of the Red states (as described by either the 2016 or 2020 election results
4. I /__/ would /__/ would not take up arms in support of the preservation of the union in the event of Red state efforts to secede.
5. I /__/ would /__/ would not take up arms in support of the preservation of the union in the event of Blue state efforts to secede.
6. I /__/ would /__/ would not take up arms in support of the preservation of the union.

B. For Reds only:

1. I am /__/ am not /__/ in favor of the Red states (as described by either the 2016 or 2020 election) seceding from the union to become a separate nation, governed in general by the same governing documents now in place, as perhaps slightly amended.
2. I /__/ would /__/ would not take up arms in support of such secession if the Blues would not agree to it.
3. I /__/ would not oppose the secession of the Blue states (as described by either the 2016 or 2020 election results).
4. I /__/ would /__/ would not take up arms in support of the preservation of the union in the event of Red state efforts to secede.
5. I /__/ would /__/ would not take up arms in support of the preservation of the union in the event of Blue state efforts to secede.
6. I /__/ would /__/ would not take up arms in support of the preservation of the union.

C. For Non-Reds and Non-Blues

1. I am /__/ am not /__/ in favor of the /__/ Red states /__/ Blue states (as described by either the 2016 or 2020 election) seceding from the union to become a separate nation, governed in general by the same governing documents now in place, as perhaps slightly amended.
2. I /__/ would /__/ would not take up arms in support of such secession if it were /__/ agreeable /__/ not agreeable to the Reds and the Blues.

3. I /__/ would not oppose the secession of the /__/ Blue states /__/ Red states (as described by either the 2016 or 2020 election results).
4. I /__/ would /__/ would not take up arms in support of the preservation of the union in the event of Red state efforts to secede.
5. I /__/ would /__/ would not take up arms in support of the preservation of the union in the event of Blue state efforts to secede.
6. I /__/ would /__/ would not take up arms in support of the preservation of the union.

I have no clear idea how people would answer this sort of poll. I would love to see Gallup or some other reputable organization with adequate resources conduct such a poll. Given the mistrust, dislike, and in some cases even hatred, of the Reds for the Blues and the Blues for the Reds, I suspect a minor minority of people on either side of the divide would see value in fighting (and risking their lives as well) for preserving a union that keeps them together with people they despise. It is less hard to imagine a group of states declaring themselves to be a country separate from the United States of America. It is easy to imagine the Reds doing this and no less difficult to imagine the Blues doing it. But for the geographic separation of certain islands of Blue, an amicable divorce would even make political (albeit not economic) sense.

On the other hand, the migratory and economic confusion that would accompany the breakup of the union might prove to be too daunting for any group to attempt to manage. But this is an interesting part of the thought experiment. If the union stays together because people just do not have the energy to bring into being a nation consistent with their policy preferences, that would itself be revealing about the overall fatigue of the nation.

Unless someone does this poll, we will never know, but my suspicion is that almost nobody would fight to save the union. But there is also, I suspect, no critical mass of people to bring about secession, so perhaps this is all wholly hypothetical. But it might not be. In a way, all of this is perhaps too bad. It could simply mean the maintenance of the status quo through indifference and fatigue, not desire. If one group really was serious about secession, serious efforts might be made by the others to unify the country. But as long as the Reds and the Blues are content to snipe and snarl at each other to no particularly good end beyond the approval of their tribe, we as a nation will continue to wallow in the mud and slip and slide our way to national mediocrity in most things and certainly governmental incompetence.

24

Societal Respect for the Rule of Law Is in Trouble

January 10, 2022

Many of our political leaders, and even more of our voting citizens, have not just lost respect for the rule of law as we have known it for centuries, but they seem committed to opposing it, even as it has proved robust in jury rooms and courthouses. This has become increasingly evident since the summer of 2020, although the attitudinal seeds for this development were sown some time ago. It is the reaping of these seeds that has become so obvious over the past two years. Worse yet, the machinery of social media, coupled with intimidating social intolerance on all sides, makes it difficult to imagine the circumstance getting better before it gets worse. The solution, if there is one, probably lies in major political change, perhaps procedural, that empowers the center and disempowers both the hard left (progressives and their fellow travelers) and the hard right (Trumpists and their fellow travelers).

The Situation

I will refer in this article to some examples of the societal, and often political, distaste for and disparagement of the rule of law and the embrace of more situationally convenient rules. These are by no means intended to be exclusive but rather more representative of this condition mainly on the left but to a degree on the right as well.

Jussie Smollett. The demand for social justice and racial equity, whatever those terms may mean in the context of any particular event, seem generally to trump the legal system on social media and in the mainstream media, most obviously with regard to criminal proceedings. Jussie Smollett's Hate Crime Hoax is a good illustrative starting point as any. The whole hoax began with a narrative that was inherently incredible. At 2 a.m. on a freezing cold morning in Chicago, Mr. Smollett purportedly felt the need to head out to Subway for a tuna sandwich. On the way, two white men with MAGA hats happened to be roaming the streets in this below-freezing weather and with a noose in hand. They supposedly attacked Mr. Smollett. This happened shortly after Smollett was supposedly the target of a racist letter threatening to lynch him. The letter was sent to his studio. It turns out he wrote the better himself. But I am getting ahead of myself. The police opened up a massive investigation into this "hate crime" and the Osundairo brothers were arrested.

In the aftermath of the purported attack, statements of support for Mr. Smollett poured in from presidential candidate Biden, then-Senator Kamala Harris, Nancy Pelosi, and a hoard of mainstream media professionals. Scores of political and media leaders echoed Nancy Pelosi's theme that the attack was "homophobic and racist and an affront to our humanity." And when the evidence mounted that this was a hoax and that Mr. Smollett had actually hired the Osundairo brothers, political leaders and media figures again lashed out at Smollett's detractors as *homophobic and racist.*

In a nutshell, the facts as designed and presented by Mr. Smollett fit perfectly into a preexisting mainstream political and media narrative thematically centered on radicalized white people, white supremacy, right-wing terrorism, structural racism, anti-Trumpism, and other such tropes that have emerged as staples of the progressive left's discourse. Given the perfect fit with this narrative, the facts were just too good for the media to check or challenge.

But even after the facts had been checked by the Chicago police and the hoax had begun to unravel, and after Mr. Smollett was indicted on sixteen felony counts, the progressive County prosecutor Kim Foxx chose to drop all charges saying: "After reviewing all of the facts and circumstances of the case, including Mr. Smollett's volunteer service in the community and agreement to forfeit his bond to the city of Chicago, we believe [dropping the charges] is a just disposition and appropriate resolution to this case." This was not the end, however. Evidently shocked by the dropping of all the charges, Judge

Sheila O'Brien appointed a special prosecutor, prominent Chicago defense lawyer Dan Webb, who was charged with investigating Mr. Smollett's claims and also why all the charges against Mr. Smollett were dropped back in March 2019. Almost a year to the day after the initial arrest, Mr. Smollett was indicted.

The trial itself turned into an effort by the defense to sell the progressive narrative to the jury and to achieve an acquittal not *because* of Mr. Smollett's innocence, but *in spite of* his guilt. In other words, as the headline in *The Hill* put it, a hate-crime hoax became a pitch for jury nullification.[187] Put most simply, Mr. Smollett and his defense team were doing everything possible to prevent the application of the rule of law and to get off in honor of the social narrative described. The entire Smollett timeline can be found here.[188] The whole episode may remind older readers of the 1987 Tawana Brawley gang rape hoax, which brought Al Sharpton into such permanent prominence, except in this case Mr. Smollett was playing the role of both Ms. Brawley and Mr. Sharpton. In that case, much as with Mr. Smollett, a spokesperson for the black community wrote that the purported victim had "been the victim of some unspeakable crime. … No matter who did it to her—and even if she did it to herself."

Meanwhile, it came out at trial that CNN anchor Don Lemon had texted Mr. Smollett early in the investigation advising that the Chicago police did not believe his story about what happened and otherwise providing general support. And after the jury found Mr. Smollett guilty (amazingly it was something of a surprise to the media that the jury followed the evidence and applied the rule of law and did not accept society's invitation to nullify the law), the media dropped the story after a day or two. The message was: *Let it go. Forget it. Leave it alone, the lesson of the event is that it* could have *been true in this country and that is the important thing.*

Kyle Rittenhouse. The anti–rule of law role of politicians, media personalities, and citizen mobs on social media had a similar, and in some ways more disturbing, visibility in the Kyle Rittenhouse affair. In the beginning, not long after the riots and shootings in Kenosha Wisconsin, presidential candidate Biden linked Rittenhouse to white supremacists and condemned him.[189] A more prudent candidate might have waited for the facts to develop or for a trial verdict, but not Joe Biden. No benefit of the doubt or presumption of innocence for him. No patience for the rule of law here. Before the verdict was handed down, the media reported that the trial would "peg" whether Rittenhouse is a "hero" or a "reckless gunman." Such a framing did not address guilt, innocence, or law, but rather treated the trial as spectacle: gladiatorial blood sport. This zero-sum coverage was typical of much reporting on the event without actually increasing public understanding. This is one reason why, especially on the left, there was such shock at the verdict. Few knew the facts or followed the actual trial, and the facts did not matter anyway. Somewhat similarly, for many on the right, including Tucker Carlson and others, this was not about the rule of law or law at all; it was about politics and theater.

President Biden did not do any better after the acquittal verdict came down. The BBC headline was "Biden Angry after Teen Cleared of Shootings."[190] Vice President Kamala Harris also condemned the verdict stating that "I've spent a majority of my career working to make the criminal-justice system more equitable, and clearly, there's a lot more work to do." When our highest elected officials express distaste for our justice system and dishonor the rule of law (while at the same time furthering the politicization of the Supreme Court by supporting the packing of the Court), it should hardly come as a shock that the narratives of the left and the right take over. Perhaps uniquely, the Rittenhouse verdict became a sort of political Rorschach test.

Post acquittal, the left media was virtually unanimous in its condemnation of the judge, Kyle Rittenhouse, and the legal system in general. Joy Reid, along with other people of color, seemed to believe that Mr. Rittenhouse had shot and killed two young black men when in fact, he shot and killed two white men. MSNBC led the pack making the strange claim that there was "nothing in place to prevent white nationalists from using the Rittenhouse verdict to attack Black Lives Matter."[191] The MSNBC host lambasted the judge for being biased and prejudiced and slammed Rittenhouse himself for using "white male tears" like Brett Kavanaugh and being a "Karen." This was unhinged rage at a verdict that was plainly correct to anyone paying attention to the facts.

The editorial board of the Madison-based *Wisconsin State Journal* slammed the Rittenhouse acquittal,[192] arguing that state law was skewed in favor of shooters who claimed self-defense and needed to be changed. The verdict, the editorial said, is "sure to embolden militant people who seek to take the law into their own hands" adding "our state should be discouraging standoffs with guns, rather than encouraging more people to arm themselves out of fear or revenge." The editorial board might well be correct in its mildly hysterical conclusions, although it should not be a surprise that if government cannot maintain social order in the streets, people will take things into their own hands. But no matter how correct the editorial board's concerns might be, finding an innocent man guilty should not be a preferred solution to those concerns in any civilized society, yet that seems to be exactly what they were saying should have happened.

All of this would seem like overblown madness absent the context of America since the summer of 2020. As Eddie Glaude Jr., chairman of the Department of African American studies at Princeton University said in an op-ed piece for the *Washington Post*: "Since he killed two men and wounded another in what he claimed was self-defense *[in this phrase rejecting the jury verdict]* Kyle Rittenhouse has become of the poster child for a general feeling among some in this country that white America is under siege. Rittenhouse defended himself, this argument goes, and white America must do the same." His larger point was "that no Black teenage boy walking around a protest with a semiautomatic rifle, no Black teenager who kills two people … would be treated, no matter what the law says about self-defense, like Rittenhouse. He would be dead." This might be correct in some instances. But it seems to frame the argument in a strange way: since young black men with guns are sometimes or often denied the benefits of the rule of law, so should white people like Kyle Rittenhouse be denied those benefits.

While Mr. Glaude may be on to something, he is certainly not calling for the primacy of the rule of law but for something quite a bit more revolutionary. He is instead accusing society—by which he means white society, and in fact all of society except a subset of people of color—of "hiding behind the law, social mores and assumptions about the capacities, moral and otherwise, of those we treat unjustly. This allows us to find a way around the evidence that reveals we are not who we say we are." To my ear this sounds like a Jacobin cry to man the barricades, start a new revolution, and upend the rule of law.

January 6. The Trump-inspired assault on the US capitol building has exposed the hard-right disrespect for the rule of law and an affection for self-help and even violence. My own initial reaction to the event was that it had more in common with the various 1968 student takeovers of collegiate administration buildings than it did with the 1923 Beer Hall Putsch in Munich, which was a failed coup d'état by Nazi Party leader Adolf Hitler. Nearly a year later, I have left that view in my rearview mirror. The communications between Republican leaders and various Trump supporters that have come out thus far are disturbing, and I am sure that the ongoing defense of those who participated in the assault (I do not think it could possibly qualify as an "insurrection") by conservatives in politics and the media represent a complete and total disregard for the rule of law. And this is true on two levels. First of all, the assault is not truly subject to any rational defense. And second of all, as best I understand it, the "defense" proffered by the hard right is a flavor of "whataboutism," in this case "what about the stolen presidential election?" In other words, much of the hard right believes, or claims to believe, that the presidential election was stolen, and therefore those who assaulted the capital were justified in trying to bring about the true and correct result of the November election. This line of argument is madness and antithetical to any semblance of a just society governed by neutral rules of law.

Abortion, Immigration, and Voting Rights. I have neither world enough nor time in this article to delve into such sensitive controversies other than to say that the debate on both sides of these issues tends to trample the rule of law. The debate on ***voting rights*** is a faux debate designed to stir up the political bases on the right and the left. The Progressives are in favor of counting harvested and unpostmarked ballots and not requiring voter identification or even in some states citizenship. Conservatives in general favor a secure voting system that has built-in indicia of trustworthiness, even at the expense of some voters who for some reason might not have identification papers. At bottom, this would seem to mean strong voter ID laws. Personally, as I have previously written, I would like to see voters demonstrate minimal citizenship knowledge, as we require from legal immigrants.

The ***immigration debates*** have been going on and in circles for decades. Progressives wish to allow illegal residents to vote, as they now can in New York and elsewhere, and are perceived by the right as wanting open borders to secure elections. Conservatives want to close the border to illegal immigration. There is much room for rational compromise, but that would take away useful political talking points and weapons that fire up the political bases.

Abortion. This is a religious war and while it is fought in the courts, where the outcome is a zero-sum game, that is because the federal legislature is unable or unwilling to legislate a political solution, as virtually all other Western democracies have done. I am not aware of any other country that has found abortion to be a fundamental legal right without legislative embrace of that notion. Absent a political resolution, which would probably look a lot like *Roe v. Wade*, the politicians and the citizens get to blame the courts, thus moving further in the direction of anti–rule of law and rule by a mobocracy.

Progressive Prosecutors. The citizens of many large cities have elected so-called progressive prosecutors, some of whose campaigns have apparently been funded by progressive billionaire George Soros. This has happened in Boston, Chicago, Detroit, Los Angeles, Milwaukee, New York, Philadelphia, San Francisco, and several other cities. One fairly obvious result has been a spectacular breakdown in law and order. It is not just the prosecutors and those who elect them, but also the legislatures, which in California have made it merely a misdemeanor to steal less than a thousand dollars' worth of goods from a store. And in a seemingly coordinated way, prosecutors have declared they will not prosecute misdemeanors. As a result, we see chilling videos of "smash and grab" gangs inundating department stores, small shops, and everything in between. This does not seem to have resulted in any prosecutions of note. This is the sort of thing that during the summer of 2020, when it occurred during riots, was described as "mostly peaceful rioting."

As a podcast I listened to recently put it, the culprits are people who "came for the social justice, but then stayed for the looting." But what may have begun as "looting for social justice" has evolved into organized crime brought into place by government policy. Actions no longer have consequences. The rule of law has been replaced by pure anarchy in many urban neighborhoods. Stores such as Walmart are closing and leaving many areas.

One might surmise that, in the beginning, the evolution of the new progressive prosecutors was an arguably good faith reaction to the over-incarceration of nonviolent black youths and the failure of many prosecutors to hold police departments accountable for shootings of civilians, especially black men. These were after all issues that even Mr. Trump sought to address during his administration. But the BLM movement accelerated the transmogrification of prosecutors from tough on crime to tough on law enforcement. And the warrant of these prosecutors has greatly expanded, as a mere perusal of the articles about them (many defending them vigorously) demonstrates.[193] Their power to ignore criminal laws they do not like is immense and very different from the run-of-the-mill prosecutorial discretion. To be sure, there is a spectrum of progressive prosecutors. Some are radical, others not so much. Some seek alternatives to massive incarceration for nonviolent crimes; others seek to undo what they see as centuries of white supremacy and racial injustice. Kimm Foxx in Chicago, Larry Krasner in Philadelphia, Karen McDonald in Detroit, George GascÓn in Los Angeles, John Chisholm in Milwaukee, and Chesa Boudin in San Francisco have all had an enormous impact in their local communities, much of it hugely negative. Recall campaigns now threaten several of these officials.

Philadelphia's Larry Krasner has become one of the poster children for progressive prosecutors run amok. He was a defense lawyer who prior to his election as Philadelphia's district attorney filed some seventy-five lawsuits against the Philadelphia Police Department. Under his regime, Philadelphia has experienced some 550 homicides so far this year, 200 more than in the entirety of 2019. Gun robberies are up almost 30%; retail theft and auto theft are up 20% and 15%, respectively. Armed robberies are occurring in the lobbies of five-star hotels such as the Four Seasons and elsewhere in the upscale center city neighborhood. Just last week, the US representative Mary Gay Scanlon was carjacked and robbed at gunpoint. Two men drove away with her personal and government cell phones, as well as her car. Mr. Krasner brags that the county jail population decreased 40% in his first three years in office. But as the *Philadelphia Inquirer* reports, Krasner's office has lost 261 attorneys out of a staff of 340, including 70 prosecutors hired under his tenure.[194]

Another poster child is San Francisco's Chesa Boudin, the son of Brink's robbery police murderers, who was raised by radical Weather Underground leaders Bill Ayers and Bernadine Dorn. Perhaps the voters of San Francisco are simply too young to remember anything about these people, or perhaps they have drunk the Kool-Aid of BLM, critical race theory, white guilt, systemic white racism, and the entire encyclopedia of progressive thought. In either case what we have seen in San Francisco, and more than a dozen other cities, is a retreat from the rule of law and the advancement of the rule of immense prosecutorial discretion to ignore law and to substitute dictatorial fiat. It is, more or less, legal autocracy superintended by people who believe in something not distant from actual anarchy.

Last week Alvin Bragg assumed the office of Manhattan's district attorney. Within days of taking office he issued a memorandum to his five hundred prosecutors creating what the *Wall Street Journal* describes as a "Sanctuary City for Crime." He has instructed prosecutors in the Manhattan VA's office that they should ask for jail or prison time only in the most serious offenses: murder, sexual assault, and economic crimes involving vast sums of money, unless the law requires them to do otherwise. Robberies and assaults will no longer result in jail time, even armed robbery. Gun possession in cases where no other crimes are involved will not involve incarceration. The actual Bragg "Day One" Memorandum is here.[195]

This is, of course, all about social justice and racial equity. If one wishes to have similar statistics for young black men as for young white men, then reclassify the crimes as non-crimes and eliminate any punishment. Voilà. Equity. While New York has gun laws that are extremely strict, it seems increasingly pointless for individuals in at-risk neighborhoods not to carry their own weapons given that those who would do citizens harm have zero incentive not to carry weapons and not to use them to engage in all manner of theft. Oddly, this places Manhattan's DA completely at odds with Erik Adams, the newly elected law-and-order Democrat mayor of New York City, which includes Manhattan. A dogfight may ensue as more Manhattanites decamp to Florida.

Most of these progressive prosecutors are elected, although some (federal US attorneys, for example) are appointed by the president. But whether elected or appointed, they are all Democrats. As a result, the Democratic Party is solidifying its reputation as the party of crime and is, for now anyway, paying a very heavy price in the polls. One result of this is that even the mainstream media, normally supportive of most things Democrat, have turned against the lawlessness engendered by progressive prosecutors. See for example *Newsweek*: "Time to Stand up to Progressive Prosecutors."[196] Although NPR is still supportive, or at least equivocal.[197]

Why This Matters. Nearly two years ago I wrote about Jonathan Sumption's book *Trials of the State and the Decline of Politics*. I adapted the following from the first paragraph of that book, which is highly pertinent in the current circumstances.

In the beginning, there was chaos and brute force, a world without law. In the mythology of ancient Athens, Agamemnon sacrificed his daughter so that the gods would allow his fleet to sail against Troy. His wife murdered him to avenge the deed, and she in turn was murdered by her son. Athena, the goddess of wisdom, put an end to the cycle of violence by creating a court to impose a solution in what today we would call the public interest: a solution based on reason, on the experience of human frailty and on fear of the alternative. Aeschylus in the Oresteia trilogy had Athena justify her intervention in the world of mortals as follows: Let no man live uncurbed by law, nor curbed by tyranny.

Is There a Way Forward? It is not clear that there is a way forward that leads back to a widely accepted rule of law in this country. But if there is, it must involve a political solution that the radical elements of both the left and the right accept more or less equally. In the absence of a political system that provides equal respect to the values of the left and the right, and some accommodation of each, it is hard to imagine the long-term survival of a stable American society. Some say we have been here before, we have returned from the brink, and we will not go over the edge this time. Perhaps, but we have never before had the radicals of the left and the right so empowered by social media and their own echo chambers. Until the late-night comedians of the left begin to take on the bloviation and hypocrisy of the left, and until the late-night comedians of the right can take on the bloviation and hypocrisy of the right, there seems to be little hope of a return to the rule of law.

But humor nonetheless goes a long way to puncture bloviation. It is therefore good fortune that Dave Barry's "Year in Review" is again broadly available.[198] While 2021 does not yield as much humor as past years it is nonetheless a good thing to read at the end of the year as a reminder that we can all laugh at most anything, including ourselves, especially when they are handled with a light and deft touch, as they are by Dave Barry.

25

Ruminations on the Need for Universal National Service

February 14, 2022

Since the inception of this twenty-first century, our citizenry has seemingly become acclimated to asking not what they can do for their country but demanding that their country do increasingly more for them. This situation has been accompanied by a steady and increasing national divisiveness. Some of this is political, some of it social, some economic: all of it is increasingly extreme. This is not a uniquely American problem, although it seems to be a problem uniquely infecting the liberal Western democracies. During the summer of 2020, German Defense Minister Annegret Kramp-Karrenbauer asked: "What keeps our society together? What is the mortar in our society? At the moment, the answer is not very much." In this country, the answer is probably more like: "Almost nothing." And really, since the end of the Vietnam War, the United States has required very little of its citizens beyond the payment of federal and state income taxes (which are paid by roughly only half of the citizenry), sales taxes, property taxes, and Social Security taxes, and also jury duty for those few who do not wriggle out of it one way or another. And even on the tax side, there has developed a very loud hue and cry for "the rich" to pay more so as to pay their "fair share." We have become a citizenry that wants more for less and something for nothing: and we want everybody else to pay for it.

In recent years, there have been many thoughtful articles advancing the rewards of universal national service in this country (see examples from the

NY Times,[199] *RealClear Markets*,[200] *Time Magazine*,[201] and even *The Harvard Crimson* [202] championing universal military service) as well as a smaller number of thoughtful and not so thoughtful articles condemning the idea as "A Bad Idea That Won't Die" (*Cato Institute* [203]) or as an idealistic but unworkable vision (*The Atlantic*[204]). The issue does not seem to pit conservatives against liberals or progressives. Indeed, many or most people of all political stripes seem to like the idea of universal national service upon graduation from high school or college. *The Tennessee Tribune* [205] published the results of an astonishing poll last year, the key elements of which were the following:

> Public opinion polling of 1000 18-24-year-old adults found near universal support for expanding National Service opportunities …. In overwhelming numbers, young people believe National Service can be part of one's civic duty (87%), help them solve problems in their communities (86%), and enable them to gain real-world experience before entering an uncertain job market (85%)

According to the *Tribune* story: "Young Americans are passionate about serving their country, whether through the military or through civilian programs like AmeriCorps. This poll shows us just how widespread that passion is." Assuming the poll is an accurate reflection of the national mood of young American men and women, it is a topic that deserves actual consideration by a purposeful leader. As always, it is useful to start with some foundational facts and to understand a little bit about how this issue has been or is being handled in other countries.

Other countries. I am going to take only a shallow dive into other countries. First of all, some basic information, which seems to be reasonably reliable, although wholly reliable data are hard to come by. In any case, around the world, there are about eighty-five countries[206] with some form of mandatory military service, and there are many other countries that mandate some form of universal national service, be it military or some other service. [207]

Among the most interesting of these is France, which made the Service National Universel (SNU) mandatory for all male and female citizens aged sixteen to twenty-five starting just last year, in 2021.[208] The compulsory service lasts just for one month, although participants are encouraged to apply their learned skills for a year or more after completion of the mandatory program. The aim of this civil conscription service is to convey French values, to strengthen social cohesion, and to promote social engagement.

Germany has introduced a slightly similar program known as "Your Year for Germany." [209] The program offers voluntary national service to young Germans. Participants will spend a year in the armed forces, but, unlike in the past, they will not simply serve in a random regiment. After six months' training, they will practice "homeland protection" in their home regions and participate in crisis operations there. This is a direct outcropping of Russian adventurism in Crimea, Georgia, and elsewhere in Europe, but equally it is the product of Germany's view that crises caused by the weather are an even greater immediate national security concern. The service program is thus designed to strengthen Germany's resilience in the face of crises of all types. The German program will also be highly selective, with initially only one thousand volunteers chosen each year based on applications. In this respect, Germany is following in the footsteps of the Nordic countries, where the selective nature of such programs has made national service (including military service) a highly attractive proposition. There is a parallel civilian service track through which young citizens can volunteer for training and work in a variety of social institutions, including care homes and hospitals.

Numbers. Perhaps the largest impediment to universal national service springs from the population of the United States and the demographics of its population. There are about 330 million people in the United States. Of those, there are about twelve million men aged nineteen to twenty-four and a similar number of women. This is a large number of individuals to manage, house, feed, assign, and supervise. And while it would surely be expensive, the trillions of dollars being thrown at infrastructure rebuilding, and the additional trillions of dollars that the administration would spend on social equity suggest that the cost of managing a universal national service program would not be enormous by comparison and would probably yield a far greater return on investment for the nation. Nonetheless, back in 1979, Milton Friedman opined in *Newsweek* that universal service (then he was speaking of military service) made sense in countries like Israel or Switzerland with populations so small that the military could readily use the temporary service of a young adult in peacetime and could muster these people into service if necessary in time of war.

In Friedman's view, that argument did not hold for the United States given that our population is so large that the military can use only a small fraction of the relevant age group. At the height of the Vietnam War, only one out of four young men in the age group subject to the draft served in the armed forces. If women were considered, it would have been only one in eight. Hence it cannot be denied that the sheer numbers of eligible people could overwhelm any system designed to manage, feed, house, assign, and supervise such a massive, conscripted workforce. It is not the purpose of this short article to address and solve that problem except to say that the program could be feathered in such a way that the problem could be solved, and that certain individuals would necessarily need to be exempted for reasons of health, disability, or otherwise. It might be universal in spirit but not necessarily in fact.

Other Factors. Friedman's essay also is a reminder that the idea of universal national service was first and perhaps most persuasively made in a work of fiction published in 1887, *Looking Backward* by Edward Bellamy, which sold in the millions and sparked a widespread national movement. In Bellamy's book, a young man falls asleep in 1887 and awakens in 2000 to find a world of perfect harmony and unity. As it happens, this is because universal service came into being. All youngsters were conscripted at age twenty-one to serve twenty-four years in the "industrial army." During the first three years, they would do the world's dirty work, and be "assigned to any work at the discretion of supervisors." These three years were a sort of school and a very strict one, in which men (women were not addressed in Bellamy's book) would be taught habits of obedience, subordination, and devotion to duty. To Friedman it had an uncanny resemblance to the Hitler Youth — battalions of happy blue-eyed Aryans marching off with shovels on their shoulders singing "Deutschland über Alles."

Friedman did not find the comparison fanciful since the young conscripted for "good" purposes would have to be given basic training. He wondered,

> Who decides what that should consist of? What ideas should they be indoctrinated with? What purposes are "good"? Someone has to assign the youngsters to various activities. Someone has to enforce discipline on them. What a power

to fall into the wrong hand. What a power for the wrong hands to seek.

Given the legitimate brouhaha today over who decides what children are taught in our school districts around the country about history, society, race, politics, literature, and a myriad of other things, Friedman's concerns ring even more legitimate today than they did when first written more than forty years ago.

Still, I am not speaking of an industrial army or a decades-long requirement but something quite more limited and benign. We are a divided country sorely in need of unity and mutual understanding. People as diverse as General Stanley McChrystal and Pete Buttigieg have weighed in in favor of creating a new rite of passage into adulthood and forging a renewed sense of citizenship. Something approaching universal national service is not only broadly popular among those who would serve, but it is easy to imagine that, after a decade of such a program, strangers meeting for the first time would be quite likely to query each other about what they each did for their national service. This sort of thing creates almost instantaneous bonding in many cases. More on this below.

Whatever the basic model or architecture for such a program, some of the features of the Civilian Conservation Core would be excellent. Citizens from diverse backgrounds sharing common housing, meals, and workspaces seems like a surefire positive in terms of creating a sense of shared citizenship. At the moment, it is not noticeably clear what it actually means to be an American. And we seem to be on the verge of being overwhelmed and sadly defeated by diversity, instead of taking advantage of its potential, including its demonstrated benefits from the past.

Ruminations and Digressions. At the risk of digressing slightly, I find it helpful to look at our country's history with military service on the assumption that nonmilitary national service could or would create similar circumstances. To me, one of the most alarming realities of the United States today is that among well-educated people, virtually nobody serves in the military. Among what one might call the "elites," my own lived experience (anecdotal evidence to be sure) suggests that such people do not know anybody who served in the military and do not know anybody whose children served or are serving in the military. There is this growing divide between military personnel and civilian personnel, and it is getting wider by the year. Some 16.5 million men and women served in the military during WWII. Virtually every family had members serving in the military.

Roughly nine million military personnel served on active duty during the official Vietnam era from August 5, 1964, to May 7, 1975. Everyone was affected in some way because of the draft, and this was the cause of much of the opposition to the war. Of these, 2.7 million served in Vietnam itself.[210] Part of the resistance to the Vietnam War was from those who never ended up serving in the military but whose families became activists against the war to protect the children. For political reasons, the universal draft was abolished and replaced by a lottery system. After the war, there was no draft, and the entire military became a volunteer service. Not unlike a Hessian army in some respects. While beyond the scope of this piece, there are major problems with an all-volunteer military, not least of which is the difficulty of filling quotas due to the limited capabilities of the pool of applicants. Something like one-third of the eligible population suffer from crippling disabilities. Today our military services comprise roughly 1.3 million active-duty personnel, less than half of 1% of the US population.

Having watched my alma mater, Harvard, throw the Reserve Officer Training Corps (ROTC) off campus back in 1968 (to demonstrate solidarity with the antiwar movement) and not allow it back on campus until 2012, it was something of surprise to see the *Harvard Crimson*, a daily newspaper published by some of the most accomplished students at Harvard, embrace national military service using the following language, which doubtless would be equally applicable to universal service whether military or not:

> That there are immense benefits to the youth of the country and to the country itself involved in the sort of training proposed, is generally conceded. These benefits are, to the individual, improved health, a larger and more national view of his relations, and wider acquaintance with his country. To the Nation, they are the creation and deepening of the sense of community interest and the breaking down of racial, religious, linguistic, and sectional differences.

This is altogether consistent with the poll results reported by the *Tennessee Tribune* referred to above. At this aspirational level, it is relatively simple to make out a good case for something like a Constitutional Bill of Responsibilities. When John F. Kennedy became president in 1961, his appeal to youth "to ask not what your country can do for you, but what you can do for your country" resonated forcefully. And citizens now in their late sixties to early eighties seem to cherish their service experience, whether military or civilian. These people have long-standing relationships with those who shared those experiences. That is certainly true for me based on my military experience, and I know equally true for my sister based on her Peace Corps experience. I know this to be true of my military friends and my sister's Peace Corps friends as well. I have no reason to believe that it is not more broadly and generally true.

Yet for those millions and millions of citizens who have never been asked to do anything for or give anything to their country beyond taxes and occasional jury duty, one gets the feeling, or at least I get the feeling, that many have some nagging regret that they missed out on some important aspect of being an American citizen.

The opponents of this kind of program argue along these lines: (1) people already delay marriage and childbearing because of modern educational and career demands, and further delay would have unintended consequences; (2) a one-size-fits-all mandate would do harm to some people in a society as diverse as ours; (3) people already fulfill obligations beyond themselves that might not be "public service" but that involve good works like supporting younger siblings, taking care of sick parents, and so forth; (4) people already commit themselves to good works for nonprofit organizations and this should count; (5) if the state is going to coerce young adults to spend a year of their lives doing something, the nation and the world would benefit more from making them spend a year living abroad somewhere; (6) compulsory national service might violate the Thirteen Amendment; (7) there is already a demand on the part of young people to serve, according to data of a decade ago, so there is no need to have a mandatory program.

Many of these criticisms seem like hogwash and nonsense and to each criticism there is a sensible response that addresses the concern stated. One among several notable facts is that there is no effort by those who criticize the idea to address a real problem: managing the millions of citizens as would be required, or bearing the immense cost of administering such a large program. To me, the reflexive criticisms also fail to bring to bear any meaningful degree of nuance to manage exemptions, exceptions which would be essential in any case given the millions of citizens who would have to be managed, housed, fed, etc. The criticisms also tend to reflect a unique twenty-first-century narcissism that denies any legal or moral obligation by any individual to the nation or any to larger unit than self or family.

Creating a template for a flexible universal national service program is not the kind of thing that can happen without strong and positive leadership from the Executive Branch, and it may be some time before we see such leadership from either party. But in this period of heightened disunity and factionalism, there may be more than a little bit of urgency to attempting a form of universal national service, or something much like it, to bring people together to serve a common purpose and in some way to bring about a healthy apolitical patriotism.

26

The Tragedy of Ukraine and the Incompetence of American Strategy and Leadership

March 14, 2022

I come at the current horror of the Russian invasion of Ukraine with a previously existing and sharply critical point of view of Mr. Biden and his administration. See my articles of September 11, 2021 (criticizing the president broadly and deeply for every aspect of his actions and inactions on Afghanistan) and October 12, 2021 (focusing on Mr. Biden's similarity to the near-sighted Mr. Magoo, but without Mr. Magoo's charm or amiability). My views on him have not much changed.

I would grudgingly give Biden credit for mobilizing the Western allies against Russia if I thought he deserved it, but frankly it would be like giving an arsonist credit for helping to put out a fire he started to bathe himself in a favorable political light. No, based on what I think I know, I give nearly all of that credit to President Zelensky of Ukraine, who has been the closest thing we have seen in this century to a Churchillian figure. Listening to him and watching him tempts me to want to take up arms and go to Ukraine myself, notwithstanding the reality that "the West" bears much blame for its blind sleepwalking into cornering Russia and Putin in a variety of needless ways. A little bit on this nuanced, complex, and hotly debated issue towards the end of this piece. For the moment I am focused not on how or why we got to where we are, but what to do now that perhaps predictable events have arrived. On that score, listening to Mr. Biden makes me weep. He is without an ounce of any Churchillian quality. But he does much resemble Neville Chamberlain, although without Chamberlain's panache, vision, courage, and will to defend England. His whispers into the microphone are very weird. A sign of something no doubt, but not something good.

The Ukrainian citizenry also has shown us something we have not seen in this country for a generation: courage, grit, extraordinary bravery, and a willingness to die for country and freedom. A stunning photograph of a nine-year-old girl standing guard with a gun and a lollipop is a remarkable photographic symbol of that courage and determination.[211] She stands in sad and stark contrast to the shocking Quinnipiac University poll released a few days ago, which was the subject of a piece in last Saturday's *Wall Street Journal*. The pollster asked: what would you do if you are in the same position as Ukrainians are now, stay and fight or leave the country? More than half of the Democrats (52%) said they would run away and not fight if the US homeland were invaded by the Russians (or anybody apparently). Only 40% say they would stand their ground and fight. More than two-thirds of Republicans (68%) said they would stand their ground. Better, but still hardly the "Don't tread on me" spirit that the author of the article was expecting. Sadly, it is pretty much what I would have expected, as was implicit in my November 1, 2021 article in these pages wondering whether anyone today would actually fight to preserve the union, although that article assumed secession, not invasion by a foreign power.

I am both at a loss for words and not at a loss for words. That is to say, words at this juncture fail me, but I do have something to try to say. Personally, it seems to me that the Biden administration has been simply dithering while the crisis was developing. This was a continuation of the dithering on Afghanistan and other things. What the administration did do was almost worse than dithering: the president, his national security advisor, and the secretary of state made multiple public statements about what they were *not* going to do in the event of a Russian invasion of Ukraine. For as much of my life as I can remember, administrations have engaged in some form of "strategic ambiguity" to avoid making a clear statement of what might or would be done in certain circumstances. But letting the enemy know what you will *not* do sends a strong signal of weakness and leaves the door open for other foes to act in a more focused and strategically disadvantageous way vis-à-vis the United States. The administration's policies have been the exact opposite: foolish strategic transparency.

I have a suspicion that the failure of Mr. Biden to approve the transfer of Polish Soviet- made fighters to Ukraine could prove decisive in any ultimate Russian "victory" over Ukraine and is certainly responsible for much of the unimaginable destruction of many Ukrainian cities and towns. We have supplied antitank and antiaircraft weapons; the Turks have supplied lethal drones. The failure to support Poland in its offer to provide Russian- made aircraft to Ukraine to be flown by Ukrainian pilots, and the Biden decision to veto the stationing of many such planes at an American air base in Germany was hardly a profile in courage. Likewise, the dithering over whether to increase domestic oil production so as, once again, to be energy independent, and so to be able to provide to Europe much of the energy that it now receives from Russia seems unbelievably foolish. To turn over to the "greens" such important geopolitical strategy cannot end well for the United States. To bow before the altar of utopian green dreams in the face of the Realpolitik on the ground is a luxury the nation cannot afford and for which we should expect to pay a very high price in the end.

I do not mean to take lightly the threat of a madman using nuclear weapons, and Putin has proved himself to be a madman. He has even allowed or encouraged his military to assault nuclear power plants in Ukraine and thereby run some nontrivial risk of a nuclear meltdown. But the very idea that we would allow ourselves to be drawn into a nuclear war with Russia over Latvia or Estonia or Lithuania (all NATO members) after Putin has secured Ukraine seems like an unnecessarily suicidal strategy and a demonstration of an internally inconsistent military policy.

I was in the Navy, not the Army. But it seems relatively obvious that the time to allow the Ukrainians to access Soviet-made aircraft (as well as US Stingers and Javelins) was before Russia had begun its campaign to destroy Ukrainian cities, before most if not all of the airfields in Ukraine had been disabled or destroyed by the Russian Air Force, and before thousands of civilians had been slaughtered and millions of women and children were forced to flee. Had American resolve been anything like that of the German resolve, the Polish resolve, or the Ukrainian resolve, we would have been ready on day one of the Russian invasion to provide the type of military hardware and logistical support that is still being kicked around as a "possibility" in the halls of the White House and Congress.

I was born in the middle of World War II. My educational years were the 1950s and the first half of the 1960s. During those years we read broadly and deeply about Hitler becoming chancellor of Germany in 1933 in a somewhat democratic process.[212] His party was elected. Hitler was appointed Chancellor by President Hindenburg. (((followed almost immediately by the burning of the German Reichstag, the Nazi boycott of Jewish-owned shops, the Nazis' book-burning projects, and the opening of the Dachau concentration camp all in that same year); the Nazis' 1934 murder of Austrian Chancellor Dollfuss; Hitler's 1935 Race Laws; the 1938 Anschluss with Austria; Neville Chamberlain's policy of appeasement that year to achieve "peace in our time"; Hitler's 1938 taking of the Sudetenland in Czechoslovakia and the subsequent resignation of the Czech government; and the onset of actual war in 1939 when the Nazis entered into a pact with Stalin (August 23, 1939), two days later Britain and Poland signed a Mutual Assistance Treaty, and on September 1 the Nazis invaded Poland. World War II began. Then the Cold War with the USSR followed, which lasted for some forty-five years from roughly 1946 until 1991.

The postwar years were followed by the *Pax Americana*, which seems to have finally ended last month, although it really ended probably some years ago when the United States lost the will to lead (e.g., leading from behind) or a willingness to fight against even the Taliban in Afghanistan, or in response to the assault on US embassies, or the use of chemical weapons by Bashir Assad against his own people when our president had publicly said that any such action would be "unacceptable." Well, it turned out to be quite acceptable indeed.

I grew up in a world in which the news media, educators, commentators, relatives, *tout le monde*, was of the view that conduct like Hitler's persistent grabbing of territory and slaughter of people "would never be allowed to happen again." But it is happening again, and it is happening right now. The current policy of the Biden administration seems to be to cross its fingers and hope that Putin will be deposed by saner powerful forces in Russia or that there will be some kind of internal uprising in that country. While perhaps possible, such events do not seem likely. Indeed, in what seems like nearly the blink of an eye, Putin has returned Russia to a Stalinesque totalitarianism into which news from the world outside of Russia can rarely be heard or found. Putin controls the internal Russian narrative with frightening effectiveness. Ukrainians stuck in bombardments of cities telephone relatives back in Russia and are told by those Russian relatives that their eyewitness reports from Ukraine are simply fake news and that the Russians are merely responding to vicious attacks by Ukrainian Nazis.

It seems to me, in short, that the time to have "done something" was a few weeks ago or a few months ago when the threat was obvious and understood by American intelligence agencies. It may not be too late, although perhaps it is. But if so, then it could be said that World War III began back on February 23 if not somewhat sooner. A decision to challenge Russia later will be more difficult than it has proved to be today given the proximity of Estonia, Latvia, and Lithuania to the Soviet Union itself.

Despite the gloom, or at least my gloom, I listened to some CNN interviews with a supposedly bipartisan group of senators visiting US troops on the Polish-Ukrainian border. Senator Blumenthal of Connecticut, who has never seemed worthy of any particular respect in my mind, made the strongest statement I have heard by a Democratic senator *against* the administration's dithering about the provision of airplanes and other war and humanitarian material to Ukraine. Senator Blumenthal is hardly a centrist, but it is clear that many senior members of the Democratic Party have been deeply troubled and influenced by what they have seen with their own eyes on television recently. Perhaps they have also been inspired by the extraordinary courage and leadership of Ukraine's President Zelensky and the Ukrainian citizenry. For whatever reason, he and other like-minded Democrats may be putting pressure on the Biden administration to do more, most especially to arrange to assist Ukraine and having access to Soviet-made aircraft now owned by former eastern bloc countries.

There is the threat of a nuclear response, but that response almost certainly would involve the use of "small" tactical nuclear weapons not large strategic nuclear weapons. The few people who purport to have insights into the Russian military psyche seem to think it improbable that the Russian military would, in the end, follow orders to launch nuclear weapons in the present circumstances.[213] That is not a guarantee, but if the bully is not stopped in Ukraine, he might be far more difficult to stop further north, where NATO countries are involved, or even further to the west or south, where other non-NATO territories could be grabbed and likely would be (Moldova and Georgia come to mind).

By the way, at present NATO has thirty members.[214] In 1949, there were twelve founding members of the Alliance: Belgium, Canada, Denmark, France, Iceland, Italy, Luxembourg, the Netherlands, Norway, Portugal, the United Kingdom, and the United States. The other member countries are Greece and Turkey (1952), Germany (1955), Spain (1982); the

Czech Republic, Hungary, and Poland (1999); Bulgaria, Estonia, Latvia, Lithuania, Romania, Slovakia, and Slovenia (2004); Albania and Croatia (2009); Montenegro (2017), and North Macedonia (2020). It is hard for me to accept that we would fight for every inch of those countries in the event of a Russian attack on any of them, while letting Ukraine fall into the hands of Russia in such a brutal and unconscionable fashion. On the other hand, I have little doubt that Mr. Biden is one of the 52% of Democrats who would flee rather than fight in the end. He does not seem like the kind of person who would fight for anything or be willing to die for any national interest (the same is likely true of many or most of our recent presidents).

On this score, today *The Atlantic* (reliably establishmentarian and literate left of center) ran a piece about the Western world being in denial. It starts with the author's understanding of why the democratic countries are reluctant to fight but expresses concern that those people simply do not understand what will happen next.[215] Meanwhile, as I am finishing this up, I see a headline that says Russia is asking China for military assistance. This tells me that the administration might once again have screwed the pooch, so to speak, by waiting too long to make the correct decision allowing Ukraine to defend itself more effectively at the outset of the war.

Finally, I am at the moment not addressing the very complicated question of how we got into our current predicament. There are many highly knowledgeable, articulate, and conflicting schools of thought on this, and part of me agrees with some part of each school of thought. This article from yesterday by Matt Taibbi is chilling for its factual accuracy in most of its details.[216] But no matter how correct the view that historical acts by the West have served to corner Russia and motivate Putin to invade Ukraine (and to a degree this is no doubt true, although to a different degree the projection of weakness by our government and military over the past many years on many fronts, most recently Afghanistan, has provided a similar and maybe more immediate incentive), fixing the blame for the current situation does not point the way to a manner of addressing it in the moment.

27

Politics, Abortion, Guns, the Economy, Foreign Policy, and more

June 27, 2022

I have been on work-enforced absence from writing ever since last March. And along the way, my brain has been overwhelmed by events such that I have been unable to muster many sustained clear thoughts. Also, too many things are heading in the wrong direction at "warp speed" for me to process them properly. So here, seeking to emerge from the fog, I present a collection of short takes on a variety of interconnected topics, without going too deeply into any of them. There is doubtless something here for everybody to disagree with and perhaps also to agree with. I should add that this was written largely before the Supreme Court's decisions on abortion and guns, which are very notable and addressed here only to a limited degree. The reversal of the constitutional right to abortion is without doubt the most important Supreme Court decision since *Bush v. Gore* in 2000 and has already spawned thousands of articles.

Politics. The primaries and the polls provide fascinating food for thought, although none of them consider the recent Supreme Court decisions on guns and abortion and so might change. On the Republican side, it seems clear that former President Trump still has influence, although a handful of candidates not supported by him have won primary elections. The Republican

Party is obviously fractured, seemingly beyond near-term repair. Trump seems to own 30% of the party and that large chunk of the party doesn't seem to care much about discreet or particular policies; they just will follow Trump anywhere. Trumpism has proved itself an actual cult.

There are others in the Republican Party who will align themselves with Trump because the alternative (e.g., Biden or the even more progressive elements of the Democratic Party) seems so unacceptable. In the circumstances, and if Mr. Trump chooses to run in 2024, it might be difficult for any traditional conservative to defeat him in many of the Republican primaries. Indeed, it is rumored that even a candidate as obviously strong as Ron DeSantis in Florida will not run against Trump if Trump chooses. On the other hand, a recent poll taken of New Hampshire voters gave DeSantis a two-point edge over Trump in a head-to-head match-up.[217] The spread last week was Trump 37% and DeSantis 39%. As the *New York Times* article at the preceding footnote explains, that is a significant change from October, when a Granite State Poll showed Mr. Trump had support from 43% of likely Republican voters; Mr. DeSantis was at 18%.

Many Republicans may want to avoid an intraparty fight and keep their powder dry for 2028. This is surprising to me given the revelations of the January 6 Committee. While that committee may lack a certain legitimacy given various manipulations attending its creation, and even presuming its partisan purpose to prevent a blue wave in 2022 or 2024, the objective facts implicating President Trump and a nontrivial number of Republican elected representatives are disturbing. But Trump's base cares not for facts of any sort, and so there we are.

The Republican Party is also burdened by its own turn to various weird forms of nationalist populism. For example, the new Texas GOP platform calls for the abolition of the Federal Reserve, the repeal of the Sixteenth Amendment (allowing a federal income tax), and the repeal of the Voting Rights Act. As one commentator put it on the Twittersphere: "The Texas GOP doesn't want to return to the 1950s. It wants to return to the 19th century." Whether DeSantis chooses to run against Trump in the primaries will have an enormous impact on the future of the Republican Party, one way or the other, and could represent a continuation of the status quo or a hinge moment not just for Republicans but for the country at large.

The Democrats are in a somewhat similar situation. The progressives seem to own some 30% or so of the Democratic electorate, although in their case it is progressive policies that bind them together rather than the cult of a particular personality (Bernie Sanders might be a slight exception to this). Biden stumbled into the presidency mainly because he was the only nonprogressive who had a shot at defeating Trump. Ousting Trump, not being a progressive, and staying out of sight so Mr. Trump could have the stage to himself (and thus remind centrists why they were frightened of him) were the main pillars of his 2020 campaign. And it all worked. He led wire to wire during the 2020 primary season, although winning only by modest pluralities in several cases. But then having governed as if he was tied to Elizabeth Warren/Bernie Sanders/Sandy Cortez and the progressives, his approval rating in the polls has fallen to the lowest level of any president in many decades. Yet his approval rating among Democrats is surprisingly high (~73%) despite the fact that he seems to suffer from serious infirmities of age wholly apart from the fact that his administration is laced with incompetence and many facets of policy incoherence.

In the regular "Direction of Country" polls (*Politico*, *Economist*, and *Reuters*), the administration is looking at 20% to 26% "wrong direction"), which suggests disaster for the Democrats in the midterms. The especially astute podcasters to whom I listen (Commentary and CNN's Harry Enten's "Margins of Error") expect a shift in the House of Representatives to decisive Republican control. But even a "red wave" midterm election does not necessarily translate into Republican control of the Senate given the weakness of a number of Republican candidates; the unknown impact of last week's contentious Supreme Court decisions; the national reaction to the distinctively horrible school shootings of recent months; the broad and deep consensus that "something" must be done to stem the plague of gun violence and death in this country; the related passage of gun control legislation just last week; and the impact if any of the January 6 Committee proceedings.

My more central observation is that in the Democratic Party there is no one other than Joe Biden at the moment who might represent a non-progressive alternative for the party. This mirrors the problem in the Republican Party: the absence of any non-Trump candidate who has demonstrated a willingness to take on Mr. Trump in the primaries should Mr. Trump run. This could change of course if the Democrats take a walloping in the upcoming November midterms. Gavin Newsome seems to be edging toward positioning himself as a candidate and beginning to pass himself off as somewhat mainstream. But for the moment, no Democratic centrist seems poised in the wings.

In this respect, things are probably more interesting in the Democratic Party. In recent days and weeks, there have been quiet whispers and murmurings among Democratic Party and media grandees that Mr. Biden should declare after the midterms that he will not seek another term. See Mark Leibovich's June 16 article in *The Atlantic* "Why Biden Shouldn't Run in 2024." But the Democrats who would like Biden to abdicate might get and regret what they wish for. The idea of a dozen or more Democratic candidates vying for the presidential nomination in 2024 would seem catastrophic for the party, especially given that it would likely involve the far left vs. the further left; at the same time all the candidates would have to condemn Kamala Harris, who was brought in to be "in the wings." And while she is worthy of condemnation, she was proudly lionized by the party as the first black female nationally elected official. And so, now to trash her inside the party carries multiple risks given the dependence of Democrats in general on heavy black female voter support. Then there is the fiasco at the southern border and the complete incoherence of any immigration policy, issues that are becoming divisive now even within the Democratic Party and could contribute to the Democrats loss of the Senate, should that in fact occur.

All things considered, the parties find themselves in a bizarre situation where Mr. Biden and Mr. Trump have an odd symbiotic relationship. As CNN's Mr. Enten put it: Mr. Trump may be the only candidate that Mr. Biden can beat, while Mr. Biden may be the only candidate that Mr. Trump can beat. The next few months will provide more interesting times for spectators. For partisans it will be nail-biting.

Abortion. To write anything about abortion in this country today invites opprobrium or even violent reaction from many or all quarters so it is with some hesitancy that I touch upon this topic. I will restate what I mentioned above: the elimination of the five-decade-long constitutional right to abortion is the most important Supreme Court decision since *Bush v. Gore*. The Supreme Court opinions (213 pages in total) can be found here.[218] Every American born in America under the age of fifty has never known a world where a woman's right to an abortion was not an established and protected right. The elimination of this right, however constitutionally flawed it may have been at inception, is uniquely unsettling. To deny this reality is to live on another planet.

In any case, there are important issues at stake, and they certainly transcend *Roe v. Wade*. But before venturing further into this minefield, I invite you to have a glance back through the lens of today at my article on these pages from March 3, 2020, about the rise of law and the decline of politics. While that article had nothing explicitly to do with *Roe v. Wade*, the article is central to the topic at hand insofar as it gets deep into the fact that legislative inaction has left the courts with some of the most nettlesome of imaginable questions.

To start with, I have been of the view since 1973 that the constitutional foundation for the decision in *Roe* was somewhere between weak and nonexistent. As everybody who has read anything about this knows, I was joined in this view in large measure by none other than Ruth Bader Ginsburg, among other strong liberals. So far as I know, no other country in the world has established the right to an abortion as a constitutional right, or as a "fundamental human right" without a legislative enactment by elected officials. Apart from dictatorships and autocracies (many of which allow abortions under various circumstances), every country that allows abortions has established and regulates those rights pursuant to a democratic legislative process. And while access to abortion is nominally protected under the European Convention on Human Rights (ECHR) [219] (which has nothing to do with the United States and under which the unborn are not regarded as "people" directly protected under the ECHR) it has been national legislatures who have implemented laws in conformance with the HCHR. It has not been unelected judges who have imposed abortion rights on societies.

Yet, while I have long felt that the constitutional foundation for *Roe* was weak or nonexistent, I have also felt that the outcome in the original case (the trimester structure) made considerable sense and would have made even better sense if it represented an outcome brought about by a democratic legislative process. While the first, second, and third trimester rules of *Roe* were long ago overtaken by our Supreme Court's current "undue burden" analysis, the trimester-driven regime is what most legislatures around the world have embraced. Most of the European countries provide an unlimited right to abortion during the first fifteen weeks, followed by varying limited forms of the right during the second, or even the third, trimester.

Our federal legislature, populated by politicians who have always shown little desire to take votes that would offend a large swath of the electorate, has had fifty years to codify the original architecture of *Roe* but has failed to do so. Indeed, little effort has been made to do so. Thus, everything has devolved to the states, a majority of which allow abortion under many circumstances, with the extreme example of New York, which arguably allows post birth abortion, if infanticide can be so described.[220] At the other end of the spectrum there is Texas, which has sought to criminalize anyone even just assisting in the procurement of an abortion by a Texas resident. While likely not enforceable, it places two of our most populous states at frighteningly distant poles on the abortion question.

Lost in the noise, as the article at the preceding footnote indicates, the overwhelming majority of abortions in this country take place during the first eight weeks of pregnancy. Putting aside, if one can, religious and moral issues, in my view the only proper way for abortion rights to be mediated in this country is through a federal or state legislative process, not a judicial process. The role of the Supreme Court in intercepting the political trend toward abortion rights in the states guaranteed the succeeding five decades of irresolvable political friction, much of which would have been muted if Congress acted legislatively or had the majority of the states embraced limited abortion rights as they have mostly done. Wholly apart from tearing the social fabric of the country, maybe even irreparably, the abortion issue, more than any other in memory, has politicized and damaged the institutional integrity of the judiciary in general and the Supreme Court in particular in scores of ways large and small. The Supreme Court especially has been almost forced into a quasi-legislative role, more by executive and legislative actions and inactions than by the court itself.

Furthermore, it is probably no overstatement to observe that the 1973 *Roe* decision itself was a hinge moment in American society. The case was decided during the Vietnam War during a time of social upheaval—and during a time when broad swaths of society (generally encouraged by the Democratic Party) championed sexual freedom and sexual liberation. Even if not immediately, the decision slowly crystallized things politically. It brought about the departure of substantial numbers of Catholics, Southern Baptists, other religious groups, and many blue-collar workers (union and nonunion) from the Democratic Party, which had long housed them. This massive political realignment was largely complete by 1980, and it brought about the landslide election of Ronald Reagan and the establishment of a strong center-right coalition that has proved quite durable, despite its drift to Trumpism.

Certainly, in hindsight, *Roe v. Wade* marked the beginning of the serious culture wars, which had been gathering and have escalated. They continue to this day. I cannot help but think that a decade or so from now people will look back on the return of abortion to democratically elected officials as a refreshment of democracy and a limitation on judicial autocracy, but that view is perhaps naïve. Activists on both sides of the abortion question tend to be maximalists: abortion should be either always legal or never legal. Public debate lacks meaningful nuance or patient reasoning. On the other hand, for fifty years, federal politicians could say whatever they wanted to about abortion without there being any consequence at all because the judiciary had taken all the heat and would continue to do so. Now, federal and state elected officials will have to vote and those votes will actually create law (or not) through a democratic legislative process. Activists will do what activists should do: lobby legislatures instead of courts. Absent superseding federal legislation, there will be a majority of states where abortion is readily available and there will be a minority of states where abortion is strictly limited or unavailable. It cannot be all bad to have these sorts of highly charged political questions decided in a political arena through a process involving elected representatives.

I cannot touch the abortion subject without mentioning the particular horror of watching abortion rights groups terrorizing the homes of Supreme Court Justices who favored the repeal of *Roe*. These groups have also terrorized various Catholic churches and cathedrals as well as others. And there has been an unsuccessful assassination attempt on the life of a Supreme Court justice at his home because of his judicial views on abortion. The indifference of the Democratic leadership to these circumstances, indeed the encouragement of this illegal activity by senior Democratic officials (CNN video here[221]; Jonathon Turley article here [222]) is shocking and demonstrates vividly the depth of the political predicament in this country. Even in the last two days, once-responsible people (including Sen. Elizabeth Warren) have shouted out that the Supreme Court "set a torch" to its last shred of legitimacy and should now be "packed."[223] Rep. Cortez has called for the impeachment of at least two justices of the Supreme Court.[224]

The utter disrespect for law and important institutions among the abortion rights advocates is mirrored in a material way by the total disrespect for law and institutions on the part of the January 6 insurrectionists. When the grievances of interest groups are reduced to insurrection, intimidation of supreme court justices, attempted assassination of one of them, and the abolition of one branch of government, the country is in a very bad place.

The echoes of summer 2020 are strong. And when the Justice Department and the administration condemn only one of these groups but not the other, things cannot be expected to get better anytime soon whatever might happen in the midterm elections. Indeed, much is being written about the permanency of the wide divisions in this country, especially by the left-leaning media. Robert Brownstein's article in *The Atlantic,* entitled "America is Growing Apart, Possibly for Good." [225] is illustrative of the genre. And while Brownstein wrongly blames only the right for the circumstances, his conclusion, and many of the stated reasons for it, sound chillingly correct. His views, minus the "blame the right" ingredient, are echoed in this piece from the *Wall Street Journal* of a few days ago entitled "Could this be an Antebellum Age?"[226]

Guns. When I was eleven or twelve years old, my uncle gave me a single-shot bolt-action .22 caliber rifle. We lived fourteen miles to the west of Boston in Concord, Massachusetts. In the mid-1950s, my younger brother and I could walk up and down the street carrying this weapon and stopping from time to time to shoot at Coke bottles, Coke cans, beer cans, or any other appealing glass or metal targets that might have been visible from the side of the road. From time to time, a police car would come by. The officer would stop, ask us how we were doing, and we would show him our plinking skills, such as they were. He would perhaps watch or take a shot or two himself as a form of education and then give us a smile and move on. Today of course our parents would be arrested for negligent parenting, and we would be sent to some kind of reeducation camp.

I served in the military in the 1960s and received excellent firearms training. I have long enjoyed shooting for sport, mostly trap or skeet. I have never been an avid hunter but have several friends who are. I own shotguns, rifles, and pistols. There are supposedly some four hundred million guns in this country now. Controlling the *use* of these guns is more than difficult as a practical matter. I live in Maryland. Maryland has some of the strictest gun laws in the country. Yet Baltimore suffers from horrific gun violence driven almost entirely by the illegal drug trade. The school shootings and mass murders that horrify us on the front pages are a rounding error on the national gun death statistics. (See Pew Research Center story: "What the Data Says about Gun Deaths in the US." [227] In general, the possession of pistols in Maryland is legal only when I am on my own property and when one is traveling to and from a place where the use of that pistol is proper and lawful. Nonresidents cannot purchase guns in Maryland. Maryland residents must have a special permit to purchase a pistol. Purchasing a pistol requires a background check, fingerprinting, and taking a prescribed test from a licensed instructor. Large magazines cannot be purchased in Maryland. Long guns are more lightly regulated to accommodate hunters (of mostly deer, geese, and ducks). Maryland does not issue concealed carry permits to any regular citizen.

The Maryland law and those of a dozen or so other states will have to change to come into compliance with the Supreme Court's decision of last week (the entire set of opinions is here).[228] That decision essentially eliminates the ability and authority of unelected bureaucrats to decide who is allowed and who is not allowed to have a permit to bear arms outside the home. The decision makes the right to bear arms a "real" right alongside the right to free speech, religious freedom, and assembly. This is not necessarily a good thing for all communities or on the highway, where road rage murders will probably occur in noticeable numbers. It is unclear how much room is left for states to regulate weaponry, but probably quite a bit.

In all events, given last week's Supreme Court decision, the United States will be an even more noticeable outlier among all the countries of the world in its allowance of the proliferation of weaponry and in its failure to regulate them. In my view, something significant must be done about gun deaths in this country given the reality that millions of people might soon be walking around carrying guns in much greater numbers than is the case today. And it can be done without doing violence to the Second Amendment. If we were serious, which plainly we are not, we could have a federal statute, for example, that requires guns to be registered, much as cars are registered, and that requires individuals to be licensed to own guns. Licenses could be issued for certain types of guns as they are for cars, motorcycles, and different classes of trucks. Magazines could be regulated (as they are in some but not all states). The impediments to these two approaches are very political. Such things will not happen in my lifetime.

Many gun rights people view the main point of the right being to protect oneself and the citizenry from governmental intrusion on personal rights, indeed from dictatorship. Such people say things like: if every Russian had a gun in 1917, the Bolsheviks never could have taken over Russia. Put simply, a main objection to these kinds of regulations is that many gun owners do not want any governmental agency or unit to *know* how many guns they have, what kinds of guns they have, where they might be located, and so forth. While this reaction may show a healthy mistrust of government, in this area we have seen enough schoolchildren killed, presidents assassinated, and innocent bystanders killed or wounded that something is needed that is more than symbolic. Something serious. Unregistered guns could be confiscated, and their owners fined. Unlicensed users could be fined. Friends tell me I am naïve and that these measures would do nothing. Maybe so, but I think over time they would have a significant impact in preventing gun crime and gun deaths. Every long journey must start with a single step in the right direction, and for me this is the right step in the right direction.

I am mindful that many of the mass school shootings have been perpetrated by young teenage boys with serious mental problems. But the red flag laws have not worked and will not work. I have little confidence that the bipartisan federal legislation just signed into law will make much difference. Families and friends seem reluctant to blow the whistle on troubled sons and neighbors before the fact of a mass shooting. The decades-long trend of increased individual rights for mentally deficient people, which can properly be blamed for the streets of our major cities being littered with mentally disturbed homeless people (and their detritus and feces) is not something that can be addressed easily or quickly. Families and authorities can no longer send mentally disturbed children to institutions run by the state, and the states no longer have the resources (or the legal authority at the moment) to operate such facilities anyway. The chickens of good (but ill-conceived) intentions have come home to roost. While the registration of guns and the licensing of gun owners are not politically realistic now, I predict it will be in the lifetime of today's young people.

Final point on this. It is annoying to hear gun opponents blaming the gun industry and more broadly "the gun lobby." The gun lobby is actually the citizenry of the United States. The views of citizens on gun ownership and regulation are complex but interesting. The article (link included in the following note) is especially interesting for those looking for granular details. At the risk of great overgeneralization, Americans are broadly OK with personal gun rights and also tight gun regulation.[229] Part of the calculus is based on all the recent "peaceful violence" from the aftermath of the George Floyd murder. No person at risk of being a victim of violence, whether urban, suburban, or rural, wants to (or can) depend on law enforcement any longer.

Self-help is the only other alternative. Our elected officials have neither the wisdom nor the courage to tackle the gun problems directly other than to appeal to their respective political bases.

The Economy. So, here we are in the first week of summer. My non–real estate portfolio is off around 30%, and I am in no way confused about who to blame. As I have observed before, I join former Secretary of Defense Robert Gates (who served under both Bush and Obama) in my belief that Mr. Biden has never been on the right side of any foreign policy issued in his entire life. I'm not sure that that statement is completely true with respect to his domestic economic policy views, but it is certainly true for the entirety of his brief but disastrous presidential administration. His main domestic economic fiascoes can probably be summed up in just a few words: stimulus payments and oil and gas.

Biden's trillions of dollars in stimulus payments put massive amounts cash in the hands of individuals and the economy with unintended but predictable consequences. The first consequence: people felt that no work was more rewarding than work. This led to sustained ongoing personnel shortages, especially in retail and food service industries. It also created a situation where employers had to pay above market rates to tease people back into the workforce. In sum, the supply side was constrained. The influx of trillions of dollars into the economy (thus among other things discouraging work) also otherwise exacerbated supply-chain issues, with the result that many more dollars were chasing fewer and fewer available goods. Thus began the inflationary spiral. Not only was this predictable, but it was also in fact predicted, particularly by former Harvard President Larry Summers, an advisor to the Obama administration.

What began as a blatant vote-buying exercise backfired spectacularly, injuring not just those whom the administration intended to benefit but everybody else as well. While perhaps a minor factor, it is worth mentioning that the Biden administration has officially favored unionized companies over nonunionized companies in all government procurement decisions, thus making 85% of the potential government contractors ineligible to bid on and win government contracts. This further greatly increases the cost of procurement but satisfies the union vote. This is just another form of "crony capitalism," a form of small "c" corruption that in truth mirrors the tendencies of the Republicans but favoring different constituencies.

Then we have oil and gas. On day one of the Biden administration, the president declared war on the oil and gas industry. This was a total capitulation to the Green and progressive wings of the Democratic Party, which substantially overlap, if not completely. The idea was to force the reduction of American production of carbon-based fuels so as to force everybody into "cleaner" fuels. This is not only disastrous as a matter of domestic economic policy, it also ceded massive power back to Saudi Arabia, Iran, and Venezuela, not to mention Russia. (More on this below under "foreign policy.") By discouraging investment in oil, gas, shale, and any other technology that did not relate to "clean energy," the administration upended the supply-side markets, the demand-side markets, and indeed entire industries and all who had invested in them. When oil prices began to shoot up (which was long before Russia invaded Ukraine), the administration paid little or no attention. After Russia invaded Ukraine, the administration blamed high oil prices on "Putin's war." Convenient, yet wrong. And the president has since had the effrontery to blame high oil and gas prices on the oil and gas industries and their CEOs. Oil industry CEOs, in a somewhat unusual move, have pushed back at the administration's blame game.[230]

IT'S THE ECONOMY STUPID said the sign President Clinton kept near his desk. Biden should get his own and keep it at hand. He has earned his low poll ratings.

Foreign Policy. Few observers have reached any conclusion other than that, in general, the Biden administration's foreign policy has been an unfocused mess. That said, there are those who give Biden credit for pulling together NATO in response to the Russian invasion of Ukraine. Frankly, I give Biden little or no credit on this score, but I do not intend to resolve that debate if there is one and so will let it pass for now. The big blunders involve Afghanistan, China, Russia, the Middle East in general, and Saudi Arabia in particular. Smaller blunders are probably everywhere.

It is unclear that the country has a policy with regard to China beyond "strategic ambiguity," an elastic term that covers all manner of incoherence but seems not to include actual deterrence. At a live press conference in Asia, Biden did say that we would go to war with China to protect the independence of Taiwan. That statement was almost instantaneously "corrected" by the White House. Statement by Biden, correction by the administration has not been a bug in this administration but rather a feature: one that has led many here and outside the country to conclude that the administration is simply incoherent and incompetent.

The administration has demonized Saudi Arabia at almost exactly the wrong moment in time. The assassination of Mr. Khashoggi continues to dominate the administration's policies toward Saudi Arabia, which is unfortunate. However horrible that assassination, it should not have become the pivot point around which Middle East policy turns. The biggest threat to Middle Eastern peace and security is Iran. The principal enemies of Iran are Saudi Arabia and Israel. That reality has brought Saudi Arabia and Israel together. The simultaneous demonization of Saudi Arabia and the administration's sucking up to Iran to make a nuclear deal at any cost seems not only shortsighted but despicable in terms of protecting legitimate American interests. Even more strange has been the US reliance on Russia as its only intermediary and protector with respect to its Iran negotiations. Luckily, the Kerry mission to Iran seems bound to fail on its own because the Iranians are not going to agree to anything. Meanwhile, the president now plans to visit Saudi Arabia begging for more oil, while at the same time begging for more oil from Iran and Venezuela. It is all very embarrassing.

Then there is Ukraine. From the beginning, the Biden administration has been advising Russia in considerable detail what it will *not* do. This has been both tactically and strategically insane. The fecklessness of President Biden has led Putin to characterize the United States as a "weak and declining power." Conversely, the administration has never made clear what it will do. What it has done is probably too little too late, if one supports the proposition that the United States should be helping Ukraine to win the war, rather than merely survive in some section of the country. One must acknowledge that there is a strong view in the country shared by many on both the left and the right that we should not be involved at all in the war between Russia and Ukraine, that the invasion is the fault of the United States and NATO for expanding recklessly too far eastward toward the Russian border, and that we should use our precious resources for domestic purposes. It is not my purpose here to take sides on that issue, other than to note that the Biden administration has itself seemed in various circumstances to be on both sides of that issue. Meanwhile, supposedly informed people are also convinced that (1) Russia will "win" the war[231] and (2) Russia will "lose" the war.[232]

Finally, while the media seem to have flushed this down the media memory hole, it was the administration's fiasco in Afghanistan, which I wrote about extensively back on September 11, that has motivated foreign enemies to be convinced of the absence of any American will or purpose internationally. The world is a dangerous place, and most everything done or not done by the current administration has made it more so. I do not mean that to be as partisan as it might sound since I have little confidence that the Republicans have a foreign policy that would be much more coherent, or that from Afghanistan to Ukraine the Republicans would have acted differently (although I am sure they would not have vowed to defenestrate the oil and gas industry and then take affirmative steps to do just that).

28

The Beginning of the End Days for Mr. Biden within His Own Party?

July 11, 2022

A few days ago, Boris Johnson declared that under no circumstances would he resign as prime minister of Great Britain. Within forty-eight hours, he was gone. Nearly a dozen cabinet ministers resigned. In effect BoJo, as he is sometimes called, was abandoned by his own ministers and his own party. Most of the press stories that I read talked about his "clown fall" and made the point, one way or another, that the Conservative Party in Britain had finally woken up to the fact that they could no longer tolerate a dishonest, crude, clownish entertainer as head of their party. Nearly all of the media ink spilled on the subject (both here and in the UK) dwelt at length on this aspect of Mr. Johnson's collapse, while at the same time hectoring American Republicans to take heed and abandon all vestiges of Donald Trump who is perceived by our mainstream media, and by the UK media, too, as largely analogous to Boris Johnson, especially in his crude and dishonest clownishness. Thus, we have these sorts of snark:

> *New York Times*: "The delightful implosion of Boris Johnson. His career is ending the way Donald Trump's should have. However, the schadenfreude brought by Johnson's collapse is mixed with envy."

> *The Independent:* "During the former president's worst excesses, there was no mass uprising against him from within his own government, as with Johnson."
>
> *Washington Post:* "The resignation of British Prime Minister Boris Johnson is testament to the power of elected politicians to hold their leaders accountable. It is a lesson that has been lost on Republican Party officials as they have weighed repeatedly how to deal with former president Donald Trump."

It is not my purpose here to suggest that there are not important analogies between Boris Johnson and his Conservative Party on the one hand, and Donald Trump and the Republicans on the other. But the commentary on it all seems banal and facile. The media raining down these analogies seems uniquely limited to stating the obvious and uniquely poorly positioned to state the less obvious but more interesting and consequential. Just two weeks ago I wrote that:

> … in recent days and weeks, there have been quiet whispers and murmurings among Democratic party and media grandees that Mr. Biden should declare after the midterms that he will not seek another term and will abdicate. See Mark Leibovich's June 16 article in The Atlantic "Why Biden Shouldn't Run in 2024." But the Democrats who would like Biden to abdicate might get and regret what they wish for.

But in the last few days, and without even a nod to Boris Johnson and his calamity, these whispers and murmurings have evolved into a grand mal panic, driven by some of the most anemic poll ratings ever seen in American politics in the last one hundred years. The whisperings and murmurings of two weeks ago have become shouts and screams. This is the most immediate and salient analogy with Boris Johnson and the British Conservative Party. Remember, what BoJo said upon resigning: "When the herd moves, it moves." Well, the Democratic herd in this country seems to be moving mainly because of oil prices, food prices, the perception that the economy is doing poorly (even though unemployment seems at an all-time low), the lack of any coherent foreign policy (whether in Asia, Afghanistan, Europe,

Ukraine, or the Middle East), the fiasco on the southern border, and now a widespread and seemingly irreversible perception that the administration is simply aimless, rudderless, and incompetent not just in devising policy but in the execution of policies.

Given the leaked *Roe* opinion last May, the administration had months of notice regarding what was going to happen in connection with *Roe v. Wade* and yet it seemed completely unprepared to take strong action of any sort in the wake of the actual opinion. The administration in particular, and the Democratic Party in general, also seemed unprepared to address the Supreme Court's decision establishing a right under the Second Amendment to possess firearms outside the home. Whether one agrees or disagrees with these Supreme Court decisions, the administration's response was bellicose, and not really connected to the underlying merits of either case. Rather, the response was to declare war on the Supreme Court, to attempt to generate enthusiasm for a court-packing scheme, and to attempt to keep the focus on the January 6 hearings so as to keep as much of the media as possible focused on the sins of Donald Trump and his White House staff, thereby distracting the electorate from life on the ground. The slowly building Hunter Biden story was altogether ghosted. And as this is written, Mr. Biden is off on a begging-for-oil trip to Saudi Arabia.

But the root problem is the president's continuing (and to many, stunning) collapse in the polls. Mr. Biden's disapproval rating now exceeds 60% in essentially all the polls. In the eight separate wrong track/right track polls, the wrong track range is from 87% to 70% with the RealClear average at 76%. This is unheard of! And a Harvard-Harris poll finds that 71% of Americans do not want President Biden to seek reelection.[233] It is thus not as large a surprise as it might otherwise be to see CNN running an article about the White House going out of its way to tamp down on whispers that he might not run for a second term in 2024. Even poor Kamala Harris was called into play to declare "Joe Biden is running for reelection, and I will be his ticket mate. Full stop." However, she later revised her remarks to say just that Biden "intends" to run.[234] Big difference.

Just yesterday, CNN ran this headline: "As worries about Biden in 2024 grow, other Democrats aren't stepping forward to challenge him."[235] This displeases CNN given the "overwhelming sense of frustration among democrats [236] …with Biden and what many in the president's party describe as mismanagement permeating the White House. Top democrats complain the

President isn't acting with — or perhaps isn't even capable of — the urgency the moment demands." [237]

At least three Democrats seem to be positioning themselves for a run if and when Mr. Biden finally exits, whether à la BoJo or otherwise: California Governor Gavin Newsome, Illinois Governor J. B. Pritzker, and Michigan Governor Gretchen Whitmer, all chief executives of states of some size and importance. Neither Pete Buttigieg nor Kamala Harris are likely to be taken seriously this time around (although a recent poll gives Buttigieg a one-point lead over Biden in New Hampshire on the order of 32% to 31%), and so it could be an interesting primary season next year. What Bernie Sanders might do could of course matter, and he and Elizabeth Warren (not to mention Sandy Cortez) could continue their roles as disruptive forces within the Democratic Party.

But given where we were just a few weeks ago, it seems increasingly clear that, like Boris Johnson, President Biden has thoroughly lost the confidence of his party and of the electorate. What remains is for him to find a face-saving way out of the next campaign lest he suffer the fate of being primaried (as Jimmy Carter was by Ted Kennedy) and watching the party splinter even further, all to the benefit of the Republicans.

I will leave for another day some comments about the Republicans, who seem to me to be on the verge of displaying a number of candidates who are not Trump but who are aiming to appeal to many Trump voters, a delicate balancing act indeed. The Democrats evidently presume that Governor Ron DeSantis has the inside track in this regard and their wannabe candidates are traveling to Florida to make speeches and generally trying to make trouble for DeSantis.

As early as it is in the presidential season, it feels a little bit like the end days for Biden and the early days for his several would-be successors.

29

How Quickly Things Change

September 6, 2022

If you have been on vacation, or otherwise taking a summer break from day-to-day news, it may surprise you to learn that the political landscape of early September, two months before the midterm elections, bears little or no resemblance to the political landscape back in May or June. My very last column was only about two months ago, and the subject was the apparent beginning of the end days for Mr. Biden within his own party. During the spring and early summer things looked beyond bleak for the president and his party. In fact, I had ruminated that the only hope for a Democratic success in 2024 would be a series of bank shots along the following lines.

> **Step One:** shortly after the Democratic shellacking at the midterms, the administration arranges for Vice President Harris to accept a lifetime appointment to some federal court or a high-paying job with George Soros or somebody similar. She resigns.

> **Step Two:** shortly thereafter, President Biden appoints Mr./Ms. X to be vice president. Gavin Newsome might be a plausible candidate, but there are other possibilities. But let's think of it for this thought experiment purpose as Mr. Newsome, the governor of the largest state, and one who easily survived a recent recall effort. Flaws notwithstanding, he is a battle-tested success in the nation's largest state

with an economy that by itself would be the fifth largest in the world.

Step Three: at some point in 2023, President Biden announces his resignation due to health concerns and the desire to spend more time with his family at this late stage of his life.

Step Four: Mr. Newsome is sworn in as president.

Step Five: The new president quickly appoints a respected man or woman, likely of color but not a full-blown progressive, and this person is the new vice president.

And voilà! Presto chango. Well in advance of the Iowa and New Hampshire primaries the Democrats have a solid ticket without the bother of a grueling primary season. They could construct a ticket certainly capable of defeating any Trump or Trump acolyte, and probably capable of defeating any Republican ticket. Through a series of unilateral actions, the Democrats could turn the Republicans into toast.

But in the brief span of just a few weeks over the late spring and summer, things have happened that appear to make it highly likely that this is already in the process of happening without the need for such fascinating machinations. Through a series of events, some well stage managed by the Democrats, and others involving multiple self-inflicted wounds by Republicans, it seems increasingly likely that the Democrats will take firmer control of the Senate, and it is at least possible that they will keep their control of the House of Representatives. The more one considers the reality of this possibility, the more astonishing it becomes. First of all, in only three midterm elections since 1930 has the president's party improved its congressional position. Those three elections were 1934 (Franklin Roosevelt in the middle of the Depression); 1998 (Bill Clinton after a full recovery from Monica Lewinski and in command of a booming economy); and 2002 (George Bush, who enjoyed extraordinarily high standing in the polls in the wake of the September 11 attacks a year earlier). Today, President Biden's standing in the polls is under water (although greatly improved since last spring, when his approval rating hit a low of 33% in the Quinnipiac and *New York Times* polls in early

July) and all of the "direction of the country" polls show a supermajority of Americans believing that the country is on the "wrong track." Yet notwithstanding these clear indications of Biden's personal weakness, the most recent *Wall Street Journal* poll shows Biden ahead of Trump in the theoretical head-to-head election 50% to 44%. And in a massive switch from just a few months ago, the *Wall Street Journal*'s most recent generic congressional ballot poll (if the election were held today would you vote for the Democrat or the Republican) shows 47% choosing the Democrat and 44% choosing the Republican.

If, like me, you have been enjoying beach/mountain reading and being pretty much unplugged from the Twittersphere and the breathless news cycle of cable television, you might feel a little bit like Rip van Winkle, awakening to an entirely new and different world. So, what that heck happened? Before I stopped paying close attention only a couple of months ago the administration seemed on the verge of collapse, having brought about the following self-inflicted policy disasters:

1. The Afghanistan debacle and its many dimensions, about which I have written a great deal in these pages. Not only did we celebrate the twentieth anniversary of 9/11 by handing over to the Taliban the most important piece of real estate in central Asia (Bagram Air Base) while at the same time gifting them billions of dollars of military equipment, making them the fifth best-equipped military force in the world. Worst of all probably, the administration's feckless Afghanistan policy doubtless played a nontrivial role in encouraging Russia to invade Ukraine and motivating China to become more aggressive than it ever has been vis-à-vis Taiwan. The administration's Afghanistan mess made the world a far more dangerous place, and that remains the case today.
2. At the inception of the new administration, Mr. Biden declared his fealty to Green progressives by declaring war on the oil and gas industry. The result of this policy was to jeopardize the United States' position as the world's largest producer of oil and gas, the dominant energy-producing country in the world, and only one of a handful of countries in the world that was truly energy independent and not under the thumb of Saudi Arabia, Iran, Russia, and Venezuela. The inflationary impact of this policy (gas prices rose to more than $5

per gallon), amplified by the reckless infusion of trillions of dollars into a recovering economy (e.g., American Rescue Plan of 2021 and follow-on legislation) has yet to run its course. Inflation in this country (over 8.5%), brought about almost single-handedly by the policies of the Biden administration, has not been this high in more than forty years.

3. The administration forced the closure of one of only four baby-food plants in the United States without considering the totally foreseeable impact of that regulatory action on baby-food supply (disastrous), an impact that was exacerbated by the continuing prohibition of the importation of European baby food.
4. There was also the administration's complete inability to deal with supply-chain disruptions that left stores empty of scores of ordinary products made overseas. Many of the administration's policies contributed to these supply-chain disruptions, including its sanctions against certain countries.
5. And then there was the cringe-worthy matter of watching a seemingly enfeebled and doddering Mr. Biden try to face off in meetings with Mr. Putin and later Xi Jinping of China. The country seemed weak and powerless to protect its interests. Worse, it seemed to be clueless as to what its interests were. That has not changed.
6. One cannot fail to forget the chaos on the southern border, about which the administration seems wholly indifferent notwithstanding that the tens of thousands of deaths of US citizens from illegal opioids (roughly twice the number of annual gun deaths) are directly related to the open southern border. If it were not so sad, it would be amusing to see the mayors of Washington, DC, and New York City shrink back in horror at the prospect of two entire busloads (!) of illegal immigrants coming into their sanctuary cities. The very idea that *they* might be asked actually to live with their own policies frightens them.

I could go on and on, but all of this has been memory-holed, and I need to move on to what the dickens happened to make all of these things seem to disappear.

For one thing, until quite recently the president spent most of the summer in Rehoboth, Delaware, or some such place, thereby keeping out of sight so as not to remind people of his impairments or general ineffectiveness as a leader. Mr. Biden out of sight is much more attractive to voters than Biden on television every day. And as occurred during the presidential campaign, this left the media and the voters to focus mostly on stories about Mr. Trump and his various supporters.

For example, there was the *drip-drip-drip* of the January 6 hearings, which went on mercilessly for much of the summer presenting some pretty horrible examples of not necessarily illegal but nonetheless horrible conduct by senior officials of the Trump administration in plotting how to "stop the steal" of the 2020 election. And while the Democrats did not play fair with the committee by disallowing the minority leader the customary privilege of appointing his chosen Republicans to the Special Committee, the Republicans made the politically idiotic decision to boycott the entire event, thereby leaving all staging and production in the hands of a very well-organized Democratic assemblage of representatives quite capable of staying focused on particular messages each session, all designed to paint Trump and his coterie as dangerous people (which it seems they indeed were). To a large extent, the strategy seems to have brought about the exact result that was intended.

Second, there was the Supreme Court's decision in *Dobbs* overruling *Roe v. Wade*. As I have written before in these pages, I believe that the *Roe* decision was wrong as a matter of constitutional law, but as I have also written, I think that the three-trimester analysis set out in *Roe* was wholly sensible and would have been just the right approach had it been established through a democratic legislative process. Indeed, virtually every other democracy in the world (and some autocracies) have embraced the trimester-by-trimester rationale of *Roe*. This includes all of the Catholic democracies. But the Republicans in many states expressed their glee at the demise of *Roe* in a distressing and dangerous way: by passing statutes making abortion illegal under all circumstances, period. This was more symbolic than real since the vast majority of states have not and will not make abortion illegal during the first trimester and will allow abortions under some circumstances much later (*viz*. New York allows post birth "abortion."). But the symbolism is itself real as it makes Republicans look like a party that people should rightly fear.

To bring the point home. the Supreme Court's abortion ruling has mobilized massive Democratic constituencies as evidenced by special elections in Nebraska, Minnesota, New York, and elsewhere. The Nebraska election was held just four days after the Supreme Court's decision. The Republican candidate emphasized his sponsorship of a law that banned abortion after twenty weeks; the Democrat criticized the *Dobbs* decision and emphasized her support for abortion rights. This was a very Republican district, and the Republican candidate won, but the Democrat outperformed the 2020 Democratic candidate by nearly 10% and outperformed Biden by more than 6%.

A special election in Minnesota was held during the second week of August. The Republican ran as a strong opponent of abortion while the Democrat again ran as a prochoice candidate with the backing of Minnesota Senator Amy Klobuchar. Again, the Republican candidate won in a heavily Republican jurisdiction. But in the last two election cycles, the Republican candidate had garnered about 60% of the vote, whereas this time the Republican candidate garnered just under 53% of the vote. Again, a Republican victory but with another yellow warning flag.

Then there was New York where Democrat Pat Ryan won a very hotly contested special congressional race in a swing district in what had been "declared" by the media as the most closely watched of the summer's special elections—one described as the county's best bellwether of the summer. Mr. Ryan won after campaigning on the protection of abortion rights (which never would be an issue in New York under any circumstances). The Democrat victory there suggests a national mood. This is strongly suggested as well by the Kansas referendum on a proposition to amend the state constitution to roll back abortion rights. The proposition went down to defeat 59–41 margin in a heavily Republican state. This appears to be a clear signal that the reversal of *Roe v. Wade* has generated much real energy among Democrats, independents, and moderate Republicans/conservatives. It feels like a Democratic Party whose voters will walk over a bed of hot tacks to get to the polls. One gets no such sense of urgency on the Republican side. This was the first time a state has actually voted on abortion post-*Dobbs*.

To make matters worse for Republicans, the GOP messaging post-*Dobbs* has been either nonexistent or execrable. The reflex of a few states (including Texas) to take the opportunity to ban abortion under any circumstances invites mistrust of all Republicans. The *Dobbs* outcome seems to be a clear example to both parties (but in this case especially the Republicans) to be careful what they wish for—getting their wish might destroy them.

While I am on special elections, just before Labor Day weekend there was an Alaska special election to fill a congressional seat held for many decades by a Republican. Sarah Palin, well known and endorsed by Trump, lost to the Democratic native Alaskan woman under a ranked choice voting mechanism. So, in five recent special elections, the Democratic candidate either won, or in losing strongly outperformed President Biden's performance in that district in the 2020 election.

The bromide to be careful what you wish for brings me to "the Trump Effect," likely the biggest threat to Republican chances in 2022 and 2024. To "level set" things for a moment, let us remember that Trump lost in 2020. While he got 74 million votes, Biden got 81 million. Those numbers do not actually mean much in some ways given our electoral system, but they do mean that by every measure Trump lost. He was a loser. And it is fair to say that he all but single-handedly caused the loss of one or both Republican seats in Georgia by turning these elections into a referendum on whether the 2020 presidential election was stolen. The Republican candidates lost; Trump lost—he was a loser there.

His interference in key Senate and House races in the upcoming midterms may well prove to be disastrous. That involvement has brought into clear focus a long-standing and deep schism within the GOP that now seems quite obviously to present an existential threat to the party. This long predicted and serious split is between Trump and his acolytes and "base" supporters (now frequently referred to as MAGA Republicans) on the one hand, and traditional conservatives on the other. The GOP itself is the victim of this now open warfare. In several races in important and contestable jurisdictions, the GOP candidate who was supported by Mr. Trump prevailed in the Republican primary but is now seemingly poised to lose in the general. These candidates supported by Mr. Trump all seem to have drunk the "2020 election was stolen" Kool-Aid. These candidates stand for little beyond fighting over 2020, demanding an investigation of Hunter Biden, demanding prosecutorial vengeance of some kind, and being both antigovernment and antiregulation on an indiscriminate scale. It is almost all anger driven; there seems little recognition that not all regulation and not all government is the enemy, and yet these Trump-backed candidates and others have no unified platform to point to and few promises to keep that would address the major economic problems of the day (other than closing the southern border). Almost as bad, politically, GOP candidates seem to have lost their talent for framing issues and policies (and there are many) that, sensibly advanced in any normal time by conservatives, would warrant a massive midterm blowout for the out-of-power party in the House and the Senate.

Key elections are those in:

Georgia (Trump-backed Georgia football star Herschel Walker is behind in the polls);

Pennsylvania (Trump-backed Dr. Oz is way behind in the polls to a Democrat who recently suffered a stroke and is barely even campaigning for want of much ability to hear or speak);

Nevada (Trump-backed Adam Laxalt polling far behind the Democrat at the moment);

Arizona (Trump-backed Blake Masters has been consistently behind in the polls since winning the primary).

To be sure, Trump-backed bestselling author J. D. Vance is ahead in Ohio, but Marco Rubio in Florida has fallen behind Val Demings 48%–44%. This might not be attributable to the "Trump Effect," but it certainly is consistent with a general weakness impacting all Republicans, both MAGA and others.

This brings me to the Mar-a-Lago "raid" and the day and night analysis and commentary about what laws Mr. Trump may have violated and so on. The power of Mr. Trump to make and break Republican candidates, especially in primaries, makes Republican politicians fearful of him. This is probably why so many Republicans do not know which way to jump in reaction to the entire Mar-a-Lago brouhaha. At first, the uniform response from the MAGA Republicans was to attack the Justice Department. And this seemed to get some traction, even in the mainstream media. But Trump's reaction to things, and the leaking of considerable information out of the administration, brought a considerable level of ambiguity into the mix.

However, the defenders of Mr. Trump were somewhat silenced last week when the pictures of top-secret materials found at Mar-a-Lago were published.[238] These were pictures of scores of documents that Mr. Trump claimed he had returned to the government and said that he did not have at his home. And so, while the statutes mentioned in the affidavit in support of the search warrant may not have been threatening, Trump's own recent conduct gives plausibility to the notion that he has been obstructing justice. I am not now suggesting that such a charge should be made (or that such a charge should not be made, although that might be a matter of prosecutorial discretion). But I am suggesting that between the January 6 hearings and the Mar-a-Lago search warrant, the Democrats have succeeded in keeping Trump and some of his most odious features front and center nearly every day for the entire summer. It may be that the search warrant was executed to achieve just this political goal, but it is just as likely that Trump, being all about Trump, tried to control an anti administration narrative, failed miserably to keep the focus on the administration's weaknesses, but instead allowed the administration and the media to keep the focus intensely and constantly on the weaknesses of Mr. Trump and his advisers. As the pundits remind us every couple of years, elections are won in November not in August. But they can be lost in August, and the Republicans seem to be doing their level best to extract defeat from the jaws of victory through political malpractice.

On top of all of that, the Biden administration seems to be demonstrating an unexpected degree of competence in making things happen that are generally popular. Moreover, for reasons that cannot be credited to any action or a policy undertaken by the Biden administration (although the administration will claim otherwise and that their release of millions and millions of gallons from the national reserve was a big factor), gas prices have been plunging all summer long (down more than 25% from highs of more than $5 per gallon), and so high gas prices have largely disappeared as a political talking point. The administration's energy policy would be a good target, but there has thus far been no effective GOP message developed.

Last fall, there was the major $1 trillion infrastructure bill, which was genuinely bipartisan (19 Senate Republicans and 13 House GOP members voted for it, although most of the MAGA Republicans voted against it and were openly critical of the non-MAGA Republicans who voted for it).

Last month, there was the misnamed Inflation Reduction Act. Not a single Republican voted for the act. The nonpartisan Congressional Budget Office has estimated that the deal would have no statistically significant effect on inflation. The real focus of the bill is to lower prescription drug prices, incentivize investment into domestic energy production while permitting clean energy, and add massive resources to the IRS so it can bash "the rich." The law will supposedly raise $737 billion and authorize $369 billion in spending on energy and climate change. The bill will also provide $80 billion to hire thousands of new IRS agents to audit more people so as to collect more taxes, fines, and penalties. The Republican messaging around this legislation also seems to be largely nonexistent. The Democratic messaging is largely limited to ballyhooing the name of the act, but more importantly, focusing upon the supposed decrease in prescription drug prices that will flow like honey from heaven. In these circumstances, there seems to be a fair amount of support for the legislation, even if not particularly well informed.

Also, just last month President Biden announced a program to cancel somewhere between $500 billion and $1 trillion of student debt. This probably cannot lawfully be achieved by executive action, but to my surprise (indeed shock), this is polling well at the moment even though noncollege graduates, college graduates who have paid their debts, and taxpayers in general might be expected to be strongly against such a program on any number of grounds, including the moral hazard problem: the underlying notion that it subsidizes irresponsibility and risk-taking at no cost to the actors and hence encourages such conduct in the future. But the polls, at least for the moment, favor the president on this by something like 52% to 48%. If this holds true (and it ought not to, but we live in interesting times), and if the Republicans are successful in having the executive action held unlawful (and this seems a likely result), the Republicans will end up being the "bad guys" who prevented something popular from happening.

And while bond and equity markets are down more than 20% this year, a special problem for retirees or others on a fixed income given the nearly 9% inflation rate, employment numbers have improved greatly in the last few months damping down the sense that the country is in a recession. According to September BLS data, total nonfarm payroll employment increased by 315,000 during August (although the unemployment rate rose by 0.2 percentage points to 3.7%, still quite a low number). The job numbers for July were even more impressive, with the economy adding some 528,000 jobs. Indeed, job creation since the inception of the Biden administration (slightly more than ten million new jobs), has brought total employment to roughly prepandemic levels, notwithstanding inflation being at a forty-year high. The increase in mortgage rates, which have nearly doubled from slightly over 2% to more than 4.5%), has not yet tanked the housing market although one feels a major market adjustment on the way.

Finally, last Thursday there was the bizarre taxpayer-funded "nonpolitical policy address" given by the president at Independence Hall in Philadelphia. He was bathed in red light and surrounded by two Marine honor guards. The entire scene was surreal: it made the president look very much like Mussolini in the 1930s. The president referred to MAGA Republicans over and over. He conflated them with the imminent prohibition of gay marriage and the nationwide disappearance of abortion. He characterized them of as representing a "clear and present danger" to democracy and indeed the United States and the Republic for which it stands. He made them enemies of the people and enemies of the country. They were characterized as "semi-Nazis" and evil. The administration, echoed and amplified by the media, has been accusing Republicans in general and Mr. Trump in particular of "breaking norms" in dangerous anti-Democratic ways that threatened the constitutional order. Yet that speech was something that not even Mr. Trump ever attempted. The speech was itself norm breaking in the extreme. The mainstream media seems to have applauded it as revelatory. But as Ross Douthat pointed out in the *New York Times*, this speech warning against eroding democratic norms

> ... was delivered a week after Biden's semi-Caesarist announcement of a $500 billion student-loan forgiveness plan without consulting Congress. And it was immediately succeeded by the news that Democrats would be pouring millions in advertising into New Hampshire's Republican Senate primary, in the hopes of making sure that the Trumpiest candidate wins—the latest example of liberal strategists deliberately elevating figures their party and president officially consider an existential threat to the Republic.

So here we are coming out of Labor Day weekend with the deck of cards seemingly reshuffled. By late spring and early summer, the establishment was ready to get past Biden one way or another. He was too old, too infirm, too ineffective, and so on. Now, suddenly, he and the Democrats have the wind at their back, the press again on their side, and the Republicans on their back foot. The Democrats have also raised far more money than the Republicans, and an undue percentage of the Republicans fundraising has been through Mr. Trump's super PAC. Those funds are not being released to the GOP in general but only to a limited number of candidates. So, one wonders whether the GOP has an act that they could ever get together between now and November. They are stuck with a handful of Trump-supported primary winners who seem unnecessarily challenged to win in November. They do not have very much money. They do not seem to appreciate that while Trump and the MAGA Republicans energize a huge number of Republican voters (perhaps even a majority of them), they energize 100% of the Democratic voters and a large percentage of independent voters to show up and vote against Republicans to make sure that Mr. Trump is denied another term as president.

In a September 1 article for *Commentary,* Noah Rothman captured what seems to be happening in his title "This Is the First True Trumpism Election, and Trumpism Is Losing." His core observations are essentially the following:

* The Justice Department's search of the president's Mar-a-Lago residence, and the GOP response to it, has provided voters with a substantive demonstration that the Republican Party is not just a generic vehicle of opposition to Democratic governance. It remains wholly dedicated to Trump's personality cult.
* Republican candidates are not only not "generic" anymore, but the party hasn't spoken with one voice in support of a set of policy preferences. To the extent that GOP lawmakers and office seekers have spoken with one voice on anything over the last several weeks, it has been to express their unequivocal endorsement of Donald Trump on a near daily basis. It is no coincidence that those same several weeks have seen the GOP's support in the polls decline and Democrats outperform expectations at the ballot box.

Lastly, it is important to note that it now feels as if the Democrats are playing the role of Lucy and Republicans that of Charlie Brown in the annual fall ritual of Lucy persuading Charlie Brown to try to kick the football. The analogy might be imperfect, but all of the administration's attacks on Mr. Trump seem to represent the administration trolling the GOP to get Republicans to take the bait of yet again defending Trump, thereby keeping close to him and keeping the focus on him, rather than keeping their focus on the disastrous impact that various Biden administration policies have brought about. As Noah Rothman seems to conclude, the administrations' political advisors have been wildly successful with this tactic.

I might be off the mark, but I have developed the view that until the GOP can shed itself of Mr. Trump and his personal miasma (while maintaining many of his important policies on China, immigration, energy, and aspects of his foreign policy), they might well be doomed to stay in the minority and force the rest of us to live in a world of policy chaos and economic decline for many more years.

30

Our Hugely Interesting 2022 Midterms

November 21, 2022

In the election finally almost concluded, the Biden administration faced hurricane-force headwinds brought on by many things, including notably: (1) the catastrophic departure from Afghanistan; (2) the declaration of war on domestic carbon fuels and the consequent spiking gasoline prices; (3) the flooding of the economy with "free cash" to politically favored groups and the consequent spiking of inflation to rates not seen since the 1970s; (4) the disastrous lack of security on the southern border and the consequential spike in deaths from opioids cum Fentanyl; (5) the toothless criminal law enforcement policies of many urban centers, driving up murders, carjackings, and burglaries; (6) the mishandling of COVID during 2021 and the caving in to the demand for lockdowns from the teachers' unions, with the effect of stunting the educational growth of millions of children; and (7) the panoply of issues surrounding wokeness in schools and elsewhere.

But bucking a nearly century-old trend, instead of receiving the voter punishment expected by most, the administration just about broke even. This was not because the electorate voted to approve the policies that generated these massive headwinds. This was because, contrary to most polling and expectations, the GOP in general, and Donald Trump in particular, handed scores of congressional seats to generic Democrats. The red wave never materialized, except in Florida, although as we shall see, normal Republicans did unusually well beneath the surface.

First, and probably most importantly, with maybe two exceptions, every normal Republican who was primaried by and lost to an ultra MAGA Trumpist candidate watched the Trumpist candidate go down to defeat. The exceptions were J. D. Vance in Ohio and Ted Budd in North Carolina. But even they garnered notably less of the electorate than the successful GOP candidates in their jurisdictions. Here is a list of the Trump-backed losers, all of whom very publicly ran on a platform of 2020 election denial out of obeisance to Trump.

Trump's losing endorsed Senate candidates

- Mehmet Oz—defeated in Pennsylvania by John Fetterman.
- Don Bolduc—defeated in New Hampshire by Sen. Maggie Hassan.
- Blake Masters – defeated in Arizona by Marc Kelley
- Leora Levy—defeated in Connecticut by Richard Blumenthal.
- Gerald Malloy—defeated in Vermont by Peter Welch.
- Herschel Walker—in a runoff against Sen. Warnock on Georgia, anticipating defeat.

Trump's losing endorsed House of Representatives candidates

- Bo Hines—defeated in North Carolina's District 13 by Wiley Nickel.
- Steve Chabot—defeated in Ohio's District 1 by Greg Landsman.
- Madison Gesiotto Gilbert—defeated in Ohio's District 13 by Emilia Sykes.
- John Gibbs—defeated in Michigan District 3 by Hillary Scholten.
- Yesli Vega—defeated in Virginia's District 7 by Abigail Spanberger.
- Karoline Leavitt—defeated in New Hampshire's District 1 by Rep. Chris Pappas.
- J. R. Majewski—defeated in Ohio's District 9 by Marcy Kaptur.
- Sandy Smith—defeated in North Carolina's District 1 by Don Davis.
- Robert Burns—defeated in New Hampshire's District 2 by Ann McLane Kuster.
- Sarah Palin—defeated in Alaska's At-Large District 2 by Mary Petlota.
- Jim Bognet—defeated in Pennsylvania's District 8 by Matt Cartwright.

Trump's losing endorsed gubernatorial candidates

- Keri Lake—lost to Katie Hobbs in the Arizona Gubernatorial race
- Tudor Dixon—lost to Governor Gretchen Whitmer in Michigan.
- Doug Mastriano—lost to Josh Shapiro in Pennsylvania.
- Lee Zeldin—lost to Governor Kathy Hochul in New York.
- Dan Cox—lost to Wes Moore in Maryland.
- Geoff Diehl—lost to Maura Healey in Massachusetts.
- Tim Michels—lost to Governor Tony Evers in Wisconsin.
- Darren Bailey—lost to Governor J. B. Pritzker in Illinois.
- Scott Jensen—lost in Minnesota to Governor Tim Walz.
- Mark Ronchetti—lost in New Mexico to Governor Michelle Lujan Grisham.
- Derek Schmidt—lost in Kansas to Governor Laura Kelly.

There was massive ticket splitting in these elections. Nearly the entire electorate stood up and in virtually one voice said to Trumpist candidates "NO. ENOUGH IS ENOUGH," while leaving regular Republicans unscathed. If you imagine looking at the outcomes via Google Earth and as a video game, the losers were hit by laser beams that hit them and them alone. There was little or no collateral damage. This debacle turned the hat trick for Mr. Trump and made him a certifiable three-time loser: the 2020 presidential election, the loss of both Georgia senate seats (and the senate) in 2021, and now the failure of the GOP to capitalize on the unprecedented weakness of the Biden administration and its slate of candidates. Whether and how the GOP processes this obvious reality will determine much about the next twenty years or more. This is also true of the Democrats.

In the weeks leading up to the election, the Democrats were frequently criticized or mocked for providing millions and millions of dollars to Trump-supported candidates for statewide office or for congressional seats. The party leadership and outside organizations spent almost $19 million across twelve races—five gubernatorial contests, two Senate races, and five congressional races. Separately, Illinois Gov. J. B. Pritzker, a billionaire, spent $9.5 million of his own money, combined with about $25 million from the Democratic Governors Association, to push Darren Bailey, a far-right, Trump-endorsed state senator, during the primary season. Pritzker won the race with an eleven-point lead over Bailey to secure his second term in office, and Bailey conceded.

An analysis by the *Washington Post* found that most of the spending was on advertising, which took one of three tacks: (1) tying a far-right Republican candidate to Trump and the MAGA movement, as Pennsylvania governor-elect Josh Shapiro did with his GOP rival Doug Mastriano in hopes that the MAGA base would turn out in the primaries; (2) attacking the more moderate candidate, as Pritzker did in Illinois; or (3) putting out advertising branding the far-right Republican candidate as "too conservative," as in the Maryland gubernatorial races. All three of these specific tactics were designed to bring out the MAGA bases to ensure the Democratic candidate would face a more beatable ultra-MAGA Republican candidate. These tactics also had plausible deniability. They generally look like they could be attack ads in the context of a general election. But it was the fact that the advertisements ran during primary season that marked them as part of a larger strategy—to give Democrats an easier shot at winning by avoiding a matchup with a much stronger Republican who they considered more electable.

In hindsight, the Democrat strategy paid major dividends and looks like money better spent than a lot of other spending by the Democratic Central Committee. It provided an extraordinary return on investment and may become an interesting feature on both sides of the aisle in the future, with each party funding what they perceive to be unelectable politicians on the other side. Bizarre, frankly. A tactic that should actually be illegal without full disclosure.

It is probably also beyond cavil that Republican absolutism on abortion rights contributed materially to the failure of the GOP to generate more than a red ripple. For political reasons that are not too difficult to grasp, the Republicans are (wrongly) perceived as being against abortion under any circumstances, ever. Yet in some states, they are. Those states become powerful poster children for Democrats to use against Republicans generally, and they did so very effectively. Indeed, five states had referenda on the ballot regarding abortion rights: California, Kentucky, Michigan, Montana, and Vermont. Voters in all five of these states voted in favor of constitutional measures protecting a right to abortion or against legislative measures designed to prohibit or restrict abortion rights. If something quite like the original trimester structure of *Roe v. Wade* were established by statute, we might de-politicize the issue. But so long as absolutists on the left treat infanticide as simply "abortion" (e.g., New York, Oregon) and so long as absolutists on the right treat all abortion as unacceptable (e.g., Alabama, Missouri), the fight will go on without end.

Much less visible, and indeed less clear, was the impact of the Tucker Carlson wing of the Republican Party and its hostility to American support for Ukraine in its war against Russia. This slice of the GOP—the "Natcons," or National Conservatives—is something of an unknown quantity with more of a social agenda than one aimed at particular economic, international, or broad-based governance policy. This is a sometimes-influential group of conservatives but one that spends most of its time opposing things, especially woke progressivism (formerly known as political correctness) in government, the military, education, culture, the media, business, and so on.

Yet, beneath at all, there were some signs of a red rebellion in, of all places, New York, California, Vermont, and other pockets of deep-blue political power. "Normal" (non-Trump-backed) Republicans flipped eighteen congressional seats in some surprising states: Arizona (2), California (1), Florida (3), Georgia (1), Iowa (1), Michigan (1), New York (4!), New Jersey (1), Oregon (1), Texas (1),Virginia (1), and Wisconsin (1). The Democrats, for their part, flipped only eight seats. Just as interesting, Republicans came very close to some massive upsets, most notably the governorship of New York and several elections in Washington state and even in California, where the Los Angeles mayoral election was just called (for the Democrat) within the last couple of days. The observable evidence suggests that these close calls were due to the persistence of high crime in many urban areas ever since 2020 and to a lesser degree inflation and allied economic concerns. And of course, we are seeing recall elections for George Soros–funded progressive prosecutors, and it is hard to imagine most of them being unsuccessful. The recall already succeeded in San Francisco (Chesa Boudin), and others are in the works.

Whether and how the Republicans will process what happened remains to be seen. But the Democrats seem to be processing what happened as if they won a stunning victory. It is worth remembering that just before the recent midterm elections, the mainstream media scribblers, senior Democratic grandees and poohbahs, and major Democratic donors were speaking quietly, and in some cases not so quietly, about how to dump Biden and Harris and the urgent need of doing so. They had about them the stench of aged losers, well past their prime. The party, many said, needed young blood and fresh leadership. The *New York Times* and the *Washington Post* were part of this chorus. They were, of course, expecting a shellacking in the midterms. They were all engaging in what *Commentary* magazine's John Podhoretz has coined as "precriminations." They were even sounding like Republicans in lambasting the administration for inflation, crime, woke policies, and such. But presto chango, because of the Biden "success" (if one can call it that, as opposed to the GOP failure) in the midterms, Biden is riding high and seems committed, even though he just turned eighty, to running for a second term in two years. The chorus of precriminations has become silent, and instead, the Democratic apparatchiks and cognoscenti seem to be salivating, for the moment, at the prospect of a Trump candidacy.

Having dodged a Trumpist bullet, they suddenly think they can dodge all bullets, like the character Neo in *The Matrix* and are hence near immortal. This could be a disastrous misreading of the electorate. Then there is the appointment of a new Special Counsel. It is hard to read the tea leaves, but this could be a catastrophe for the Democrats if it drives the Republicans away from Mr. Trump. Surely it was intended to do the opposite: to solidify support for Mr. Trump and weaken support for stronger opponents such as Mr. DeSantis thus permitting Mr. Biden to have a presidential contest against the only Republican he could defeat.

In all events, unlike the Republicans (and as I wrote a few weeks ago), the Democrats have a tricky billiard shot up their sleeve that could serve as an emergency parachute: (1) Kamala Harris is persuaded to take a lifetime federal judgeship or a multimillion-dollar-a-year job working for George Soros; (2) President Biden appoints a vice president, somebody with demonstrated voter appeal (perhaps Gavin Newsome, governor of California); (3) in early 2024, Mr. Biden resigns on health grounds, explaining that he wants to spend more time with his family; (4) the vice president (Mr. Newsome, say) is sworn in as president (he maybe even issues a pardon for Mr. Biden); (5) Mr. Newsome appoints as vice president a woman, a woman of color, a man of color, or some other person no Democrat could vote against and who some Independents (or even moderate Republicans) could vote for. Voilà! The Democratic ticket is established early in 2024, and there is no need for troublesome fractious primaries or the expenditure of billions of dollars.

Back in the real world of the present, it remains to be seen whether Kevin McCarthy has anything close to the skills of Nancy Pelosi to hold together his raucous Republican Caucus or to devise a legislative agenda that would capture votes while serving the public interest. I would wager that Kevin McCarthy will be a weak and ineffective House Speaker, unable to control the Republican Caucus and unable to resist spending two years investigating Hunter Biden, Joe Biden's connection with monies brought in by Hunter

Biden, the FBI, and other things political and vengeful. While some topics might be worthy of House investigations (for me it would be the Afghanistan debacle and maybe the Fauci/China connection) one doubts that the GOP leadership is capable of stopping the cycle of political vengeance and trying to focus instead on the vital business of the people, including the topics detailed below.

So, with Mr. Trump last week having announced his candidacy, and with Florida's governor Ron DeSantis looking like the winner Mr. Trump has always claimed to be, we are in for an interesting time. One can read about all this in most any newspaper or in any Twitter feed. So, I will poke around for a moment in the shadows. First of all, Trump's announcement so early in the game seems to me to carry a bit of danger for him and great opportunity for the GOP as a whole. Having become a declared candidate, he has certain reporting obligations for each quarter. Among those obligations is to report contributions. One wonders whether he will get many contributions. If he does not, then there is the risk of public humiliation through loss of financial support. It seems unlikely that he would put any meaningful amount of his own money into his campaign.

Secondly, the one attack made upon Governor DeSantis by Mr. Trump seems to have backfired, and Mr. DeSantis seems to have the self-discipline, much lacking in Mr. Trump, to ignore Trump's insults and to respond softly while carrying a big stick. His response last week was as simple as it was elegant and probably quite effective. When asked to respond to Trump's criticism and characterization of him as Ron DeSanctimonious, DeSantis quietly shrugged and said that as one who has run for office several times he was accustomed to criticism from opponents, the press, the networks, and that it was all just noise that came with the territory. But, he added, if one wished to compare him with others, "at the end of the day, I would just tell people to go check out the scoreboard from last Tuesday night." This was a brilliant answer, lumping Trump in with the media, not mentioning his name, and just pointing to the Florida outcome, where DeSantis carried every county including Miami-Dade County, which had not been carried by a Republican for a hundred years.

But back to the next election. If the GOP expects to reform itself in time to be competitive in 2024, the party leadership needs to come to grips with many realities, among them:

1. Trump is doubtless the only Republican candidate who could lose to Biden in 2024. Therefore, the party must find a way to get him away from the public eye and out of the public mind without alienating most of his base.

2. There are literally dozens of strong non-Trump Republican candidates as sitting or former governors (Abbott, DeSantis DeWine, Haley, Hogan, and Youngkin, for example) as well as present and former senators and members of Congress in the House who could be attractive to most Republicans, most Independents, and some Democrats. The GOP has a deep and strong bench if Trump is certifiably out of the picture. If he is on the ballot, the GOP should expect another defeat.

3. There are very few notable Democratic candidates waiting in the wings to take over from Biden, Pelosi, and Schumer. The Democratic Party has a shallow and weak bench. There is not any Democrat who would seriously say that Kamala Harris could be a viable candidate for anything.

4. The GOP is very good at opposing things, but it has proved terrible when governing at the national level. The party needs to stop looking in the rearview mirror, complaining about the past, and trying to get even. It needs to provide the country with its vision of a sustainable and positive future. Among many other things, this means:

    a. Addressing the immigration fiasco with a program that could in fact be implemented. Achieving border security, implementing a path to legal citizenship, and creating a priority immigration system that matches immigrants with national needs would be three main pillars of an achievable immigration policy.

    b. Addressing economic policy in a way that does not mean just lowering taxes. I have been stunned, frankly, to see that some 53% of the people polled seem to approve of the student debt "forgiveness." One suspects that the polling question itself may have been loaded and failed to disclose that we the taxpayers would bear the burden of the hundreds of billions of dollars of debt transfer. A GOP-controlled Congress would be wise to enact legislation that would prevent the executive branch from doling out such political favors without congressional approval. It is certainly difficult for me to see the tuition "forgiveness" scheme as anything more than a vote buying gambit aimed at young people increasingly feeling entitled to "free stuff."

Yet student debt is a problem worthy of being addressed and the GOP could address it in any number of sensible ways. For example, national service, military or otherwise, could be a condition of debt relief with the length of time in service bearing some objective relationship to the amount of debt canceled. Another approach, as I have previously written, would be to permit student debt to be discharged in bankruptcy, which is not now the case. Moreover, if students declare bankruptcy with outstanding student debt, the colleges and universities who took the money ought to bear some responsibility for repayment of a material portion of the debt. The student debt problem is just a symptom. The more serious problem is that the cost of tuition, room, and board has far outstripped the inflation rate for the last sixty years.

c. Unleashing American industry to provide oil and gas for the country to become independent and able to supply much of Europe with oil and gas. The idea that we can make and power electric vehicles and create the necessary infrastructure by fiat and diktat is and has always been a progressive pipedream. This would do much to contain inflation and bring the country back to prepandemic normal. It would also back off from the phony crony capitalism of the Democratic Party, which has always been inclined away from free markets and toward industrial engineering with a strong flavor of central planning.

In this connection, I have found it beyond offensive that the president, without the approval of Congress, has used up most of the American strategic petroleum reserve purely for the political purpose of trying to bring down gasoline prices in the weeks and months preceding the midterm elections. The strategic petroleum reserve is intended for use in wartime or other such critical circumstances. The GOP would be wise to pass a law making it impossible for the sitting president to release fuel from the strategic petroleum reserve during peacetime without some form of congressional approval.

d. Making a serious effort to confront the somewhat frightening international landscape, including China (with a newly empowered dictator in charge) with its designs on Taiwan, Russia with its designs on Ukraine, North Korea with its designs on who knows what, and other autocracies in Europe, Asia, and South America. One has a sense (or at least I have the sense) that neither the Democratic Party nor the Republican Party have given serious attention to these matters for quite some time, putting Ukraine aside for a moment. It would be an extraordinarily refreshing change to see a GOP with a foreign (and military) policy designed to deter aggression rather than one designed mainly or only to react to it.

One vital but obscure example where action is needed has to do with tactical nuclear weapons. Years ago, pursuant to a treaty with the USSR, the United States agreed to eliminate most of its tactical nuclear weapons. The USSR agreed as well. The United States complied with the agreement. The Soviet Union did not. One result is that Russia today has some two thousand tactical nuclear weapons at its disposal, while the United States has slightly more than two hundred. This imbalance becomes especially interesting and risky, for example, given the situation in Ukraine. The ten-to-one imbalance could well tempt Russia into utilizing such weapons in Ukraine, especially given the absence of a reliable US delivery system for tactical nuclear weapons.

e. Finding a way to bring our schools and colleges back to teaching and to draw them away from indoctrination. There is of course a fine line between these things, but it is a line that should be drawn and respected. The increasing trend away from objective standards (such as the SATs and other such tests) is concerning. Once objective standards disappear, one worries that merit might, too. The role of government in creating objective standards is difficult and tricky, especially inasmuch as it collides with various flavors of affirmative action. But a society that has no objective standards becomes a society that has few standards at all, and this is something most people should be concerned about, especially the GOP.

f. It has been painful for me, as a veteran, to see so many trillions of dollars frittered away for reasons that are either not readily apparent or that are overtly political. The COVID relief program threw money at people young and old indiscriminately. Yet we have a population of wounded veterans that, according to various internet sources, numbers around two million people. A GOP program to provide special care, in some cases by providing suitable housing, to disabled veterans, especially amputees, is something that should be seriously considered. We are bombarded almost every night by advertisements asking us to give to the Wounded Warrior Project, the Tunnel to Towers Project, and other such organizations that appear to provide some basic needs for veterans who seem worthy of them. It strikes me that it should be far more politically acceptable to both Republicans and Democrats that these people who have served and been grievously injured should be the object of our bounty before we give $800 billion to students who chose to borrow money to go to college and have not served the country at all.

Extra Credit Reading

Christopher DeMuth published a brilliant article in the November 18 issue of the *Wall Street Journal* entitled "America's Right Confronts the 21st Century."[239] It is a trenchant analysis of the origins of political conservatism, its development, its essential purposes, and a short to-do list suited to serving those purposes. It is behind a paywall, so apologies for that.

Matt Taibbi's November 19 article on Substack provides an original and entertaining view of both Trump and the left entitled "No, *New York Times*, You Don't "Deserve Better" Than Donald Trump."[240] I do not think this is behind a paywall, and it is both short and entertaining. The subtitle is "Trump Should Spare Us All and Retire. But His Antagonists' Lack of Self-awareness Keeps Giving Him Oxygen." As a bonus, embedded in the article is a clip (2:20) of Dave Chapelle doing a riff on why Trump was so popular in the early days. It is quite priceless and very much on the money.

Today (November 22) brings an excellent, albeit for some controversial, article in *Common Sense*, the Substack publication run by Bari Weiss: "Bill Barr: Trump Will Burn Down the GOP. Time for New Leadership."[241]

31

A Year of Dark Clouds, Silver Linings, and Mysteries

January 10, 2023

As Dave Barry said in introducing his 2022 Year in Review: "The best thing we can say about 2022 is: It could have been worse."

> For example, we could have had nuclear Armageddon. This briefly appeared to be a possibility, at least according to the President, who broke the news in October at (Why not?) a Democratic Party fundraiser at the home of a wealthy donor in New York City. That must have been an exciting event! One moment everybody's standing around chewing hors d'oeuvres, and the next moment WHOA WHAT DID HE JUST SAY?
>
> The next day, after the news media ran a bunch of scary headlines, the White House Office of Explaining What the President Actually Meant explained that the president wasn't suggesting that we were facing Armageddon per se, but was merely, as is his wont, emitting words, one of which happened to be "Armageddon."

No year, and this has been especially true of recent years, should end without lifting a glass to Dave Barry and his ability to find humor in all things.[242]

The year 2022 may have been mostly bad in many ways, but there were some significant silver linings in some of the dark clouds, and I touch upon them in no special order other than as they occur to me.

Russia and Ukraine.

The first war in Europe since 1937–38 is no small thing. In a sense it was not a surprise. Russia, under Putin, had been nibbling at the fringes of NATO for many years, including incursions into Estonia, Georgia, the seizing of Crimea, and incursions into the Donbas region in eastern Ukraine. Then came the Biden catastrophe in Afghanistan. I am not speaking of the incompetence of the execution of the withdrawal but the decision to withdraw at all and to abandon billions of dollars of weaponry, along with the most strategically important real estate in all of central Asia: Bagram Air Force Base. That event, as I wrote at the time (see Chapter 21), invited aggressive mischief on the part of Russia, China, and Iran, among others. And aggressive mischief is what we got.

It is not difficult to imagine, and I expect it is true, that Mr. Putin (and Xi Jinping in China, too) had reasonably reached the conclusion that the West was a rotten structure preoccupied with national fringe issues and lacking the resources or will to stand up against consistent but limited aggression in eastern Europe. Angela Merkel and other European leaders, not to mention Presidents Bush, Obama, and Trump, had all preappeased Mr. Putin consistently from the beginning of this century. Thus, when Putin's large-scale invasion actually came, supported by his mini-me Alexander Lukashenko from Belarus, the political class in this country and elsewhere presumed that the invasion would take a matter of weeks, if not days.

At the outset, there was no sentiment to do very much and certainly not to send any American money or troops to die for the Donbas. But what we saw on our television screens and our media, no matter what news silo we inhabited, was as extraordinary as it was unexpected. Inspired by the leadership of Mr. Zelensky and the heroics of the Ukrainian citizenry, we witnessed the relatively rapid unification of NATO; the renewed commitment of NATO members large and small to the founding principles of NATO; the expansion of NATO shortly to include Finland and Sweden; increases in military budgets throughout the NATO territories (and in Japan and South Korea, too);

and an overall strengthening in general of the NATO alliance. The support for Ukraine, while slow to develop, and almost certainly more limited than it should have been even today, nonetheless sent a strong message not only to Russia but also to China and Iran that the West had stopped sleepwalking.

Indeed, the failure of the Russian military across the entire battlefront exposed not the rot of the West, but the rot, corruption, and incompetence of the Russian military. It is Russia that proved to be the paper tiger, not the United States and the West. This is not to say that Russia cannot prevail in the end against Ukraine should the West continue to withhold more effective weaponry that could reach into Russian staging areas inside of Russia itself. Even so, the world is in a different and better place because of the West's response to Russia.

To be sure, the internal politics of the war and the national response to it have exposed some strange bedfellows, most notably the far right and the far left both aligning themselves with an anti-Ukraine/pro-Russia message. Indeed, it has been shocking to watch people like Tucker Carlson and others on Fox News align themselves with Russia in this war. And as a commentary by Adrian Karatnycky published by the *Wall Street Journal* in early January 2023 revealed, Russia's airwaves are no longer free of supporting US voices, with clips by Ukraine critics such as Tulsi Gabbard, Tucker Carlson, and Representative Marjorie Taylor Greene. But more surprising are the appearances of various establishment figures, including Columbia University economist Jeffrey Sachs; the National Interest's former national security correspondent, Mark Episkopos; and Dimitri Simes, until recently president of the Center for the National Interest. All three of these men appear on the programs of what the *Wall Street Journal* commentary calls Russia's most odious state propagandist, Vladimir Solovyov, and generally support not just Russia but the very rationale advanced by Russian nationalists for the "special military operation" in Ukraine.

China.

The Having mishandled COVID by avoiding any vaccinations and engaging in massive lockdowns for nearly three years now, Xi Jinping has throttled the Chinese economy in the midst of the largest military buildup the world was ever seen. And in the face of a powerless United States and Europe, China simply took over Hong Kong with barely a peep from the West, just as it expects eventually to take over Taiwan. China has also been overtly supporting the Russian war against Ukraine, although as Russia has proved itself incompetent and Ukraine has proved itself highly competent and heroic, the Chinese support has become increasingly muted.

To back up just a bit, on the eve of having himself proclaimed emperor for life, so to speak, Xi Jinping was gifted by President Biden with the Afghanistan withdrawal, thus signaling a lack of will on the part of the United States to maintain or exercise power in Asia. For several weeks, right up until the beginning of Russia's humiliation at the hands of Ukraine, China seemed poised to follow the lead of Russia and simply take over Taiwan straightaway. One suspects that the American and Western response to the Russian invasion of Ukraine preempted such Chinese adventurism, at least for now.

Yet President Biden and the entire domestic foreign policy establishment maintain our incoherent "One China" policy, a policy that itself suggests a US willingness to see the People's Republic of China take over the Republic of China, even by force eventually. But for now, the silver lining is that China is in economic trouble; the United States and its major corporations have "discovered" the perils of a supply chain dominated by a dictatorship as to which companies, and indeed nations, have little or no negotiating power, and whose government has interests that are materially adverse to those of the United States.

In short, China is finally being recognized as a longer-term and more challenging threat to the United States and the West than Russia or any other country. One senses that the foreign policy establishment and the political classes have finally recognized that seeking to bring China and Russia into the international order through economic integration might have been in certain respects a fool's errand.

The Midterm Elections and the Aftermath

My last column took on the subject pretty extensively, so I will be shorter than usual. The bad news is that the Republicans supposedly "took control" of the House of Representatives by a minuscule margin of four seats. But the good news is that the center of the bell curve in this country rejected the crazies on the right overwhelmingly and with laser-like precision. Suburban voters, independent voters, and moderate Republican voters all said no to Trump and most of his acolytes and dependents. Trump is now a certifiable loser in many dimensions including but not limited to: the 2020 election; his potentially treasonous involvement in the January 6, 2021 assault on the Capitol, the Republican loss of the Senate in 2020, the Republican loss of the Senate in 2022, the near-Republican loss of the House of Representatives in 2022, his theft of documents from the White House and transport of them to Mar-a-Lago, his dinner with Kanye West and Mick Fuentes (both raging antisemites), and his legal woes piling up like sand in the desert.

Right up until the midterm elections, much of the GOP feared his ability to mobilize his base against them in primaries. But the electoral catastrophes (for Republicans) of 2020 and 2022 have perhaps finally caused the GOP to wake up to the real-world consequences of being in bed with Donald Trump. As my mother said long ago (and maybe yours did, too): if you lie down with dogs, you get up with fleas. With any luck, the GOP will take less than a generation or two to recover from Donald Trump. The left should not take too much comfort in the public exposure of Republican incompetence and nihilism. Should the Democratic Party persist in its strong tilt to progressive radicalism in all facets of business regulation and in the regulation of personal conduct, the Democratic Party will have its own problem of comparable and perhaps even greater magnitude. They really are, for example, coming after your gas stove.

As to the four-day drama relating to the election of Kevin McCarthy as Speaker of the House, suffice it to say that what he gave away in negotiations with the crazies of the radical right makes the House Speakership itself powerless and almost ceremonial. Still, these are interesting times for watchers of politics and policy. The Democrats are very good at governing but govern through policies that are anathema to many people and to many segments of the economy. Democratic economic policies and behavioral policies are nothing if not autocratic and antidemocratic. These policies have trickled down not just to the universities but also to corporate America—and they are dangerous. The animating principles seem to have at their center the spending of vast sums of money on favored identity groups in the hope of buying votes sufficient to keep the game going.

Conversely, absent a strong Republican president, the Republican Party seems incapable of actual governance and seems to revel more naturally in performance politics designed to gain reelection but not designed to advance any useful national policies. This is partly because the right-of-center coalition in this country has no vision of government as to which there is either conference or consensus. As a matter of prurient interest, it might be fascinating to watch all of the investigations that the Republican House has in mind, but it is hard to imagine that those investigations (with a thimbleful of exceptions) will do much to advance the national interest.

In the end, Kevin McCarthy will prove to be no Nancy Pelosi. He will not be able to command the fealty of his thin majority to achieve material legislative success the way Ms. Pelosi did. Like her or not, it is Ms. Pelosi who will go down in history is one of the most accomplished people ever to hold the job of House Speaker, whereas Mr. McCarthy will be unremembered by history other than being a historical footnote by virtue of going through some fifteen ballots to procure the job. George Santos, who invented an entire fictional persona to win a Republican congressional seat on Long Island, is likely to be more remembered by history than Kevin McCarthy.

Iran and China (Again).

One of the most amazing events of 2022 was observing the people of China and Iran rising up against their leaders in circumstances that may well bring about the execution of many of them. These Chinese and Iranians have demonstrated the type of large-scale bravery that has not been seen in this country since the 1960s or so. The bravery of these dissidents is comparable to the bravery we have been privileged to witness on the part of the citizens of Ukraine. They may not succeed in the end, but to watch people yearning for a measure of freedom and liberty against the state machinery of China and the theocratic machinery of Iran is stirring.

It is beyond sad that the people in this country do not appreciate their liberties and freedoms. One cannot help but take note of the fact that so many in this country seem to be engaged in various flavors of loathing. Yet many citizens throughout the rest of the world look to the United States as a symbol of the freedom and liberty for which they are willing to die. But here in America, this national loathing, class loathing, race loathing, gender loathing, self-loathing, and other loathing is quite capable of destroying irreparably the fabric of the country. We are in urgent need of a leader capable of understanding all of this and gaining a leadership position through actions in the national interest rather than through actions in the interest of one or two national factions.

Power and Energy—Fusion.

I might be burying the lede here, but perhaps the most important event of the last five hundred years may have gotten lost in the shuffle of all of the breathless news about Harry, Meghan, the Kardashians, and the other woke and not woke things that capture the national attention for a minute or two at a time. I am speaking of the successful nuclear fusion experiment at Livermore Labs in California. That experiment proved that for a fraction of a second bombarding a single hydrogen isotope with more than 190 laser beams produced more energy from hydrogen fusion that it consumed. This is the very reaction that powers the sun and the hydrogen bomb and yet energy produced by nuclear fusion is clean, so inexpensive that it need hardly be metered, and capable of transforming the world even more than the transformation of the world that occurred when steam engines and carbon fuels provided the power to replace animals and humans as sources of power. Ever since World War II scientists have been exploring nuclear fusion as an energy source. It is long been said in the industry that "fusion is the energy of the future… And always will be." Maybe during the lives of some living souls, that line will no longer be a joke.

It may take many decades to commercialize the technique but at some point, perhaps even during this very century, it will come into existence and transform life on this planet in ways that truly cannot be imagined.

Power and Energy—Carbon Fuels and Electricity.

I bought an electric vehicle three years ago; I sold it three weeks ago. It had eight thousand miles on it and was a wonderful car. Yet it opened my eyes to the absolute recklessness of national policies here and elsewhere basically mandating electric vehicles, subsidizing electric vehicles, and all but prohibiting gasoline or diesel-powered vehicles. During my three years of owning an electric vehicle I came to realize a few things. First, one cannot drive a long distance with confidence. The maximum range is something like 270 miles. In very cold weather it is half of that. The super-charging stations one finds here and there take at least thirty minutes to charge the battery but only up to 80%. And they do not always work, either, or there is a long line of cars waiting.

But second, and more important than mere inconvenience is the reality that the electric grid in this country has nothing close to the capacity to charge all of the electric vehicles that the Biden administration is effectively mandating over the next decade. It would take trillions of dollars of public or private investment to re-create a far more robust electric grid. The cost of doing this would include an unknown but extraordinary environmental cost. Moreover, some of the raw materials required to build out the grid, to make electric cars, and to make batteries, are in short supply at the moment and are supplied mainly by China or in many cases by countries using child labor to extract the raw materials.

Third, the political forces behind electric vehicles are for the most part naïve and engaging in performance politics and virtue signaling more than sensible economic or industrial policy. Those forces also ignore that electricity is created in this country almost exclusively by carbon fuels, so there is a kind of bait-and-switch feature to the EV sing-along chorus. Nuclear fusion may change all this in the long run, but for now, the administration's policies are selling a slow-motion disaster.

Tesla, which makes the overwhelming majority of electric vehicles sold in this country, has its own proprietary charging network—which, by all accounts, is far superior to the not-very-robust charging network available to all other EV producers. I do not provide financial or investment advice, but I personally would not hesitate to invest in Tesla or Elon Musk in general (Twitter notwithstanding), or in the producers focusing on plug-in hybrids work that use a technology not unlike the Prius that permits batteries to be charged while driving. But I would sell short and bet against those gasoline car producers who are betting the farm on electric vehicles and getting largely out of the production of gasoline- powered vehicles. Recent comments of Toyota's CEO are congruent with this view.[243]

It is well beyond the scope of this article to take on the boneheaded policies of the Biden administration with regard to carbon fuels in general. Suffice it for the moment simply to say that it should be unlawful to use millions of gallons of the country's emergency strategic oil reserve for the purpose of temporarily bringing down the price of gasoline on the eve of an important election. The emergency oil reserve of this nation is not intended to be reserved for political emergencies but for emergencies of a more urgent national character, such as war. It is also execrable that the administration's policies with respect to oil and gas were themselves responsible for the enormous increase in price (not to mention triggering an inflation rate not seen in fifty years) that were then temporarily mitigated for political reasons through use of the strategic reserve. Carbon fuel prices are on the rise again, which should be a surprise to nobody who is paying attention. It is too bad that neither party has the common sense or courage to do the one thing that would make enormous sense, and that nearly all other democratic countries have done: impose a carbon tax.

The Economy and the Markets.

I will be the first to admit that I do not understand what is going on with the equity and bond markets on the one hand and the real economy on the other. My retirement assets are down since January 1, 2022, by around 23% or so, a slight improvement over last month. I refinanced a mortgage for 1.62% on December 27, 2021. Mortgage rates today are around 7%. Inflation is running at a little more than that on an annual basis.

Yet down on the ground, unemployment stands at less than 3.5%, a historic low. Nearly half a million jobs were created during the month of December 2022. I am old enough to have lived through the 1970s and early 1980s when mortgage rates hit 18% or so, and a 9% mortgage was a "good deal." But this does not feel like the 1970s or early 1980s. In the best case, perhaps there will be no recession or a very mild recession in 2023, followed by a robust recovery. I wish I knew.

Bernie Madoff and Sam Bankman-Fried.

Not much to say here except that I just watched the four-part Netflix series on Bernie Madoff, which is very good. His arrest in December of 2008 capped that awful financial collapse, one even worse than what we have seen this year. The Netflix series was timed almost perfectly to be a foil to the Sam Bankman-Fried conundrum. Madoff was a respected icon of Wall Street for decades. His life and downfall were Shakesperean in dimension inasmuch as he was turned in by his sons, one of whom thereafter committed suicide. The other died of cancer while Madoff was in jail. His wife was estranged from him most of the time he was in prison, and several of those who ran the funds that fed him the Ponzi dollars also committed suicide or otherwise came to a tragic (even if deserved) end.

Sam Bankman-Fried, or "SBF" as he likes to call himself, is a thirty-year-old little boy who had a net worth of $26 billion before it all disappeared into thin air leaving his (mostly very wealthy) investors holding the bag. Nobody seems yet to understand how this could have happened. In the same way that Bernie Madoff was a symbol of the excesses of his time, so is SBF a symbol of the regulatory and political dysfunction of his time. And the fact that he made (and lost) his billions on a technology (cryptocurrency) that almost nobody understands seems also emblematic of our confusing digital era.

32

Forward to the Past with the GOP

March 7, 2023

Since shortly after the midterm elections of last November, I have been ruminating about the Republican Party, what it stands for, and whether it has or deserves to have a future in anything resembling its current form. But last month I stumbled across two very different reviews (one from the *Wall Street Journal*, the other from *New York Times*) of a new book: *The Ghost at the Feast,* by Robert Kagan. These prompted me to peruse the book itself, although I have by no means plowed through it all yet. But these modest readings did focus me on the eerie parallels between the GOP now and the GOP a century ago. Those parallels do not auger well for the future of the GOP.

 At the beginning of the twentieth century, the United States kept largely to itself notwithstanding that it had become, over the prior century, the pre-eminent economic power in the world. It possessed the economic strength of several of its rivals combined. And while its rivals had huge standing armies numbering in the millions of soldiers, and very large navies, the United States had a standing army measuring in the tens of thousands and hardly any Navy at all. It stood apart as a distant island in geopolitical terms, on a huge continent surrounded on two sides by vast oceans, thousands of miles from all the other great powers of the world. The Americans' physical location gave them both wealth and a remarkable degree of economic independence. Americans led the world in the production of copper, coal, zinc, iron ore, lead, and other valuable minerals. They produced half of the world's oil and the third of its pig iron, silver, and gold. They had surpassed the British in the production of steel and coal, the two greatest measures of economic power at that time, as well as in industrial manufacturing. The Americans' international passivity (the United States generally declined membership in international bodies and security arrangements) puzzled European leaders. Harold Nicolson, a British diplomat, described the United States as "the ghost at all our feasts," which supplied Kagan with the title for his book.

Americans were also largely self-sufficient and hence did not depend on trade in the same way that European countries did. And while President Teddy Roosevelt was an internationalist and championed the building of the Panama Canal between 1903 and 1914, that was done not just to facilitate free trade internationally but also to facilitate ocean transportation of goods between the West and East Coasts of the United States.

Nonetheless, until the end of the Wilson administration in 1921, the GOP had been the outward looking, internationalist, even imperialist party. Consider, for example, the Spanish-American War and, thereafter, the Philippine-American War to subdue that colony. But that internationalist view of America ended with the onset of American participation in World War I. Woodrow Wilson, a Democrat, was an internationalist thorough and through. His Fourteen Points speech issued in 1918 during the war, his use of those points as the basis for negotiating the Treaty of Versailles, and his creation of the League of Nations all put the United States at the head of an emerging world order.

Yet the GOP reacted to all of this by retreating into fortress America. The leaders of the Republican Party in 1919 wanted nothing to do with the League of Nations. Led by Henry Cabot Lodge, they abruptly aligned themselves with isolationist policies presented most strongly by people like Sen. William Borah, who served as the Republican senator from Idaho from 1907 until 1940 and was Chairman of the Senate Foreign Relations Committee from and after 1924. The isolationism of that era represented the foreign policy stance of the Republican Party, but it was also politically popular in general and operated as a material restraint on the ability or willingness of the Roosevelt administration during the 1930s to become more engaged with England, France, Poland, and other targets of the Hitler regime, especially the Jews of Europe who were essentially ignored even after *Kristallnacht* in the fall of 1938. Indeed, it is not likely wrong to state that then, as now, American foreign policy was driven less by the strategic interests of the United States than by partisan politics. Being against all things foreign has always garnered more votes than it loses. And now, given the extreme polarization of the country, being against all things Obama or Biden has become the defining characteristic of Republican politics and hence Republican policies.

Today we are seeing the splintering of the GOP in ways that harken back a century. A hundred years ago, the GOP was dominated by isolationists, but the "America First" part of the GOP, while isolationist, also was more than tinged with fascism of the type represented by Charles Lindbergh. The America First branch of the GOP, while small, was influential because of Lindbergh. It fulminated in favor of neutrality but sympathized with Hitler and the German Reich. Germany alone, Lindbergh argued, could "dam the Asiatic hordes" and prevent the overrunning of Europe. The GOP was also influenced by Father Coughlin, the sort of Rush Limbaugh of his day, who embraced Lindbergh's message of white supremacy and supported the establishment of the America First Committee in 1940. That group, which numbered almost a million members, opposed American aid to the allies and relied upon Lindbergh and Coughlin to deliver its message to the wider public.

Today, the GOP splinters are most clearly revealed through the prism of the Russian invasion of Ukraine. While I have seen no meaningful polling on this, my sense from what I read is that there are at least these four groups or "lanes" of Republicans:

First, there are those who generally support the current US position vis-à-vis Russia and Ukraine. These seem to represent a strong but steadily declining minority of Republicans. Republicans who take this position do so somewhat quietly since it requires nontrivial support for the Biden administration. This view is that American credibility with other dictators and autocrats depends on doing everything practicable to ensure that Russia does not "win." This view is probably best represented by Brett Stevens, in his recent *New York Times* column (February 28, 2023). Nikki Haley seems to be the only GOP presidential candidate who has come down clearly in favor of support for Ukraine ("This is a war about freedom, not just Ukraine").

Second, there is what appears to be the Trump/Tucker Carlson/MAGA/Glenn Greenwald view that: (1) the war in Ukraine is largely the fault of the United States and the West for allowing NATO to expand eastward and threaten Russia; (2) the United States is dominated by elite military and commercial interests that favor endless wars; and (3) the war-making regime in the United States is morally repellant. Trump has said "that war has to stop, and it has to stop now, it's easy to do." Harking back to President Nixon's "secret plan to end the Vietnam war," Trump says he must keep his solution to himself.

Third, there is the view that the country is urgently in need of an Asia First foreign policy, and we should leave Ukraine to the Europeans so that we can "focus everything on Asia and the defense of Taiwan." Missouri Sen. Josh Hawley is probably the most visible spokesperson for this lane as of this writing but it is a view that seems to be gaining steam even if for all the wrong reasons.

Fourth, there is the view that there should be no "blank check" for Ukraine. Republican Speaker of the House Kevin McCarthy has been making this point, although it is hard to tell whether this is intended as a critique of Mr. Biden for having done just that, or whether it is a placeholder position intended to avoid taking any actual position.

Now, I may have caricatured these groups unfairly, and other variations no doubt exist. I'm also not today flogging any of the views summarized in general or in particular. The larger point here is simply that apparently a majority of the Republicans in this country identify with one or more of the last three groups, which collectively are gaining supporters from the first group. Notably, while the GOP is splintered more or less as described, the Democrats by a margin of some 77% to 23% support the administration's policies in Ukraine. Combined with a minority of Republicans, there is at least for the moment a clear majority in this country who support the US backing of Ukraine.

Former President Trump does not seem to have a coherent view on Ukraine or a coherent set of foreign policy views in general. Governor DeSantis is clearly hedging his bets. While he has engineered a "soft launch" of his presidential campaign, he has been very coy about his position on Ukraine. In the past he expressed strong support for Ukraine, but as the Republican primary voters have drifted away from such support so has DeSantis drifted toward some vague combination of the last three GOP lanes described.

This GOP instinct to withdraw from the world, to be indifferent to matters outside our borders, to disengage as much as possible from other nations so as to be self-sufficient in all important things has a direct link to the 1920s and 1930s. This brings to mind three sayings:

- ★ Those who forget history are condemned to repeat it (George Santayana),
- ★ History repeats itself, first as tragedy and then as farce (Karl Marx); and
- ★ History repeats itself but with differences (Anonymous).

The splintering of the GOP this year, and the rise of a strong isolationist sentiment, could well lead to another four years of Biden and his administration, even should President Biden not personally survive his old age and health issues. And who knows when if ever the MAGA machine will wear out. Perhaps the (as of this writing) seemingly imminent fall of Bakhmut may have an impact on things, but no one event in Ukraine seems to have the capacity to support a hinge movement. And so, as the isolationists and America Firsters of the 1930s generally supported Germany, so today do their twenty-first-century counterparts generally seem to support Russia. In any case, the war in Ukraine is now definitely "Biden's War," and the Republicans seem generally to be as infected by a Biden Derangement Syndrome as were the Democrats infected with their own Trump Derangement Syndrome just a few years ago.

All of this will have immense implications for the next generation. First it could enshrine a relatively progressive Democratic Party, at least in the executive branch, and second, it may result in the withering away of the Republican Party itself, which no longer seems to stand for any particular policies beyond blind opposition to all things Biden and all things woke. Things might change, and there is still a long time between now and the first primaries, but we are still waiting for the adults in the Republican Party, if there are any left, to assert themselves. But so long as Trump wields power sufficient to control much of the Republican agenda, this does not seem likely to happen. It is thus up to the primary voters, whose collective instinct for supporting policies that could win a broad mandate has proved nearly nonexistent over the past few years.

Extra Credit Reading

I am new to Mark Halperin, who puts out a daily email called "Wide World of News." On Saturday he did a short piece on Trump's nearly two-hour stemwinder at the annual Conservative Political Action Committee CPAC conference. Then on Sunday he did an equally short piece critiquing DeSantis's performance in his first "major" speech, which was at the Reagan Center. Spoiler alert: he thinks Trump did way better than expected and that DeSantis did worse than expected. He seems like a thoughtful and nuanced writer.

Last weekend's (March 4, 2023) *Wall Street Journal* interview was really a highly favorable summary and review of Philip Howard's new book *Public Unions vs. The People*. I had not appreciated that all presidents, even the sainted FDR, opposed public unions. It was JFK who legislated them into existence supposedly "as a payback for union support." The book's author, a lawyer, has concluded that the public union problem has become so entrenched that it cannot be solved politically but must be attacked through the courts as an unconstitutional limitation on the executive power to terminate employees, a proposition that has strong constitutional precedent. I was persuaded to buy the book.

ENDNOTES

1. https://www.usdebtclock.org/. The numbers cited were as of September 2019. As of the publication date of this book, the numbers will have changed as the debt clock keeps ticking.
2. Kimberley Amadeo, "US Federal Tax Revenue," *The Balance*, Updated on December 12, 2022, https://www.thebalance.com/current-u-s-federal-government-tax-revenue-3305762
3. Robert Bellafiore, "Latest Federal Income Tax Data 2018 Update," Tax Foundation, November 13, 2018, https://taxfoundation.org/summary-latest-federal-income-tax-data-2018-update/.
4. D'Vera Cohn and Andrea Caumont, "10 Demographic Trends That Are Shaping the US and the World," Pew Research Center, March 31, 2016, https://www.pewresearch.org/fact-tank/2016/03/31/10-demographic-trends-that-are-shaping-the-u-s-and-the-world/.
5. Federal Election Commission, "Election and Voting Information," accessed April 28, 2023, https://www.fec.gov/introduction-campaign-finance/election-and-voting-information/.
6. Justin Song, "Average Cost of College in America," Value Penguin, accessed April 28, 2023, https://www.valuepenguin.com/student-loans/average-cost-of-college#history.
7. Finaid, "Yuition Inflation," Finaid, accessed April 28, 2023, https://finaid.org/savings/tuition-inflation/#targetText=On%20average%2C%20tuition%20tends%20to,the%20child%20matriculates%20in%20college.
8. Anna Helhoski, "How to Take Out Student Loans without Your Parents," Nerd Wallet, July 24, 2020, https://www.nerdwallet.com/article/loans/student-loans/take-student-loans-without-parents.
9. Kimberley Amadeo, "Historical US Unemployment Rate by Year," *The Balance*, December 6, 2022, https://www.thebalance.com/unemployment-rate-by-year-3305506
10. Gloria G. Guzman, "Household Income 2018," United States Census Bureau, September 26, 2019, https://www.census.gov/library/publications/2019/acs/acsbr18-01.html.
11. Ashley Edwards, "Poverty Rate Drops for Third Consecutive Year," United States Census Bureau, September 12, 2018, https://www.census.gov/library/

stories/2018/09/poverty-rate-drops-third-consecutive-year-2017.html#targetText=Poverty%20Rate%20at%2012.3%20Percent%2C%20Down%20From%2014.8%20in%202014&targetText=The%20poverty%20rate%20dropped%20consistently,Economic%20Supplement%20(CPS%20ASEC).

12. Committee for a Responsible Federal Budget, "Analysis of the 2019 Social Security Trustees Report," CRFB, April 22, 2019, https://www.crfb.org/papers/analysis-2019-social-security-trustees-report.

13. Office of the Inspector General, "Review of Four FISA Applications," US Department of Justice, December 2019, https://www.justice.gov/storage/120919-examination.pdf

14. Dave Barry, "Dave Barry's Year in Review 2019," *Washington Post*, December 28, 2019, https://www.washingtonpost.com/magazine/2019/12/29/dave-barrys-year-review/?arc404=true.

15. Craig Whitlock, "At War with the Truth," *Washington Post*, December 9, 2019, https://www.washingtonpost.com/graphics/2019/investigations/afghanistan-papers/afghanistan-war-confidential-documents/.

16. Ross Douthat, Michelle Goldberg, and David Leonhardt, "Why Hasn't Impeachment Changed Minds?," *New York Times*, editorial, December 19, 2019, https://www.nytimes.com/2019/12/19/opinion/the-argument-impeachment-trump-brexit.html.

17. Ross Douthat, "Lies Have Kept Us in Afghanistan," *New York Times*, December 10, 2019, https://www.nytimes.com/2019/12/10/opinion/afghanistan-washington-post.html.

18. Ross Douthat, "Laughing through the Trump Era," *New York Times*, December 17, 2019, https://www.nytimes.com/2019/12/17/opinion/trump-coen-brothers.html.

19. https://www.washingtonpost.com/opinions/2019-was-the-year-of-inequality/2019/12/29/3ebc6f4a-28b9-11ea-9c21-2c2a4d2c2166_story.html?arc404=true

20. Robert J. Samuelson, "Our Lopsided Prosperity," *Washington Post*, December 30, 2019, https://www.washingtonpost.com/lifestyle/style/the-decade-has-ended-but-it-will-never-be-over/2019/12/30/2915636e-1b9d-11ea-8d58-5ac3600967a1_story.html.

21. "The 2010s Were the Decade of…" *Washington Post*, editorial, December 26, 2019, https://www.washingtonpost.com/opinions/2019/12/26/s-were-decade-what-exactly-six-columnists-tell-us/?arc404=true.

22. Ross Douthat, "Decade of Disillusionment," *New York Times*, editorial, December 28, 2019, https://www.nytimes.com/2019/12/28/opinion/sunday/2010s-decade-disillusionment.html

23. Dave Barry, "Dave's Year in Review," davebarry.com, accessed April 28, 2023, https://www.davebarry.com/columns-year-in-review.php.

24. Wikipedia, s.v. "The Closing of the American Mind," accessed April 28, 2023, https://en.wikipedia.org/wiki/The_Closing_of_the_American_Mind.

25 Greg Lukianoff and Jonathan Haidt, "The Coddling of the American Mind," *The Atlantic*, September 2015, https://www.theatlantic.com/magazine/archive/2015/09/the-coddling-of-the-american-mind/399356/.
26 Anthony Kronman, "The Downside of Diversity," *Wall Street Journal*, August 2, 2019, https://www.wsj.com/articles/the-downside-of-diversity-11564758009.
27 Peggy Noonan, "A Progressive Defends Liberal Education," *Wall Street Journal*, August 29, 2019, https://www.wsj.com/articles/a-progressive-defends-liberal-education-11567121394?mod=e2tw.
28 Nicholas Lemann, "Two Views of the Tumult on American Campuses," *New York Times*, August 20, 2019, https://www.nytimes.com/2019/08/20/books/review/assault-on-american-excellence-anthony-kronman.html.
29 US Debt Clock, https://usdebtclock.org/.
30 Eric Boehm, "Most Politicians Are Disingenuous Opportunists," March 25, 2020, https://reason.com/2020/03/25/most-politicians-are-disingenuous-opportunists-the-coronavirus-outbreak-only-makes-that-more-obvious/
31 Wikipedia, s.v. "Qing Dynasty," accessed April 28, 2023, https://en.wikipedia.org/wiki/Qing_dynasty.
32 Lars Jonung and Steve H. Hanke, "Freedom and Sweden's Constitution," *Wall Street Journal*, May 20, 2020, https://www.wsj.com/articles/freedom-and-swedens-constitution-11589993183?emailToken=e244ba05c5effb5d3748e9878353c5a4aWOx-1l4++dq3hB8Fz5wp2UqHDr5AM03spCKajQ/ibP9zKHCODVBTwqxVIrT0rH-8dijmv9p6GMCbIh9wOJukDNQ%3D%3D&reflink=article_email_share.
33 CJ Hopkins, "Virus of Mass Destruction," Consent Factory, Inc., May 4, 2020, https://consentfactory.org/2020/05/04/virus-of-mass-destruction/.
34 Rebeca Ibarra, "'The Death of a City': New York Coty Restaurants Fear the Pandemic Will Wipe Them Out," *Gothamist*, April 25, 2020, https://gothamist.com/food/nyc-restaurants-fear-the-pandemic-will-wipe-them-out.
35 Kate Taylor, "3 Million Out of Work, $25 Billion Lost," Business Insider.com, March 21, 2020, https://www.businessinsider.com/how-coronavirus-devastating-restaurants-across-us-2020-3.
36 "*1984*," CliffsNotes.com, https://www.cliffsnotes.com/literature/n/1984/book-summary.
37 Wikipedia, s.v., "*The Bonfire of the Vanities*," accessed April 28, 2023, https://en.wikipedia.org/wiki/The_Bonfire_of_the_Vanities.
38 Wikipedia, s.v., "Dreyfus Affair," accessed April 28, 2023, https://en.wikipedia.org/wiki/Dreyfus_affair.
39 Wikipedia, s.v., "Reign of Terror," accessed April 28, 2023, ohttps://en.wikipedia.org/wiki/Reign_of_Terror.
40 *Encyclopedia Britannica Online*, s.v., "Committee of Public Safety," accessed April 28, 2023, https://www.britannica.com/topic/Committee-of-Public-Safety.
41 *Encyclopedia Britannica Online*, s.v., "Maximilien Robespierre," https://www.britannica.com/biography/Maximilien-Robespierre.

42 *Encyclopedia Britannica Online*, s.v. "Jaccuse," accessed April 28, 2023, https://www.britannica.com/topic/Jaccuse.

43 Wikipedia, s.v., "Emmet G. Sullivan," accessed April 28, 2023, https://en.wikipedia.org/wiki/Emmet_G._Sullivan.

44 Michael Rubin. "Michael Flynn's Vindication Doesn't Fix His Bad Judgment," AEI.org, May 10, 2020, https://www.aei.org/op-eds/michael-flynns-vindication-doesnt-fix-his-bad-judgment/.

45 Paul Waldman, "Michael Flynn Isn't a Martyr: He's a Crook and a Crackpot," *Washington Post*, May 15, 2020, https://www.washingtonpost.com/opinions/2020/05/15/michael-flynn-isnt-martyr-hes-crook-crackpot/.

46 Wikipedia, s.v., "Schrödinger's cat," accessed April 28, 2023, https://en.wikipedia.org/wiki/Schr%C3%B6dinger's_cat.

47 Dictionary.com, "Cognitive Dissonance," https://www.dictionary.com/browse/cognitive-dissonance.

48 United States Court of Appeals, "On Petition for a Writ of Mandamus to the United States District Court for the District of Columbia," https://www.documentcloud.org/documents/6894721-Petition-Filed.html.

49 Wikipedia, s.v., "All Writs Act," accessed April 28, 2023, https://en.wikipedia.org/wiki/All_Writs_Act.

50 Carol D. Leonnig and Spencer S. Hsu, "Federal Judge Hires High-Powered D.C. Attorney to Defend His Actions in Flynn Case," May 23, 2020, https://www.washingtonpost.com/politics/federal-judge-hires-high-powered-dc-attorney-to-defend-his-actions-in-flynn-case/2020/05/23/9cae4d5e-9d0c-11ea-ac72-3841fc-c9b35f_story.html.

51 See Sophia Ankel, "Pain and Anger: 19 Powerful Photos Show the Fury of US Protests over the Death of George Floyd," Insider.com, May 31, 2020, https://www.insider.com/george-floyd-death-15-powerful-images-of-nationwide-protests-2020-5; and Mike Gonzalez, "For Five Months BLM Protestors Trashed America's Cities: After the Election Things May Only Get Worse," The Heritage Foundation, November 6, 2020, https://www.heritage.org/progressivism/commentary/five-months-blm-protestors-trashed-americas-cities-after-the-election.

52 Wikipedia, s.v., "Watts Riots," accessed April 28, 2023, https://en.wikipedia.org/wiki/Watts_riots

53 Wikipedia, s.v., "1967 Detroit Riots," accessed April 28, 2023, https://en.wikipedia.org/wiki/1967_Detroit_riot.

54 Wikipedia, s.v., "1968 Riots," accessed April 28, 2023, https://en.wikipedia.org/wiki/1968_riots.

55 Wikipedia, s.v., "1992 Los Angeles Riots," accessed April 28, 2023, https://en.wikipedia.org/wiki/1992_Los_Angeles_riots.

56 *Encyclopedia Britannica Online*, s.v., "Commune of Paris 1871," accessed April 28, 2023, https://www.britannica.com/event/Commune-of-Paris-1871.

57 John Daniel Davison, "Monument-Destroying Mobs Don't Hate the Confederacy, They Hate America," *The Federalist*, June 15, 2020, https://thefederalist.

com/2020/06/15/the-monument-destroying-mobs-dont-hate-the-confederacy-they-hate-america/.

58　William McGurn, "Cy Vance's Broken Window," *Wall Street Journal*, June 15, 2020, https://www.wsj.com/articles/cy-vances-broken-window-11592263910?emailToken=877947dea29889a1c86d4d148d757b62q33hskLQbHaBL5i8kCm8osAtLfGlskDi1WLRt3EizEx1q09VY8fZtmt4ESKMou66khX4siMEqj0Cn-5rEsKOKvg%3D%3D&reflink=article_email_share.

59　Mark Judge, "The Ecstasy of the Mob," First Things, December 24, 2019, https://www.firstthings.com/web-exclusives/2019/12/the-ecstasy-of-the-mob.

60　Matt Taibbi, "The American Press Is Destroying Itself," Substack.com, June 12, 2020, https://taibbi.substack.com/p/the-news-media-is-destroying-itself.

61　Andrew Sullivan, "Is there Still Room for Debate," *The Intelligencer*, June 12, 2020, https://nymag.com/intelligencer/2020/06/andrew-sullivan-is-there-still-room-for-debate.html.

62　Yaron Steinbuch, "Claudia Eller, Variety Editor in Chief, Placed on Leave After Twitter Spat," *New York Post*, June 5, 2020, https://nypost.com/2020/06/05/claudia-eller-variety-editor-in-chief-placed-on-leave-after-twitter-spat/?utm_campaign=SocialFlow&utm_source=NYPTwitter&utm_medium=SocialFlow.

63　Tom Cotton, "Send in the Troops," *New York Times*, June 3, 2020, https://www.nytimes.com/2020/06/03/opinion/tom-cotton-protests-military.html.

64　David Marcus, "Tom Cotton Hysteria Shows Cowardice from the *New York Times*," June 5, 2020, https://nypost.com/2020/06/05/tom-cotton-hysteria-shows-cowardice-from-the-new-york-times/.

65　65 Zack Beauchamp, "The *New York Times* Staff Revolt over Tom Cotton's Op-Ed, Explained," June 7, 2020, https://www.vox.com/2020/6/5/21280425/new-york-times-tom-cotton-send-troops-staff-revolt.

66　Tom Cotton, "Send in the Troops," *New York Times*, June 3, 2020, https://www.nytimes.com/2020/06/03/opinion/tom-cotton-protests-military.html.

67　Wesley Lowery, "Why Minneapolis Was the Breaking Point," *The Atlantic*, June 10. 2020, https://www.theatlantic.com/politics/archive/2020/06/wesley-lowery-george-floyd-minneapolis-black-lives/612391/.

68　68 US Debt Clock, https://www.usdebtclock.org/

69　John DeQ. Briggs, "Thinking about Things," *The Chesapeake Observer*, September 17, 2019, https://chesob.org/2019/09/17/thinking-about-things-money-demographics-and-politics/.

70　Lily Batchelder, "Tax the Rich and Their Heirs," *New York Times*, June 24, 2020, https://www.nytimes.com/2020/06/24/opinion/sunday/inheritance-tax-inequality.html.

71　Wikipedia, s.v., "Capital Gains Tax in the United States," accessed April 29, 2023, https://en.wikipedia.org/wiki/Capital_gains_tax_in_the_United_States.

72　"An Overview of Capital Gains Taxes | Tax Foundation," Tax Foundation, February 10, 2023, https://taxfoundation.org/capital-gains-taxes/.

73. Alan Gomez, "Who Are the DACA Dreamers and How Many Are Here?," *USA TODAY*, February 13, 2018, https://www.usatoday.com/story/news/politics/2018/02/13/who-daca-dreamers-and-how-many-here/333045002/.
74. Richard Gonzales, "For 7th Consecutive Year, Visa Overstays Exceeded Illegal Border Crossings," *NPR*, January 17, 2019, https://www.npr.org/2019/01/16/686056668/for-seventh-consecutive-year-visa-overstays-exceeded-illegal-border-crossings.
75. Definition here. *Oxford English Dictionary*, s.v. "Racism," accessed May 19, 2023, https://www.oxfordreference.com/display/10.1093/acref/9780199599868.001.0001/acref-9780199599868-e-1499;jsessionid=D829E2E76152100D612DD255CAC7D914.
76. Definition here. *Merriam-Webster*, s.v. "Determinant," accessed April 29, 2023, https://www.merriam-webster.com/dictionary/determinant.
77. ABC News selection of film clips, https://www.youtube.com/watch?v=eRC9Iuy4gPQ.
78. "Protestors Criticized for Looting Businesses without Forming Private Equity Firm First," *The Onion*, May 28, 2020, https://www.theonion.com/protestors-criticized-for-looting-businesses-without-fo-1843735351.
79. "The Gun Sales of June," *Wall Street Journal*, July 2, 2020, https://www.wsj.com/articles/the-gun-sales-of-june-11593730985?st=xjizepgio2rkmga&reflink=article_email_share.
80. John DeQ. Briggs, "Thinking about Things: The Rise of Law and Decline of Politics," *Chesapeake Observer*, March 3, 2020, https://chesob.org/2020/03/03/thinking-about-things-the-rise-of-law-and-decline-of-politics/.
81. Wikipedia, s.v., "List of Landmark Court Decisions in the United States," accessed April 28, 2023, https://en.wikipedia.org/wiki/List_of_landmark_court_decisions_in_the_United_States#Discrimination_based_on_race_and_ethnicity.WpWiki
82. Wikipedia, s.v., "Greenhouse Effect (United States Supreme Court)," accessed April 29, 2023, https://en.wikipedia.org/wiki/Greenhouse_effect_(United_States_Supreme_Court).
83. Leandra Bernstein, "House Dems Call for Supreme Court Term Limits: Here Are the Pros and Cons," *WJLA*, September 26, 2020, https://wjla.com/news/nation-world/house-dems-call-for-supreme-court-term-limits-here-are-the-pros-and-cons.
84. "Democrats Introduce Unconstitutional Act to Limit the Tenure of Supreme Court Justices," Jonathanturley.org., September 25, 2020, https://jonathanturley.org/2020/09/25/democrats-introduce-unconstitutional-act-to-limit-the-tenure-of-supreme-court-justices/#more-163316.
85. Ronald Brownstein, "Why the Senate Filibuster Could Be Gone in 2021," *The Atlantic*, September 11, 2020, https://www.theatlantic.com/politics/archive/2020/07/why-senate-filibuster-could-be-gone-2021/614278/.
86. "Bobulinski Transcript" Google Search," n.d., https://www.google.com/search?q=-Bobulinski+transcript&sxsrf=ALeKk0156B8H683MsIXshEXZNTQurtjJAQ:1604166008763&ei=eKGdX-6HLq-p_QbE-ZiIAw&start=20&sa=N&ved=2ahUKEwjuo_OIsN_sAhWvVN8KHcQ8BjE4ChDw0wN6BAgFEEM&biw=1244&bih=551.

87. John DeQ. Briggs, "Thinking about Things," *Chesapeake Observer*, June 21, 2020, https://chesob.org/2020/06/20/thinking-about-things/.
88. "NBC Finally Responds To Hunter Biden Story . . . With an Exhaustive Expose of an Unknown and Unrelated Document," Jonathanturley.org., October 31, 2020, https://jonathanturley.org/2020/10/31/nbc-finally-responds-to-hunter-biden-story-with-an-exhaustive-expose-of-an-unknown-and-unrelated-document/.
89. Jeremy B. White, "The Bitter Feud Behind the Law That Could Keep Jared Kushner Out of the White House," POLITICO, November 19, 2016, https://www.politico.com/magazine/story/2016/11/1976-nepotism-law-lyndon-johnson-bobby-kennedy-trump-kushner-214465/.
90. Wikipedia, s.v., "William Barr," accessed April 29, 2023, https://en.wikipedia.org/wiki/William_Barr.
91. Jerry Nadler, "Chairman Nadler Statement on Appointment of U.S. Attorney John Durham as Special Counsel," press release, December 1, 2020, https://nadler.house.gov/news/documentsingle.aspx?DocumentID=394466.
92. Ronn Blitzer, "Adam Schiff Flip-Flops on Special Counsels after Durham Appointment," *Fox News*, December 2, 2020, https://www.foxnews.com/politics/adam-schiff-special-counsel-flip-flop-durham-appointment.
93. "Barr's Appointment of Special Counsel Leaves Biden and Democrats in a Muddle," Jonathanturley.org., December 4, 2020, https://jonathanturley.org/2020/12/04/barrs-appointment-of-special-counsel-leaves-biden-and-democrats-in-a-muddle/.
94. Perry Bacon Jr., "The Cabinet Appointments That Really Matter in the Incoming Biden Administration," *FiveThirtyEight*, November 19, 2020, https://fivethirtyeight.com/features/the-cabinet-appointments-that-really-matter-in-the-incoming-biden-administration/.
95. Dave Barry, "Dave Barry's Year in Review 2020," *Washington Post*, December 27, 2020, https://www.washingtonpost.com/magazine/2020/12/27/dave-barrys-year-review-2020/?arc404=true.
96. Frank Bruni, "Can Joe Biden Make American Politics Decent Again?," *New York Times*, editorial, December 23, 2020, https://www.nytimes.com/2020/12/23/opinion/biden-mcconnell-republicans.html?referringSource=articleShare.
97. "'Treason Is a Matter of Dates': Democrats Denounce Republicans for the Same Challenge They Previously Made to Republican Presidents," Jonathanturley.org., January 1, 2021, https://jonathanturley.org/2021/01/01/treason-is-a-matter-of-dates-boxer-and-democrats-denounce-republicans-for-the-same-challenge-previously-raised-against-republican-presidents/.
98. Chilton Williamson Jr., "The Woke See No Evil—and Nothing but Evil," *Wall Street Journal*, December 25, 2020, https://www.wsj.com/articles/the-woke-see-no-eviland-nothing-but-evil-11608925768?st=26tpmpk6igzj61o&reflink=article_email_share.
99. James Lindsay, "The Woke Breaking Point," *New Discourses*, June 25, 2020, https://newdiscourses.com/2020/06/woke-breaking-point/

100. James Lindsay, "The Woke Make Biden's 'Moderation' Irrelevant," *New Discourses*, March 25, 2021, https://newdiscourses.com/2021/01/woke-make-bidens-moderation-irrelevant/
101. Wikipedia, s.v. "Substack," accessed April 29, 2023, https://en.wikipedia.org/wiki/Substack.
102. Ben Smith, "Why We're Freaking Out about Substack," *New York Times*, editorial, October 5, 2021, https://www.nytimes.com/2021/04/11/business/media/substack-newsletter-competition.html.
103. "De Blasio's Dance and the Delusional Politics Of 2021," Jonathanturley.org., January 4, 2021, https://jonathanturley.org/2021/01/04/de-blasios-dance-and-the-delusional-politics-of-2021/.
104. Jonathan Turley, Muckrack.com, https://muckrack.com/jonathanturley/articles.
105. Wikipedia, s.v., "Andrew Sullivan," accessed April 29, 2023, https://en.wikipedia.org/wiki/Andrew_Sullivan.
106. Andrew Sullivan, "Our Politics And The English Language," June 4, 2021, https://andrewsullivan.substack.com/p/our-politics-and-the-english-language.
107. Wikipedia, s.v. "Matt Taibbi," accessed April 29, 2023, https://en.wikipedia.org/wiki/Matt_Taibbi.
108. Matt Taibbi, "Congratulations, Elitists: Liberals and Conservatives Do Have Common Interests Now, " https://taibbi.substack.com/p/congratulations-elitists-liberals.
109. "Full Interview: Journalist Matt Taibbi on the Need for Change in American Media," YouTube video, 25:53, https://www.youtube.com/watch?v=sGz2GzaxF6s.
110. "Media and the Death of Objectivity: Matt Taibbi with John Wood Jr. and Ciaran O'Connor," YouTube video, 1:01:55, https://www.youtube.com/watch?v=Zx_-JxTEsTo.
111. Matt Taibbi, "So Much for Transformational Joe Biden," *Racket News*, May 28, 2021, https://taibbi.substack.com/p/so-much-for-transformational-joe.
112. Wikipedia, s.v. "Glenn Greenwald," accessed April 29, 2023, https://en.wikipedia.org/wiki/Glenn_Greenwald.
113. Common Dreams, "Glenn Greenwald," Runner, n.d., https://www.commondreams.org/author/glenn-greenwald?gclid=Cj0KCQjwweyFBhDvARIsAA67M72xTziffy-HfvVVZeRZ91Vo5wmbdqeGWig5bLklrXw2I9lssryFV-DgaAgeXEALw_wcB.
114. Glenn Greenwald, Substack.com, https://greenwald.substack.com/.
115. "Sam Harris | Home of the Making Sense Podcast," Sam Harris, accessed April 30, 2023, https://www.samharris.org/.
116. Wikipedia, s.v. "CJ Hopkins," accessed April 29, 2023, https://en.wikipedia.org/wiki/CJ_Hopkins.
117. CJ Hopkins, "Articles & Essays," https://cjhopkins.com/articles-essays-fiction/./
118. Hopkins, "Interviews and Reviews." https://cjhopkins.com/interviews-reviews-etc/./
119. Wikipedia, s.v. "Bari Weiss," accessed April 29, 2023, https://en.wikipedia.org/wiki/Bari_Weiss.
120. Bari Weiss, "Resignation Letter," accessed April 29, 2023, https://www.bariweiss.com/resignation-letter.

121 Wikipedia, s.v. "John Podhoretz," accessed April 29, 2023, https://en.wikipedia.org/wiki/John_Podhoretz.
122 Wikipedia, s.v. Noah Rothman," accessed April 29, 2023, https://en.wikipedia.org/wiki/Noah_Rothman.
123 Christine Rosen, "Christine Rosen, Author at Commentary Magazine," *Commentary*, accessed April 29, 2023, https://www.commentary.org/author/christine-rosen/. See also "Christine Rosen," Encyclopedia.com, accessed April 29, 2023, https://www.encyclopedia.com/arts/educational-magazines/rosen-christine-1973.
124 Abe Greenwald, "Abe Greenwald, Author at Commentary Magazine," *Commentary*, accessed April 29, 2023, https://www.commentary.org/author/abe-greenwald/.
125 Bill Maher, "New Rule: Losing to China," YouTube video, 6:12, https://www.youtube.com/watch?v=2DH4v6FnbvM.
126 Matt Taibbi, "Afghanistan: We Never Learn," *Racket News*, August 16, 2021, https://taibbi.substack.com/p/afghanistan-we-never-learn.
127 "Decline Is a Choice: And We're Choosing It," *Commentary* podcast, August 13, 2021,Decline Is a Choice: And https://podcasts.google.com/feed/aHR0cHM6Ly9mZWVkcy5zb3VuZGNsb3VkLmNvbS91c2Vycy9zb-3VuZGNsb3VkOnVzZXJzOjIwMzQzNDU2MC9zb3VuZHMucnNz/episode/dGFnOnNvdW5kY2xvdWQsMjAxMDp0cmFja3MvMTEwNTM-5MzE0MQ?hl=en&ved=2ahUKEwj37sr02LDyAhXUGs0KHS8WAzUQjrkEegQIEhAF&ep=3.
128 "Images of Saigon, Vietnam in 1975, and Afghanistan in 2021. " PBS.com, https://pbs.twimg.com/media/E83YH7ZXMAI4pmk?format=jpg&name=small.
129 Colum Lynch and Robbie Gramer, "Afghanistan Withdrawal: China, Russia Move to Outflank U.S. with Taliban," *Foreign Policy*, September 2, 2021, https://foreignpolicy.com/2021/09/02/afghanistan-withdrawal-china-russia-outflank-geopolitics-united-nations/. See also other overseas reactions here: https://www.wilsoncenter.org/event/hindsight-front-implications-afghanistan-withdrawal-china-and-russia. And here, regarding European feelings of disbelief and betrayal https://www.politico.eu/article/europe-reacts-bidens-afghanistan-withdrawal/.
130 "Canceling the Constitution: Biden Hailed for Violating Rule of Law to Extend Eviction Moratorium," Jonathanturley.org., August 9, 2021, https://jonathanturley.org/2021/08/09/canceling-the-constitution-biden-hailed-for-violating-rule-of-law-to-extend-eviction-moratorium/.
131 David Von Drehle, "The Eviction Moratorium Mess Exposes the Decay in American Politics," *Washington Post*, August 6, 2021, https://www.washingtonpost.com/opinions/2021/08/06/eviction-moratorium-mess-biden-cdc/.
132 YCharts, "Moderna, Inc.," https://ycharts.com/companies/MRNA/market_cap.
133 Greg Bump, "What a Rock Has to Do with Racism," Office of the Chancellor, September 16, 2021, https://chancellor.wisc.edu/blog/what-a-rock-has-to-do-with-racism/.
134 Christine Rosen, "'Pregnant People' and the Erasure of Motherhood: Christine Rosen, Commentary Magazine," *Commentary,* August 13, 2021. https://www.commentary.org/christine-rosen/pregnant-people-and-the-erasure-of-motherhood/.

135. Tyler Durden, "Named and Shamed: IRS Lists the Record Number of Wealthy Americans Becoming Ex-Americans in 2020," ZeroHedge, August 15, 2021, https://www.zerohedge.com/political/named-shamed-irs-lists-record-number-wealthy-americans-becoming-ex-americans-2020.
136. Glenn Greenwald, "The NSA's Inspector General into Allegations of Illegal Spying on Tucker Carlson," Substack.com, August 10, 2021, https://greenwald.substack.com/p/the-nsas-inspector-general-opens.
137. Greg Sargent, "Tucker Carlson's Fawning New Orban Interview Shows the Right's Dream Future," *Washington Post*, August 6, 2021, https://www.washingtonpost.com/opinions/2021/08/06/tucker-carlson-orban-interview-right-dream-future/.
138. Ross Douthat, "Why Hungary Inspires So Much Fear and Fascination," *New York Times*, editorial, August 8, 2021, https://www.nytimes.com/2021/08/07/opinion/sunday/hungary-orban-conservatives-free-speech.html?referringSource=articleShare.
139. "Oregon Suspends Need for High School Graduates to Be Proficient in Reading, Writing, and Math," Jonathanturley.org., September 3, 2021, https://jonathanturley.org/2021/08/10/oregon-suspends-need-for-high-school-graduates-to-be-proficient-in-reading-writing-and-math/.
140. "Mass Psychosis: How an Entire Population Becomes Mentally Ill," YouTube video, 28:41, https://www.youtube.com/watch?v=09maaUaRT4M.
141. Hanna Trudo and Amie Parnes, "Harris's Bad Polls Trigger Democratic Worries," *The Hill*, August 27, 2021, https://thehill.com/homenews/administration/565336-harriss-bad-polls-trigger-democratic-worries/.
142. "Trump Announces 2024 Run," *Le Monde Diplomatique*, August 6, 2021, https://mondediplo.com/2021/08/06usa.
143. Thomas B. Edsall, "Have Trump's Lies Wrecked Free Speech?," *New York Times*, January 6, 2021, https://www.nytimes.com/2021/01/06/opinion/trump-lies-free-speech.html.
144. "Corporate America Got More 'Woke.' Will It Last?," *Politico*, May 25, 2021, https://www.politico.com/news/2021/05/25/george-floyd-death-corporate-america-diversity-490016.
145. "Lockheed Martin's Woke-Industrial Complex," *City Journal*, March 23, 2023, https://www.city-journal.org/lockheed-martins-woke-industrial-complex?wallit_nosession=1.
146. Glenn Greenwald, "Congress, in a Five-Hour Hearing, Demands Tech CEOs Censor Internet Even More Aggressively," Substack.com, March 21, 2021, https://greenwald.substack.com/p/congress-in-a-five-hour-hearing-demands-0cf.
147. Matt Taibbi, "The Vanishing Legacy of Barack Obama," *Racket News*, August 13, 2021, https://taibbi.substack.com/p/the-vanishing-legacy-of-barack-obama-147.
148. Maureen Dowd, "Behold Barack Antionette," *New York Times*, August 14, 2021, https://www.nytimes.com/2021/08/14/opinion/barack-obama-birthday.html.

149 Video and story here. "That Time Joe Biden Lied about His Academic Credentials," *Mother Jones*, May 2019, https://www.motherjones.com/politics/2019/05/that-time-joe-biden-lied-about-his-academic-credentials/.

150 "Biden Admits Plagiarism in School But Says It Was Not 'Malevolent,'" *New York Times*, September 18, 1987, https://www.nytimes.com/1987/09/18/us/biden-admits-plagiarism-in-school-but-says-it-was-not-malevolent.html.

151 Neena Satija, "Echoes of Biden's 1987 Plagiarism Scandal Continue to Reverberate," *Washington Post*, June 5, 2019, https://www.washingtonpost.com/investigations/echoes-of-bidens-1987-plagiarism-scandal-continue-to-reverberate/2019/06/05/dbaf3716-7292-11e9-9eb4-0828f5389013_story.html.

152 "Top 10 Joe Biden Gaffes," *Time*, accessed April 30, 2023, http://content.time.com/time/specials/packages/article/0,28804,1895156_1894977_1895081,00.html.

153 "A Timeline of U.S. Troop Levels in Afghanistan since 2001," *Military Times*, August 17, 2022, https://www.militarytimes.com/news/your-military/2016/07/06/a-timeline-of-u-s-troop-levels-in-afghanistan-since-2001/.

154 Associated Press, "A Timeline of the US Military Presence in Afghanistan," *AP News*, September 8, 2019, https://apnews.com/article/fd2ec2085b0b4fd3ae0a3b03c6de9478.

155 Wikipedia, s.v. "Withdrawal of United States Troops from Afghanistan (2020–2021)," accessed April 30, 2023, https://en.wikipedia.org/wiki/Withdrawal_of_United_States_troops_from_Afghanistan_(2020%E2%80%932021).

156 Jen Kirby, "The Afghanistan Withdrawal Is Making Europe Nervous about US NATO Leadership," *Vox*, August 31, 2021, https://www.vox.com/22639474/afghanistan-nato-europe-refugees-germany-uk.

157 Michael Hirsh, "Biden's Denial of Error in Afghanistan Dismays U.S. Allies," *Foreign Policy*, August 22, 2021, https://foreignpolicy.com/2021/08/20/lessons-biden-afghanistan-withdrawal/.

158 US Debt Clock, https://www.usdebtclock.org/.

159 "Afghanistan: Tony Blair Says Withdrawal Was Driven by Imbecilic Slogan," *BBC News*, August 23, 2021, https://www.bbc.com/news/uk-58295384.

160 Matt Taibbi, "We Failed Afghanistan, Not the Other Way Around," *Racket News*, August 19, 2021, https://taibbi.substack.com/p/we-failed-afghanistan-not-the-other.

161 Marc A. Thiessen, "Biden's Afghan Retreat Has Done Irreparable Damage to Our Alliances," *Washington Post*, September 2, 2021, https://www.washingtonpost.com/opinions/2021/09/02/bidens-afghan-retreat-has-done-irreparable-damage-our-alliances/.

162 Robert Burns, "US Vacates Key Afghan Base; Pullout Target Now 'Late August,'" *AP News*, July 3, 2021, https://apnews.com/article/taliban-afghanistan-f6da97f3bde5b50b6d029185c9eb385d.

163 Maureen Dowd, "Opinion | Blunder on the Mountain," *New York Times*, December 19, 2009, https://www.nytimes.com/2009/12/20/opinion/20dowd.html.

164 "Remarks by President Biden on the Drawdown of U.S. Forces in Afghanistan," White House.gov., July 8, 2021, https://www.whitehouse.gov/briefing-room/

speeches-remarks/2021/07/08/remarks-by-president-biden-on-the-drawdown-of-u-s-forces-in-afghanistan/.

165 "How Biden Broke NATO," editorial, *Wall Street Journal*, August 19, 2021, https://www.wsj.com/articles/how-joe-biden-broke-nato-allies-boris-johnson-angela-merkel-emmanuel-macron-11629406300?st=5gfxm3k2t7xq3hd&reflink=article_email_share.

166 Rory Stewart, "Rory Stewart: The Allies' Retreat from Afghanistan Is a Monstrous Act of Self-Harm," *Mail Online*, August 14, 2021, https://www.dailymail.co.uk/debate/article-9892183/RORY-STEWART-Allies-retreat-Afghanistan-monstrous-act-self-harm.html.

167 Matt Viser, "'Don't You Ever Forget That Name': Biden's Tough Meeting with Grieving Relatives," *Washington Post*, August 30, 2021, https://www.washingtonpost.com/politics/biden-meeting-fallen-americans-families/2021/08/30/07ecff7c-09ac-11ec-a6dd-296ba7fb2dce_story.html.; Zachary Evans, "Families of Fallen Marines Lash Out at Biden after Meeting: 'This Isn't about You," Yahoo! News, August 31, 2021, https://www.yahoo.com/now/families-fallen-marines-lash-biden-140152624.html?guce_referrer=aHR0cHM6Ly93d3cuZ29vZ2xlLmNvbS8&guce_referrer_sig=AQAAAIOG211HQT2w5fcJz7OYqgWkvQywn-4yTryeP4Gv5MTvaMLmlLz7WMSkc0X22WgQIlXH8qWMEDh1nxgObW0s-k9l6zgfWCA6EIWnHv7OuV0a9csby8Xi84hF1SImmroTPGJx5YxlbayA7QC-c9dUDwGV0bdjWLB-eYKLSgyhbmsSVW1&guccounter=2.

168 Jon Simkins, "Taliban Photo Appears to Mock Iwo Jima Flag Raising in Latest Propaganda Push," *Military Times*, August 19, 2022, https://www.militarytimes.com/off-duty/military-culture/2021/08/21/taliban-photo-appears-to-mock-iwo-jima-flag-raising-in-latest-propaganda-push/.

169 Andrew Doran, "A Reckoning for U.S. Foreign Policy Elites Is Long Overdue," *The National Interest*, September 9, 2021, https://nationalinterest.org/feature/reckoning-us-foreign-policy-elites-long-overdue-193280.

170 "Team Biden's Lies Pile up as Taliban Hold Abandoned Americans Hostage," editorial, *New York Post*, September 8, 2021, https://nypost.com/2021/09/08/team-bidens-lies-pile-up-as-taliban-hold-abandoned-americans-hostage/.

171 "Biden on Afghanistan Fact-Checked," *BBC News*, August 19, 2021, https://www.bbc.com/news/58243158.

172 Sam Harris, "#260—The Second Plane," in *Making Sense*, September 9, 2021, podcast, https://www.samharris.org/podcasts/making-sense-episodes/260-second-plane. 9/11 image here https://images.news18.com/ibnlive/uploads/2011/09/reuters13_RTXKQQP.jpg?impolicy=website&width=0&height=0.

173 Image of Mr. Biden bearing striking likeness to MR. Magoo. Compare with next image. https://c8mediaforum.afp.com/CacheServer/Cache.svc/g?hid=622A4730AF-1B82A4C433221C3141921EB4C17498119C7DA3B18D64CF91478A62.

174 Image of Mr. Magoo, cartoongoodies.com, accessed April 30, 2023, https://img.cartoongoodies.com/wp-content/uploads/2021/04/Mr.-Magoo-New-glasses.png.

175 "Monthly Inflation Rate U.S. 2023," Statista, April 17, 2023, https://www.statista.com/statistics/273418/unadjusted-monthly-inflation-rate-in-the-us/.

176 Paul Krugman, "Opinion | Wonking Out: Coins and Credibility," *New York Times*, October 9, 2021, https://www.nytimes.com/2021/10/08/opinion/coins-debt-ceiling-default.html?searchResultPosition=1.

177 Brian Riedl, "Here's How Schumer Is Trying to Gaslight the GOP on Debt," *The Daily Beast*, September 19, 2021, https://www.thedailybeast.com/heres-how-schumer-is-trying-to-gaslight-the-gop-on-debt.

178 John Gramlich, "Monthly Encounters with Migrants at U.S.-Mexico Border Remain near Record Highs," *Pew Research Center*, January 13, 2023, https://www.pewresearch.org/fact-tank/2021/08/13/migrant-encounters-at-u-s-mexico-border-are-at-a-21-year-high/.

179 "Consumer Price Index Summary: 2023 M03 Results," accessed April 20, 2023, https://www.bls.gov/news.release/cpi.nr0.htm.

180 See this apt image portraying Mr. Magoo and his recklessness with energy: https://encrypted-tbn0.gstatic.com/images?q=tbn:ANd9GcQlMjgcwrIHMgpAzQmoD-3BggQMTP6N2TSOCpQ&usqp=CAU

181 "Help Wanted Crisis: Real Causes of the Worker Shortage," YouTube video, 7:10, https://www.youtube.com/watch?v=p8yoM2ESOK8.

182 Matt Taibbi, "The Cult of the Vaccine Neurotic," *News Racket*, October 7, 2021, https://taibbi.substack.com/p/the-cult-of-the-vaccine-neurotic.

183 "I Am Part of the Resistance Inside the Trump Administration," editorial, *New York Times*, October 28, 2020, https://www.nytimes.com/2018/09/05/opinion/trump-white-house-anonymous-resistance.html.

184 David French, "Yes, America Could Split Apart," *The Dispatch*, September 20, 2020, https://frenchpress.thedispatch.com/p/yes-america-could-split-apart?triedSigningIn=true.

185 Wikipedia, s.v. "Secession in the United States/ Supreme Court Rulings," accessed April 30, 2023, https://en.wikipedia.org/wiki/Secession_in_the_United_States#Supreme_Court_rulings.

186 Madison Hall and Shayanne Gal, "How the 2020 Election Results Compare to 2016, in 9 Maps and Charts," *Business Insider*, November 20, 2020, https://www.businessinsider.com/2016-2020-electoral-maps-exit-polls-compared-2020-11#the-electoral-vote-count-from-2016-to-2020-basically-flipped-1

187 Jonathan Turley, "Jussie Smollett's Final Act: How a Hate Crime Hoax Became a Pitch for Jury Nullification," *The Hill*, December 8, 2021, https://thehill.com/opinion/criminal-justice/584870-jussie-smolletts-final-act-how-a-hate-crime-hoax-became-a-pitch-for/.

188 "Jussie Smollett: A Complete Timeline from Actor's 2019 Arrest to Jail Time," *BBC News*, March 11, https://www.bbc.com/news/newsbeat-47317701.

189 Douglas Ernst, "Biden Links Kyle Rittenhouse to White Supremacists; Lin Wood Vows to 'Rip Joe into Shreds'," *Washington Times*, September 30, 2020, https://www.washingtontimes.com/news/2020/sep/30/biden-links-kyle-ritten-

190. "Kyle Rittenhouse: Biden Angry after Teen Cleared of Shootings," *BBC News*, November 20, 2021, https://www.bbc.com/news/world-us-canada-59356081.

191. "Joy Reid: Nothing In Place To Prevent White Nationalists from Using Rittenhouse Verdict to Attack Black Lives Matter," RealClearPolitics, November 19, 2021, video, 1: 23, https://www.realclearpolitics.com/video/2021/11/19/joy_reid_nothing_in_place_to_prevent_white_nationalists_from_using_rittenhouse_verdict_to_attack_black_lives_matter.html.

192. "Kyle Rittenhouse Verdict Sends a Chilling Message to Wisconsin and the Rest of the Country," *Wisconsin State Journal*, editorial, November 21, 2021, https://madison.com/wsj/opinion/editorial/kyle-rittenhouse-verdict-sends-a-chilling-message-to-wisconsin-and-the-rest-of-the-country/article_7299e869-82f2-5a38-b7b2-2f078a57b0ab.html#tracking-source=home-trending.

193. Selection of articles about "Progressive Prosecutors," accessed on Google April 29, 2023, may be found here. https://www.google.com/search?q=Progressive+Prosecutors&sxsrf=AOaemvKygxL8oqWvuR6KZ14HIbF89zYAyg%3A1640542436895&source=hp&ei=5LDIYYWHNN6UwbkPsMOPQA&iflsig=ALs-wAMAAAAAYci-9IfaEWs-VHLOfBMaCgRkPNHM7VBE&ved=0ahUKEwiFicDpiIL1AhVeSjABHbDhAwgQ4dUDCAk&uact=5&oq=Progressive+Prosecutors&gs_lcp=Cgdnd3Mtd2l6EAMyBAgjECcyBQgAEIAEMgUIABCABDIFCAAQgAQyBQgAEIAEMgYIABAWEB4yBggAEBYQHjIGCAAQFhAeMgYIABAWEB4yBggAEBYQHjoKCC4QxwEQrwEQJzoFCAAQkQI6BAgAEEM6CguEMcBEKMCEEM6DgguEIAEELEDEMcBEKMCOg0ILhCxAxDHARCjAhBDOggILhCABBCxAzoHCAAQsQMQQzoICAAQgAQQsQM6BQgAELEDOg4ILhCABBCxAxDHARDRAzoLCC4QgAQQxwEQrwE6CggAEIAEEIcCEBRQAFikKGCCR2gAcAB4AIABsAGIAa0PkgEEMjEuMpgBAKABAQ&sclient=gws-wiz.

194. Jonathan Turley, "Exodus: Philadelphia Prosecutors Are Leaving Larry Krasner in Droves." https://jonathanturley.org/2021/12/23/exodus-261-philadelphia-prosecutors-quit-under-larry-krasner/

195. https://www.manhattanda.org/wp-content/uploads/2022/01/Day-One-Factsheet-Final-1.6.22.pdf.

196. Pedro L. Gonzalez, "It's Time to Stand up to Progressive Prosecutors," *Newsweek*, December 3, 2021, https://www.newsweek.com/its-time-stand-progressive-prosecutors-opinion-1655026.

197. Eric Westervelt, "Behind the Loud Pushback against Progressive District Attorneys across the Country," *NPR*, November 26, 2021, https://www.npr.org/2021/11/26/1059391712/behind-the-loud-pushback-against-progressive-district-attorneys-across-the-count.

198 Dave Barry, "Dave Barry's 2021 Year in Review," *Washington Post*, December 26, 2021, https://www.washingtonpost.com/magazine/2021/12/26/dave-barrys-year-review-2021/.

199 Jonathan Holloway, "Compulsory National Service Could Unite America," *New York Times*, October 29, 2021, https://www.nytimes.com/2021/07/02/opinion/compulsory-national-service-america.html./

200 "It's Time to Make National Service a Universal Commitment," RealClearMarkets, November 30, 2017, https://www.realclearmarkets.com/articles/2017/11/30/its_time_to_make_national_service_a_universal_commitment_103011.html.

201 Stanley McChrystal, "Joe Biden Should Make National Service the Cornerstone of His Legacy: Here's How He Can Achieve That," *Time*, March 24, 2021, https://time.com/5949436/joe-biden-national-service/.

202 Newton D. Baker and Secretary of War, "Universal Military Service of Immense Benefit to Youth of America and to National Interests," *Harvard Crimson*, April 2, 1920, https://www.thecrimson.com/article/1920/4/2/universal-military-service-of-immense-benefit/.

203 Doug Bandow, "Mandatory National Service: A Bad Idea That Won't Die," Cato Institute, August 8, 2019, https://www.cato.org/commentary/mandatory-national-service-bad-idea-wont-die.

204 Conor Friedersdorf, "The Case against Universal National Service," *The Atlantic*, June 27, 2013, https://www.theatlantic.com/politics/archive/2013/06/the-case-against-universal-national-service/277230/.

205 "New Poll Finds Near Universal Interest among Young People," *Tennessee Tribune*, May 24, 2021, https://tntribune.com/new-poll-finds-near-universal-interest-among-young-people-in-national-service/.

206 "Countries with Mandatory Military Service 2023," *World Population Review*, accessed April 30, 2023, https://worldpopulationreview.com/country-rankings/countries-with-mandatory-military-service.

207 National Commission on Service, "Mandatory Service around the Globe," Medium.com, December 6, 2018, https://medium.com/@inspire2serveUS/mandatory-service-around-the-globe-c05e11810cfc.

208 Wikipedia, s.v. "Service National Universel," accessed April 20, 2023, https://en.wikipedia.org/wiki/Service_national_universel#:~:text=French%20President%20Emmanuel%20Macron%20implemented%20the%20Service%20national,be%20performed%20in%20both%20civil%20and%20military%20facilities.

209 Elisabeth Braw, "Western Democracies Need National Service. They Should Follow Germany's Lead.," *Foreign Policy*, August 4, 2020, https://foreignpolicy.com/2020/08/04/national-service-germany-usa-ask-what-you-can-do-for-your-country/.

210 "Vietnam War Facts, Stats and Myths," *US Wings*, September 28, 2019, https://www.uswings.com/about-us-wings/vietnam-war-facts/.

211 David Nelson, "Photo of Ukrainian Girl with a Lollipop and a Rifle Goes Viral," *Diario AS*, March 12, 2022, https://en.as.com/en/2022/03/12/latest_news/1647049220_819544.html

212 According to my sometimes-reliable chatGPT, which accords with my memory of learning this back in 1960, Hitler came to be appointed Chancellor through a combination of political maneuvering, propaganda, and the support of military leaders and business elites. In the July 1932 elections, Hitler's Nazi Party won the biggest share of votes in the German Reichstag, but they did not win a majority. President Paul von Hindenburg appointed Franz von Papen as Chancellor, but von Papen was unable to garner the support of the Reichstag. Thus, new elections were held in November 1932, and the Nazi Party lost seats.

Nonetheless, in January 1933, von Papen convinced Hindenburg to appoint Hitler as Chancellor despite the Nazis having only a minority of the Reichstag. Von Papen and others believed they could control Hitler to their own ends. The rest, as they say, is history.

213 Sam Harris, "Episode 275: The Russian War in Ukraine," in *Making Sense*, podcast, March 10, 2022, https://www.samharris.org/podcasts/making-sense-episodes/275-the-russian-war-in-ukraine

214 North American Treaty Organization, "Member Countries," last updated April 5, 2023, https://www.nato.int/cps/en/natolive/topics_52044.htm.

215 Veronika Melkozerova, "The Western World Is in Denial About Putin," *The Atlantic*, March 14, 2022, https://www.theatlantic.com/ideas/archive/2022/03/what-if-world-war-iii-has-already-started/627054/.

216 Matt Taibbi, "Orwell Was Right," *Racket News*, March 13, 2022, https://taibbi.substack.com/p/orwell-was-right?s=r.

217 Azi Paybarah, "New Hampshire Poll Points to Trouble for Trump; Growing Support for DeSantis," *New York Times*, June 23, 2022, https://www.nytimes.com/2022/06/23/us/politics/trump-desantis-new-hampshire-poll.html?auth=login-google1tap&login=google1tap.

218 United States Supreme Court, "Dobbs, State Health Officer of the Mississippi Department of Health, et al. v. Jackson Women's Health Organization, et al.," Syllabus, October term 2021, https://www.supremecourt.gov/opinions/21pdf/19-1392_6j37.pdf.

219 Spyridoula Katsoni, "The Right to Abortion and the European Convention on Human Rights," *Völkerrechtsblog*, March 19, 2021, https://voelkerrechtsblog.org/the-right-to-abortion-and-the-european-convention-on-human-rights/#:~:text=Precisely%2C%20it%20highlighted%20that%20the,interests'%20(para%2080).

220 Angelo Fichera, "Addressing New York's New Abortion Law," FactCheck.org, May 23, 2019, https://www.factcheck.org/2019/02/addressing-new-yorks-new-abortion-law/

221 "Schumer Tells Justices They Will 'Pay the Price' in Angry Rebuke," CNN.com, March 4, 2020, https://www.cnn.com/videos/politics/2020/03/04/schumer-gorsuch-kavanaugh-supreme-court-abortion-lead-vpx.cnn.

222 "The Kavanaugh Murder Attempt Is Shocking But Not Surprising," Jonathanturley.com, September 13, 2022, https://jonathanturley.org/2022/06/12/the-kavanaugh-murder-attempt-is-shocking-but-not-surprising/.

223 "In Op-Ed, Senator Warren Calls for Supreme Court Expansion to Protect Democracy and Restore Independent Judiciary," Elizabeth Warren, December 15, 2021, https://www.warren.senate.gov/newsroom/press-releases/in-op-ed-senator-warren-calls-for-supreme-court-expansion-to-protect-democracy-and-restore-independent-judiciary.

224 Ramon Antonio Vargas, "Alexandria Ocasio-Cortez Calls for Supreme Court Justices to Be Impeached," *The Guardian*, June 28, 2022, https://www.theguardian.com/us-news/2022/jun/27/alexandria-ocasio-cortez-supreme-court-justices-impeach-kavanaugh-gorsuch-thomas.

225 Ronald Brownstein, "America Is Growing Apart, Possibly for Good," *The Atlantic*, June 26, 2022, https://www.theatlantic.com/politics/archive/2022/06/red-and-blue-state-divide-is-growing-michael-podhorzer-newsletter/661377/.

226 Lance Morrow, "Could This Be an Antebellum Age?," *WSJ*, June 23, 2022, https://www.wsj.com/articles/political-violence-jan-6-capitol-hill-riot-2020-summer-rioting-looting-kavanaugh-assassin-abortion-guns-civil-war-11655997537.

227 John Gramlich, "What the Data Says about Gun Deaths in the U.S.," *Pew Research Center*, April 26, 2023, https://www.pewresearch.org/fact-tank/2022/02/03/what-the-data-says-about-gun-deaths-in-the-u-s/.

228 Supreme Court of the United States, "New York State Rifle and Pistol Association, Inc. et al v. Bruen Superintendent of New York State Police, et al.," Syllabus, October term 2021, https://www.supremecourt.gov/opinions/21pdf/20-843_7j80.pdf.

229 Rani Molla, "Polls Show a Solid Majority of Americans Want Gun Control," *Vox*, June 1, 2022, https://www.vox.com/policy-and-politics/23141651/gun-control-american-approval-polling.

230 Lexi Lonas, "Exxon Mobil, Chevron Push Back on Biden Blaming Industry for Oil Prices," *The Hill*, June 16, 2022, https://thehill.com/business-a-lobbying/business-lobbying/3526290-exxon-mobil-chevron-push-back-on-biden-blaming-industry-for-oil-prices/.

231 Tulsi Gabbard and Daniel L. Davis, "Biden's Endgame Shouldn't Be Victory for Ukraine," *Foreign Policy*, January 12, 2023, https://foreignpolicy.com/2022/06/27/us-ukraine-russia-war-endgame-victory-settlement-negotiation-biden-putin-zelensky/?utm_source=PostUp&utm_medium=email&utm_campaign=Editors%20Picks%20OC&utm_term=43912&tpcc=Editors%20Picks%20OC.

232 Liz Sly, "Russia Will Soon Exhaust Its Combat Capabilities, Western Assessments Predict," *Washington Post*, June 26, 2022, https://www.washingtonpost.com/world/2022/06/25/ukraine-russia-balance-of-forces/.

233 Brittany Bernstein, "Over 70 Percent of Americans Don't Want Biden to Seek a Second Term: Poll," *National Review*, July 2, 2022, https://www.nationalreview.com/news/over-70-percent-of-americans-dont-want-biden-to-seek-a-second-term-poll/.

234 Chris Cillizza, "Will Joe Biden Face a 2024 Primary Challenge?," *CNN*, July 2, 2022, https://www.cnn.com/2022/07/01/politics/joe-biden-2024-primary-challenge/index.html.

235 Edward-Isaac Dovere, "As Worries about Biden in 2024 Grow, Other Democrats Aren't Stepping Forward to Challenge Him," *CNN*, July 11, 2022, https://www.cnn.com/2022/07/11/politics/biden-democratic-primary-challenge-2024/index.html.

236 Phil Mattingly, "'Give Us a Plan or Give Us Someone to Blame': Inside a White House Consumed by Problems Biden Can't Fix," *CNN*, June 26, 2022, https://www.cnn.com/2022/06/26/politics/joe-biden-white-house-economic-problems/index.html.

237 Edward-Isaac Dovere, "After String of Supreme Court Setbacks, Democrats Wonder Whether Biden White House Is Capable of Urgency Moment Demands," *CNN*, July 6, 2022, https://www.cnn.com/2022/07/05/politics/democrats-frustrated-biden-lack-of-urgency-supreme-court-setbacks/index.html.

238 Philip Bump, "The Photo of Classified Documents at Trump's Mar-a-Lago Resort, Annotated," *Washington Post*, August 31, 2022, https://www.washingtonpost.com/politics/2022/08/31/trump-mar-a-lago-fbi-search-classified-documents/.

239 Christopher DeMuth, "America's Right Confronts the 21st Century," *Wall Street Journal*, November 18, 2022, https://www.wsj.com/articles/how-the-american-right-is-changing-conservative-natcon-trump-founders-great-awakening-tradition-woke-progressive.

240 Matt Taibbi, "No, New York Times, You Don't Deserve Better Than Donald Trump," *Racket News*, November 19, 2022, https://www.racket.news/p/no-new-york-times-you-dont-deserve.

241 Bill Barr, "Trump Will Burn Down the GOP. Time for New Leadership," The Free Press, November 21, 2022 *https://www.thefp.com/p/bill-barr-trump-will-burn-down-the*

242 The entire column can be found at this link among many others: Dave Barry, "Dave Barry's 2022 Year in Review," *Washington Post*, December 25, 2022, https://www.washingtonpost.com/magazine/2022/12/25/dave-barrys-2022-year-review/.

243 See Michael Wayland, "Toyota CEO Akio Toyoda Talks about Why He Isn't All-in on EVs — and What Made Him Do a 'Happy Dance,'" *CNBC*, October 3, 2022, https://www.cnbc.com/2022/10/02/toyota-ceo-akio-toyoda-electric-vehicles-happy-dance.html.

www.ingramcontent.com/pod-product-compliance
Lightning Source LLC
Chambersburg PA
CBHW070803040426
42333CB00061B/1832